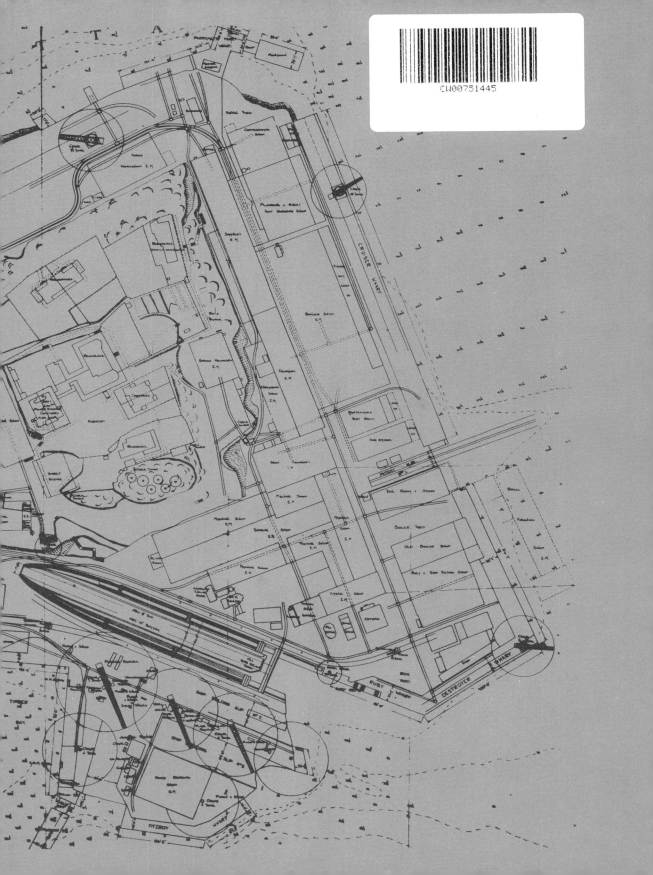

COCKATOO ISLAND

COCKATOO ISLAND

SYDNEY'S HISTORIC DOCKYARD

JOHN JEREMY

A UNSW Press book

Published by
University of New South Wales Press Ltd
University of New South Wales
Sydney 2052 Australia

© JC Jeremy
First published in 1998

National Library of Australia
Cataloguing-in-Publication entry:

Jeremy, John C. (John Christopher), 1942–
Cockatoo Island: Sydney's Historic Dockyard.

Includes index.
ISBN 0 86840 640 6.
1. Shipbuilding—New South Wales—Cockatoo Island
Dockyard—History. 2. Cockatoo Island Dockyard
(NSW)—History. I. Title.

623.83099441

A catalog record for this book is available from the Library of
Congress. Library of Congress Catalog number: 98–60221

Designed by *Dana Lundmark*
Printed by Kyodo Printing, Singapore

Dimensions and tonnages are in imperial or metric
measurements as used at the relevant time.

Photographs and illustrations are from Cockatoo Dockyard
collection unless otherwise credited.
The following abbreviations are used:
PWD: NSW Department of Public Works and Services
Tyrell Collection: Trustees of the Museum of Applied Arts
and Sciences, Sydney

Front cover: The Battle class destroyer HMAS *Anzac* in the
Fitzroy Dock in April 1970. The turbines and boilers in
Anzac, which was built at the Williamstown Naval Dockyard
in Victoria, were made at Cockatoo Island.
Back cover: *Arunta* during sea trials in early 1942.
Title page: HMAS *Australia* stemming the Sutherland
Dock in 1914.

CONTENTS

This book is dedicated to the people of Cockatoo Dockyard.

I am often told that Australia is a big country — I have indeed noticed that myself in the last three years — but vast as it may be, it is still an island, enjoying the same advantages that Great Britain has enjoyed as an island and subject to the same disadvantages. Every ton of oil brought into this country, every ton of wool or wheat taken out of it, goes by ship, at some hazard in peace, in deadly peril of war. An island which does not provide itself with the ships and with the means to protect them gives, as tragic hostages to fortune, its own people.

That is why, to Australia, a shipbuilding and ship repair industry is not a luxury but a necessity, and those who, against many difficulties, maintain it effectively and efficiently, as do the builders of *Vampire*, deserve well of this country.

Field-Marshall Sir William Slim
Governor-General of Australia
proposing the toast to the builders
after the launching of HMAS *Vampire*
Saturday 27 October 1956

The Daring class destroyer *Vampire* entering the water on 27 October 1956. (News Limited)

FOREWORD

Cockatoo Island is the largest of the eight islands that grace the most beautiful harbour in the world — Sydney Harbour. Once forested with tall red gums that were home to many thousands of sulphur crested cockatoos, the island has been host to a wide range of important and sometimes unusual activities since European settlement.

From the early 1830s, Cockatoo Island has been at various times a convict prison, a quarry, an industrial school for girls, a grain storage site, a reformatory and a base for the boys training ships *Vernon* and *Sobraon*. From the 1850s, with the construction of the first dry dock on the island, ship repair and from 1870 shipbuilding co-existed with these other various activities, until 1908, when the whole island was dedicated to a dockyard role.

In the years since, and until its demise as a dockyard in recent years, Cockatoo has served our nation with distinction through times of peace and war. Successive generations of its skilled workforce have enabled the dockyard to expand its construction and repair activities to include merchant and warships of all descriptions, including submarines and at one time aircraft — Sir Charles Kingsford Smith's famous aircraft *Southern Cross* was extensively repaired on the island and a new design of aircraft, appropriately named *Codock*, was built there. There would be few dockyards anywhere in the world that could boast such a wide range of marine and general engineering activities as Cockatoo Dockyard.

My first contact with Cockatoo was during the years of World War II when as a youngster, I accompanied my father to the launching of one of the great many warships that were built there over those critical years. I was not aware then that Cockatoo would become a familiar place for me in my later naval career. Some of the ships I served in were built or refitted there. I also spent over two years as gunnery trials officer working on the ships under construction or being repaired on the island. During those years, the trials team worked from rooms in the old convict prison. So I had ample opportunity to become familiar with life on Cockatoo Island and the people who became part of its history.

What always impressed me about Cockatoo Island was the deep sense of history and heritage that was always present there. The ghosts of the past were always close by — for me at least! I was always conscious that the ship or weapons system that I might have been working on, although important at the time, was only a small, perhaps minute part of the overall Codock story.

Australia is an island continent whose discovery, founding, exploration, economic development and security has been largely dependent upon ships and the use of the sea. Our nation therefore boasts a rich and colourful maritime heritage, and for over 140 years Codock has played a prominent, indeed critical role in that history. It is a story that is worthy of the telling and I am delighted that John Jeremy, who was the last of the dockyard's managing directors, has taken on that important duty.

Previous books on Cockatoo Island have concentrated on its convict and prison history, and the earlier dockyard activities. John Jeremy's book complements these works, in providing a detailed and comprehensive account of the achievements of the dockyard leading to its development in the twentieth century and its ship-building, ship repair, submarine, ship design and other engineering roles. Importantly, the people of Cockatoo Island, who made it all happen, are also featured. His book also covers the sad and often traumatic events leading to the closure of the dockyard in 1991.

In his Preface the author writes:

> Perhaps now we can say that the story of Cockatoo Dockyard, if not Cockatoo Island, is complete, and this history can be finished.

I doubt that history can ever be 'finished' as such, but John Jeremy has produced a comprehensive coverage of Codock which will stand the test of time.

I commend his book to all who have been involved in the making of the Codock story over the years, or have an interest in our nation's maritime heritage.

Rear Admiral Peter Sinclair AC AO RAN (Retd)

PREFACE

I first visited Cockatoo Dockyard in late 1958 as a schoolboy. My main memories of that visit are of the new destroyer *Vampire*, then lying at the Cruiser Wharf having just completed sea trials. I came back to Cockatoo Island a few months later to see the frigate *Parramatta* launched on a sunny summer Saturday morning. That was my first experience of the thrill of seeing a new ship start on its way to the water for the first time.

That day in January 1959 I had no idea what lay ahead of me in years to come. I had always (it seemed) been interested in ships but had no idea what direction my future career might take. Later that year my father happened to meet Engineer Rear Admiral A B Doyle in the city, and described to him his son's dilemma and mad obsession with ships — particularly warships. 'Send him up to Cockatoo to see Hutch. He'll sort him out' was Admiral Doyle's suggestion.

My father contacted Captain Hutcheson, the managing director of Cockatoo Dockyard and in due course I was on the ferry on my way to an interview. As promised, I was sorted out. On 4 January 1960 I got off the 8:00 ferry and found my way up the hill to the ship drawing office where I was to start my apprenticeship as ship draughtsman.

Cockatoo Island from the north-west, January 1986. HMAS *Adelaide* is in the Sutherland Dock, HMAS *Success* (with the port main engine running) at the Sutherland Wharf, HMAS *Tobruk* at the Destroyer Wharf, HMAS *Oxley* on the slave dock at the Bolt Shop Wharf and the floating crane *Titan* at the Cruiser Wharf.

That day was the start of more than thirty years of challenge and intense interest. During my early years I hardly ever took leave in case I missed something, and I must have been something of a nuisance because I always wanted to know what was going on. This interest in all the dockyard's activities probably led to me being directed towards planning work, but in the meantime I had to learn the basics in the drawing office. This often required me to look for plans that had gone astray in the strong room, searches that introduced me to the treasure chest of plans and other records of the work done at the island. A short spell as temporary dockyard photographer served the same purpose with the photographic records. As the years passed, I acquired the task of updating the short dockyard histories that were used as handouts for visitors, and began to accumulate information about the wide variety of work that had been done over the years.

In 1971 the then managing director Roger Parker retired, and shortly thereafter the chairman, Ted Harty persuaded him to write a history of the dockyard. There had been no complete history written until then, although there was a popular and rare record of World War II work which had been published by the Company in about 1950. Roger took on the challenge, and in due course asked me to help him by checking facts and finding information, but mainly to gather and caption photographs to illustrate his work. It was a task I took on with great pleasure. *Cockatoo Island, a history* by R G Parker, was published in 1977.

In 1977 there was, of course, more history to be made. Cockatoo was heavily involved in the refit and modernisation of the Royal Australian Navy's Oberon class submarines, its principal task for the last 20 years of its operation. This was demanding and rewarding high quality work, but we keenly wanted to get back into naval shipbuilding. Within a few years we were building the replenishment ship that was to become HMAS *Success*, a project that had its full share of problems and controversy.

In 1981 Roger Parker's successor, Dick Humbley retired, and it was my privilege to succeed him and to move into the 'front office' as managing director. By 1984, when we launched *Success*, we had finally resolved the problems of that contract and had reached the highest employment level for many years, about 2650 people, including more than 400 apprentices.

A second replenishment ship to follow *Success* on the slipway proved elusive, and our management effort was directed towards trying to get some involvement for our people in either the new submarine construction project or the new destroyer project (which became the ANZAC frigate project). With that and concentrating on completing HMAS *Success*, and the continuing submarine refit and modernisation programme we did not see what was coming. When, in early 1987, I received a telephone call from Canberra to warn me of an impending statement by the Minister for Defence, it came as a surprise. It was unfortunate that our landlord and principal customer chose not to confer with the Company before announcing their intention not to renew the Company's lease of Cockatoo Island after its expiry in 1992. Had they done so, the consequences of the decision might have been different.

It became our task to bring the industry that was Cockatoo Dockyard to an end. That task was a sad one. The island dockyard was only stone, bricks and steel; it was old and expensive to keep operating. The people were the real asset and it was not a pleasant task to have to end the employment of so many and to stop the training of new generations of naval architects, engineers, technicians and tradesmen.

The closure of Cockatoo Dockyard became inevitable when the government decided in June 1990 not to send the last two submarine refits to the island. Our last refit, of HMAS *Orion*, was completed in June the following year, by which time all other work had also been completed. Over the following eighteen months, stores and equipment were sold and dispersed. At the Commonwealth's request, auctions were arranged for the sale of machine tools and equipment, cranes, boats, and even buildings.

It was a considerable task as the accumulation of material gathered on the island over more than a century was identified and sold. Throughout this project I was particularly concerned that the unique collection of records of the dockyard and its work not be lost. It was my hope that a Cockatoo Dockyard collection might be established in the same way the records of famous shipbuilders like William Denny & Brothers of Dumbarton, Scotland, are preserved by the National Maritime Museum at Greenwich.

Many of the documents remaining on the island in 1990 related to the period between 1913 and 1933, when the dockyard was operated by the Commonwealth. These records belonged in Australian Archives, who quickly saw the opportunity that was presented by the closure of the dockyard. Agreement was soon reached for the Company to donate to National Archives of Australia, and hence the nation, those of the Company's records which were worthy of permanent retention.

The work of identifying, preserving and packing the records was done over nearly a year by a dedicated team of people from National Archives of Australia, professionally led by Margaret Chambers. Letters, files, drawings, plans and many thousands of photographs now comprise a unique collection of the work of one of Australia's oldest dockyards. The collection also includes drawings of the Alfred Graving Dock in Melbourne, and drawings of the aircraft designed by Wing Commander (later Sir Lawrence) Wackett and his team in the Aircraft Department between 1929 and 1934.

There were also many items like ship half-models, remains of old ships like the destroyer *Warrego* of 1912 and the steel beam that had held the stern of the cruiser USS *Portland* together as the ship came to Cockatoo for repairs in 1942. These and small things like ship's badges and crests were transferred to the RAN museum on Spectacle Island.

Ever since Roger Parker's book was published in 1977 I had hoped to see the story of the work of the dockyard further expanded and brought up to date. With a strong sense of personal identification with the dockyard, I have always been sensitive to the achievements of Cockatoo being credited to others, as sometimes happens. The gathering together of all the dockyard records presented a unique opportunity to explore this history and help set the record straight, and this book was born at that time.

I have not tried to retell in any detail the convict and prison history of the island. Roger Parker told much of this story in his book, and James Kerr prepared a most detailed and fascinating account of the influence of that period on the fabric of the island in *Cockatoo Island penal and institutional remains* in 1984. This work was a report prepared for the Department of Housing and Construction, which was published by the National Trust of Australia.

I have only touched upon the part played by the dockyard and its workforce in the industrial relations history of the Australia. That could be a long story in itself, some of which has been told by others like Susanna Short in her book *Laurie Short, a political life* and Issy Wyner in *With banner unfurled, the early years of the Ship Painters and Dockers Union*.

It is inevitable, however, that I must cover some of the same ground that Roger Parker covered in 1977. This book is intended to tell the story of the work done at Cockatoo Island. It is primarily based on the dockyard's own records, but in some areas these were incomplete. Apart from drawings of the docks and other facilities little remains in the dockyard collection from the period the yard was operated by the New South Wales Government. There is not much available for this period from other sources either. The early records of the Commonwealth Naval Dockyard are also patchy. The hungry Cockatoo Island white ants were known to have destroyed some files, and finally a memorandum was found that recorded the damage by water and subsequent destruction in 1941 of the files for all the major projects in the period from 1913 to about 1930. Luckily, the drawing offices kept quite complete records, and the excellent work of others has helped to fill in many of the gaps. I have also made reference to the books by Robert Hyslop and John Bach, who with others such as Bob Nicholls have set out much of the early Australian naval history in great detail.

Amongst the papers that now occupy the shelves of National Archives of Australia, are several books of newspaper cuttings covering most of the period from 1913 to the late 1930s. These cuttings have also filled some gaps. However, I have been very cautious about relying on this material because in my own experience what we read in the newspapers often bears but a tenuous relationship to the truth.

I must also acknowledge the help of many Cockatoo people (and others like Ross Gillett) who, over the years, have helped put this history together, by giving me bits of information or old photographs that they have unearthed. There would be too many to name, even if I could remember them all. I would, however, particularly like to thank Alan Mitchell, who made available to me the papers of his father, David Mitchell. David Mitchell was also deeply interested in the history of the dockyard and its place in the history of Australian shipbuilding, and his papers have been a most fruitful source of information.

The first draft of this book was completed by the end of 1991, and set aside for time to mellow the perception of recent events. Over the next year, a major dispute developed between the Company and the Commonwealth over the circumstances of the early end of the submarine refit work and the consequences of the government's decisions of 1987. Arbitration of these disputes began in early 1993, with some hope that it would be over relatively quickly. In the event this difficult process and associated visits to the New South Wales Supreme Court and Court of Appeal continued for nearly four and a half years until finally settled.

Perhaps now we can say that the story of Cockatoo Dockyard, if not Cockatoo Island, is complete, and this history can be finished.

The story in these pages is told from a dockyard perspective. I have tried to be as objective as possible, but my close involvement with the dockyard for 37 years is likely to have influenced my perceptions of what happened, and why.

Cockatoo Dockyard is no more. I can still visit *Vampire*, now a popular exhibit at the Australian National Maritime Museum in Sydney, and I do from time to time. She looks older than she did when I first walked her decks in 1958, but then, I dare say, so do I.

John C Jeremy

Chapter One

A CONVICT PRISON

There is no evidence of Aboriginal use of Cockatoo Island, and there was no permanent European settlement there until 1839. Some reports mention the construction of buildings by convicts as early as 1833, but they probably relate to Goat Island, as some early maps of the harbour show Goat Island as 'Cockatoo Island', and Cockatoo as 'Banks Island'.

On Saturday 23 February 1839, the *Sydney Gazette and New South Wales Advertiser* reported:

COCKATOO ISLAND — The island known by this name is situated at the mouth of the Parramatta River, and is of the form of a triangle. It contains about four acres (sic) of land. It is without water, and is said to abound with snakes. On this island it is known by all persons at all acquainted with it, that there are places where a man might effectually conceal himself for days together, notwithstanding the strictest search. It is very rocky and the stone is said to be of an excellent description. The sixty commuted prisoners from Norfolk Island, were forwarded to the island on Thursday morning under a military escort. The men were removed there chained together. They are placed under the charge of Lieutenant Bentley, of the 50th Regiment, the officer commanding on Goat Island. This gentleman will not reside on the island, but in his absence the men will be in the custody of a sergeant's guard. There are two working overseers stationed on the island. The works are to be carried on under the superintendence of the person who now holds, or lately held, the office of Ranger of the Government Domain at Parramatta. The men on their arrival were placed in tents, huts being erected for the overseers. The first employment that will be furnished the men will be the construction of a wharf on the southern side of the island, after which they will proceed with the quarrying. The stone is not intended for sale as formerly stated, but is intended to be applied for the erection of the New Circular Wharf. To remedy the want of water, a party is now employed in boring a well. The view from the island is one of the finest near Sydney.[1]

The convicts may have had a larger island than reported — the original area was about 32 acres — but it is doubtful that any of them had much opportunity to enjoy the view.

Early work for the convicts included the building of a barracks block and a guard house and kitchen for the military personnel. The design and technical supervision of the buildings was the responsibility of the Commanding Royal Engineer, Captain George Barney, whilst the discipline of the convicts was the responsibility of the superintendent of Convicts, Captain MacLean. The first superintendent of the prison, Thomas Rawson, was appointed in February 1841. Charles Ormsby replaced him in September, becoming the assistant superintendent. By October 1841, work was sufficiently advanced for the main body of prisoners to be transferred to the island.[2]

The Governor, Sir George Gipps, had originally intended only doubly convicted prisoners to be transferred to Cockatoo Island from Norfolk Island. However, orders to end transportation of convicts from New South Wales to Norfolk Island, and the refusal of Governor Franklin to allow any New South Wales transportees to be received in Tasmania, placed considerable pressure on prison accommodation in New South Wales and Gipps decided to move all transportees to Cockatoo Island.

The prison buildings on Cockatoo were soon overcrowded, and although construction continued for a number of years, at first under Ormsby, and later under the Civil Engineer, Cockatoo Island, Captain Gother Kerr Mann, overcrowding was to be a continuing problem on the island. Mann was appointed civil engineer in 1847, and in 1859 engineer in chief and superintendent of Cockatoo Island.

In 1842, 323 men were imprisoned on the island; 165 iron gang men, 84 Norfolk Island expirees, and 74 under colonial sentences. The island location made escape unlikely, although there were a number of attempts. In 1842, William Westwood, known as 'Jackie Jackie', attempted a mass escape with 20 other men, but they were soon recaptured. Westwood was later hanged on Norfolk Island for the murder of a prison warder. The only successful escape from Cockatoo was that of Frederick Ward. He had been sentenced to life for cattle stealing, and on 11 September 1863, with another convict, swam from Cockatoo Island in a heavy fog. The other man drowned, but Ward got ashore and escaped. He became famous in the north-west of New South Wales as the bushranger 'Thunderbolt', until a police constable shot him at Uralla in May 1870.

In addition to constructing their own prison buildings, the first convicts on Cockatoo Island were employed quarrying the excellent sandstone of the island for use in public works, including the sea wall of Sydney Cove. Very early work also included the digging of silos in the solid rock.

During the severe drought from 1837 to 1841, the colony suffered from frequent shortages of grain, and the silos on Cockatoo Island were intended to store surpluses in the good times for later use. Seventeen silos were dug by hand from the rock of the island. They were bottle shaped, and the largest was 21 feet in diameter and 23 feet deep. The only access was by a man-hole about 2 feet square. They could hold up to about 6000 bushels of grain, and when sealed proved to be very satisfactory. Governor Gipps had intended that storage for up to 100,000 bushels be provided, but the Imperial Government in London put a stop to his plans in 1841, declaring that the storage of grain by the government interfered with free market forces. The silos were later used as water tanks. Most remain today, although some were lost during excavations for new workshops during World War II.

As a prison, Cockatoo Island was not a nice place. Prisoners of all kinds were crowded together in inadequate accommodation. The solitary confinement cells were frequently occupied, and one of the cells was so small its occupant could only stand. The overlapping responsibilities of Barney and Ormsby also caused much friction, until it was resolved by the appointment of Mann as superintendent in 1859.

The poor conditions of the prisoners on the island prompted calls for a public inquiry into the operation of the prison. Henry Parkes (later Sir Henry), proprietor of the 'Empire', agitated successfully for the appointment of the 1858 Board of Enquiry into the management of the Cockatoo Island Penal Establishment. Parkes was also a member of parliament, and chaired the 1861 Select Committee of Inquiry into Sydney prisons. The report of this committee gives an insight into the conditions on Cockatoo Island at the time:

> On the occasion of your Committee's first visit to Cockatoo Island, on February 1, 1861, there were 167 prisoners in that establishment, 63 of whom, on the previous night, had been confined in one dormitory. The men engaged in productive labour on the day in question were only 68 out of the whole number, and 10 of these were set down as overseers; they were employed on the works of the Fitzroy Docks. The buildings assigned for the prisoners, especially for their confinement at night, are of a deplorable description. There are, in all, five dormitories, which have been built with very imperfect ventilation; on either side of each there are double tiers of double sleeping berths, with coffin-like apertures opening upon a narrow central passage. In this passage are placed night-tubs for the common use of the men during the 12 hours they are locked up. Two of the dormitories contain 88 berths each, two contain 52 each, and one contains 48. In all, there are 328 berths of the character described. But as many as 500 prisoners have been upon the island at one time, though nothing like so large a number appear to have been confined there lately.

Boys from the *Vernon* school on parade on Cockatoo Island. (The *Vernon* can be seen in the background.) The school maintained a swimming pool, parade ground and a small farm on the island. (J C Jeremy Collection)

While the physical suffering from this inadequate night accommodation must aggravate the sentence of the law to many men to an extent beyond all calculation, the moral results of such a state of existence are, as might have been expected, of the very worst description.

Your Committee would direct particular attention in this respect to the evidence of the chaplains of the island, and Mr Inspector Lane. The latter witness, who has been in charge of the police force on the island for the last 13 months, says he has paid much attention to the condition of the prisoners at night. He has often seen them at the iron gratings gasping for fresh air from without, and he 'wonders how they live'. The brutalising effect upon the prisoners is admitted by all, and it is described by some as terrible in depravity. Crimes of the deepest dye are committed. The clergymen in attendance complain that as the prisoners are never alone for a single hour during the whole of their sentence, they literally have no opportunity for the practice of religion, even if they are so disposed, and similar complaints are made by the men themselves. It is almost unnecessary to add that there is no attempt at classification of prisoners in this establishment.[3]

Although there were some improvements in the administration of the prison after this report, little further development of the prison buildings took place. In October 1859, Mann had commented on the inadequacy of the accommodation, but did not recommend extensive alterations in view of the possibility that Cockatoo might become entirely a dockyard and store.

Ten years later, in July 1869, the breaking up of the penal establishment on Cockatoo Island was approved and the prisoners were transferred to Darlinghurst. In 1871, an industrial school for girls was set up on the island, with a separate reformatory for girls under the age of 16 who had been convicted of a crime. Both establishments were transferred from Newcastle, and Cockatoo had been chosen because of its isolated location. The establishment was named 'Biloela' to remove some of the image of the old prison, but little was done to improve the buildings.

The girls were separated from the rest of the island by a high corrugated iron fence, although just who was being protected is debatable.

In 1871 Henry Parkes, then Minister for Education, had been instrumental in the purchase by the government of the sailing ship *Vernon*, of 911 tons, for conversion for use as a training ship for wayward and orphaned teenage boys. Administered by the Department of Education, *Vernon* was moored to the east of Cockatoo Island, and a recreation area and small farm were set up on the eastern side of the island. In October 1871 the superintendent of the *Vernon* school, I V S Mein, complained to the Principal Under Secretary:

> Three girls came down abreast of the ship, in a semi nude state, throwing stones at the windows of the workshops — blaspheming dreadfully and conducting themselves more like fiends than human beings. I was compelled to send our boys onto the lower deck to prevent them viewing such a contaminatory exhibition.[4]

Up to 500 boys were accommodated in *Vernon*, and they were taught under strict discipline. In 1890, *Vernon*, then nearly fifty years old, was replaced by the famous clipper ship *Sobraon*, of 2131 tons, built in 1866. (*Sobraon* remained off Cockatoo until 1911, when she was taken over by the Commonwealth Government for use as a naval training ship. She was converted by Mort's Dock and commissioned as HMAS *Tingira*. She was paid off in 1927.)

The school ship
Vernon.
(J C Jeremy Collection)

By 1874, it had become clear that Biloela was an unsuitable place for the reformatory and industrial school, but the establishment was not closed until 1888. In June that year Biloela was again proclaimed a prison, despite its disadvantages, in order to ease the overcrowding at Darlinghurst. The gaol was then used to house petty offenders, vagrants and prostitutes. As the arrangement was intended to be temporary, little work was done to improve the prison accommodation, although in the 1890s staff accommodation and service facilities were improved and daytime segregation was increased.

The Biloela Gaol was finally closed in 1908, when the new Long Bay Gaol was completed. In the final years the gaol housed only female prisoners, in the original convict-built prison buildings. Some effort

The training ship *Sobraon* at her mooring off Cockatoo Island. (J C Jeremy Collection)

HMAS *Tingira* (ex-*Sobraon*) in the Sutherland Dock in December 1924. (J C Jeremy Collection)

had been made to improve conditions for the eighty-odd prisoners, and most of the space was used for workrooms, where clothing was manufactured for industrial schools and other government institutions.

After 1908, the whole island was taken over by the dockyard, and the old prison buildings, which had been declared unsuitable for use over half a century before, took on a new role as dockyard offices, a role which was to continue for another 83 years.

A newspaper report of 1 February 1908, headed 'The Last of Biloela', reported the final closing of the gaol, and ended with a prophetic paragraph:

> Most likely in a few years from now the historic Biloela will have given place to Government residences and offices on the spurs of the picturesque heights, and Cockatoo Island will one day become the hub of a great ship-repairing centre second to none in the Southern Hemisphere.[5]

Chapter Two

THE GRAVING DOCKS

On 31 October 1845, the Legislative Council adopted an Address to the Governor, Sir George Gipps, asking him 'to represent to Her Majesty's Government the advantages, which would accrue to this Colony and to the Empire at large, were a Dry Dock to be constructed at Sydney for Men of War'. The proposal was supported by Gipps, who forwarded the Address to London to the Secretary of State for the Colonies, Mr William Gladstone (the future Liberal Prime Minister of Britain), adding, 'Cockatoo Island is the best place in Sydney Harbour, which I consider best adapted for a Naval Establishment'.[6]

Gladstone forwarded the proposal to the Admiralty for an expression of opinion. The Secretary of the Admiralty replied on 28 May 1846, saying:

> I am commanded by their Lordships to request you will state to Mr Secretary Gladstone that my Lords consider the situation at Cockatoo Island, which has been indicated, as well adapted to the construction of a dry dock, and that great accommodation would doubtless be derived from such a work; but that if it is intended by the Colonial Legislature that the expense should be borne by the Naval Department, they are not prepared at present to recommend the Treasury to undertake it.[7]

This setback did not lessen the interest of the Colonial authorities, and on 18 May 1847, the Commanding Royal Engineer, Lieutenant Colonel James Gordon (who had succeeded Barney in 1843) submitted an estimate for the construction of a dock 266 feet long, 90 feet wide, and with a depth at the entrance at high water of 17 feet. The estimated cost for tools, implements and materials, including an iron plate cais-

A plan of Cockatoo
Island, dated 1860,
showing the Fitzroy
Dock as completed and
the outline of the first
extension.

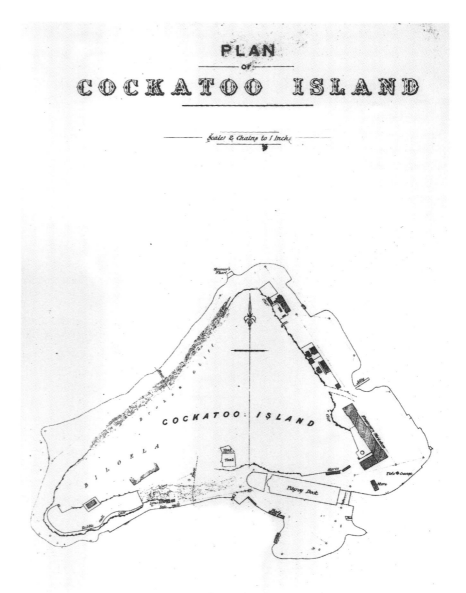

son, was £4085. If prison labour was used, it was estimated that 100
men would be required for 470 days. The estimate using non-convict
labour was 100 men for 365 days, at a wages cost of £5262.

The Governor, then Sir Charles Fitz Roy, submitted the plan and
estimate to the Legislative Council on 10 June 1846, and sought the
sum of £1000 so that work could start. The Council referred the proposal to a select committee, which reported in 1847, recommending
that the work should go ahead with only minor modifications. On 29
October 1847, Gordon was advised that £500 had been provided for

the construction of the dock, and he was instructed to proceed with the work.

Having been told that the dock was to be built, the Admiralty, on 29 May 1847, indicated that they would be prepared to bear part of the cost 'on condition that it is of such dimensions as will be sufficient for a large frigate or steamer, and that Her Majesty's ships have preference when required for its use'.[8]

The Admiralty finally paid £3094 towards the cost of the dock. It was designed by Captain Mann, and made large enough to comply with the Admiralty's wishes. Work proceeded only slowly, using convict labour, under Mann's direction. The dock was excavated from the solid

A very early photograph of the Fitzroy Dock.

rock of the island by blasting using gunpowder charges fired by electricity.[9] By July 1853, 1.5 million cubic feet of rock had been excavated, including 580,000 cubic feet to form the dock itself. Governor Fitz Roy laid the first stone for the inverted arch lining on 5 June 1854. Progress was slow using convict labour, and Mann acknowledged that non-convict labour would have been faster, but that free stonemasons and quarrymen would not work alongside prisoners.

Mann prepared the preliminary design for the dock caisson and the detailed design and prefabrication (in galvanised wrought iron) was carried out by Rennie and Waterman of Blackwall, London. It was assembled at Cockatoo by Mann.[10] The steam-driven dock pumping machinery was built in London by George and Sir John Rennie, and arrived in Sydney in July 1853. Its installation was supervised by Henry Broderick, who came to Sydney for the purpose, and who went on to be the dock master and chief engineer. Gother Mann became the engineer in chief of the Civil Engineering, Dry Docks and Cockatoo Island Department within the Public Works Branch of the Department of Land and Public Works when it was formed in October 1857.

The new dock was named Fitz Roy Dock after the former Governor. In later years the dock became known as the 'Fitzroy Dock'. It is a graving dock. The term 'graving' is said to be derived from the French word 'grève', meaning a flat beach or shore, where in times past, simple excavations in the shore, open to the tide and possibly lined with timber, were built to enable ships to be worked on in dry conditions at low tide. Fitzroy Dock was first occupied by a punt of the Colonial steam dredger *Hercules* between 8 September and 8 October 1857.[11] The ship credited as being the first to use the dock was the survey frigate HMS *Herald*, which docked on 1 December 1857.

When *Herald* was docked the dock itself was not complete, and work continued for some time. In 1857 the dock was 284 feet long. It was lengthened by 1870 to 400 feet, and again in 1880 to its final length of 475 feet. By then, the total cost of the dock and associated works had risen to £95,550.

The matter of priority for Royal Navy ships remained unclear. In a Minute dated 26 February 1869, the Under Secretary for Public Works, Mr John Rae, stated:

> There is nothing in the papers to show any obligation on the part of the Colonial Government to give any preference for Her Majesty's Ships in the order of admittance to the dock.[12]

In the published conditions[13] for the use of the dock, the government reserved the right to determine the order of priority for its use, but it was usual to consult the naval authorities on the docking programme and to give preference to navy ships when a booking was made.

The Fitzroy Dock was not the first graving dock to be completed in Sydney, although it was the first started. The privately owned Mort's Dock in Waterview Bay, Balmain was completed a year earlier. It had been built with non-convict labour in 12 months.

The need for a larger dock soon became apparent. Shortly before he retired in 1870, at the age of 61,[14] Gother Mann proposed further extension of the Fitzroy Dock. He pointed out that new docks had recently been built at the Cape of Good Hope, San Francisco, and Hong Kong, and a new dock was being built in Melbourne. He urged that if the maritime prestige of Sydney was to be maintained it was imperative that the facilities provided in the port should be at least equal to those provided elsewhere. His recommendation was favourably received, and in 1871 a sum of £20,000 was placed in the estimates for the enlargement of the Fitzroy Dock, but it was apparently not approved.

In May 1872, Mr E O Moriarty, Engineer in Chief for Harbours and Rivers, stated that the sum had been submitted to Parliament pending the completion of surveys and an assessment of the relative merits of extending the Fitzroy Dock, or building a new larger dock. He prepared estimates of £65,000 for the extension of the Fitzroy Dock, or £83,000 for a new one. In due course the Secretary for Public Works directed Moriarty to report on proposals to construct a new dock at Cockatoo.

His report was submitted to the Legislative Assembly in March 1874.[15] It comprehensively reviewed the various types of docks, and the size and cost of existing docks throughout the world. Moriarty said:

> On first considering the subject of a first class dock at Cockatoo, I was disposed to think it would be better to enlarge the present dock than to construct a new one altogether; but after maturely considering the subject in all its bearings, I have been compelled to change my opinion, and I am now satisfied ... that it will be better to construct a new dock at the western end of the Island, with its head pointing eastward toward the present dock.[16]

He concluded:

> In determining the dimensions of the new dock, I have been guided by those of the new first-class docks at Chatham, Portsmouth and Malta, and the Alfred Dock, Melbourne; but as any increased dimensions in our proposed dock would be simply a matter of a little more or less excavation, involving little or no masonry, I have thought it should slightly exceed the dimensions of those other docks described, so that we may truly boast of having in Port Jackson the largest single dock in existence.[17]

Nothing happened for some years, yet the problems at Cockatoo mounted as the management tried to meet demand with the facilities they had available. In a memorandum to the engineer in chief, dated 3 October 1879, the dock master reported:

> I docked HIMS *Bismark* last night at 9 pm, and I only had one half-inch of water to spare; and unless the ship is lightened, she will have to remain in dock until the 15th of the month.[18]

The *Bismark* was a third rate protected corvette cruiser completed in Kiel in 1878. Fully rigged with a sail area of 2721 square metres, the ship was also fitted with a steam engine of 2530 indicated horsepower (IHP), for a maximum speed of 12.5 knots. Her overall length was 82.5 metres and the beam 13.8 metres.[19]

The German corvette *Bismark* in the Fitzroy Dock. The *Bismark* was the only ship of her class fitted with two bow-mounted 35-centimetre torpedo tubes, which can be seen just above the waterline. (Sydney Water Heritage Collection)

The Sutherland Dock
as completed. The
photograph was taken
in about 1893. (PWD)

Just what the dock master meant by 'one half-inch of water to spare' is not clear. If he meant that there was only half an inch between the top of the blocks and the keel then the docking of the *Bismark*, particularly at night, was a dangerous operation. The atmospheric pressure and wind speed and direction have considerable influence on the actual depth of water over the blocks, and it is probable that he felt that he was within half an inch of his minimum nominal safe clearance. In the twentieth century it was normal to abandon a docking in the Fitzroy Dock unless there could reasonably be expected to be at least 9 inches of water between the top of the blocks and the keel.

The last extension of the Fitzroy Dock was completed by January 1880, when Moriarty reported that the dock:

> ... is now long enough to take in any ship in the world but one, but the depth of water on the sill is not sufficient for very large vessels such as the *Orient* and others of her class, and this cannot be altered without throwing the dock out of use for at least twelve months and incurring considerable expense.[20]

The *Orient* was the first steam ship built specifically for a regular Australian service. Completed by John Elder & Company in 1879 for the Orient Steam Navigation Company, she was 460 feet long, 46 feet in the beam and 5400 tons gross. Accommodation was provided for 200 first class, 130 second class and 300 steerage passengers. Whilst a small ship by today's standards, when built the *Orient* was a large ship and second only in size to the *Great Eastern*, which was then the largest ship afloat in the world. The *Orient* was the first ship to be equipped with electric light, and the first in the Australian trade with refrigeration facilities.[21]

Finally, in 1880 the Parliament decided to build a new first class graving dock at Cockatoo, suitable for the largest classes of vessels, including ironclads, and larger than any then existing in the world. A sum of £150,000 was approved for the purpose.

THE SUTHERLAND DOCK

Mr J B Mackenzie designed the dock under the direction of Moriarty. An early drawing of the dock, dated 1882, shows how it was designed to be capable of docking the largest ships then in service (see Appendix 1). The dock entrance is shown with the cross sections of three ships—the *Great Eastern*, the battleship HMS *Inflexible*, and the Inman liner *City of Rome*. The latter is also shown in profile in the longitudinal section of the proposed dock.

The *Great Eastern*, conceived by Isambard Kingdom Brunel in 1851, and built between 1854 and 1859, was, for 50 years, the largest ship ever built. By 1882 she had been laid up at Milford Haven UK for seven years, and would never have fitted in the new dock at Cockatoo. She was 680 feet long overall, and had a breadth over the paddle wheel sponsons of 120 feet. However her midship section moulded dimensions (a beam of 82 feet, depth of 58 feet and draught of 30 feet) would have been a useful guide for the dock design.

HMS *Inflexible* was a notable British battleship, designed by the Admiralty's chief constructor, Nathaniel Barnaby, between 1873 and 1874, and was built between 1874 and 1881. The ship was a complete departure from previous standards of design, gun power and disposition and armour thickness. Not particularly successful, *Inflexible* was the 'fattest' battleship built so far, for although only 320 feet long, her beam was 75 feet and draught 26 feet 6 inches.[22]

The *City of Rome* was the longest ship then in service.

A contract for preliminary work for the new dock was awarded in October 1882 to Keogh and Johnston. Between February 1883 and December 1884, some 50,000 cubic yards of rock, 17,000 cubic yards of soft soil, and 2700 yards of scabbling were removed at a cost of £10,500.[23] The material was used to reclaim an area to the south of the site. The original cell block from 1839 was also demolished as part of this work.

The second and major contract was awarded to a young civil engineer, Mr Louis Samuel, who submitted the lowest of 14 tenders, with a schedule of prices working out to a little over £135,000. Samuel was only 23 at the time. Born in Sydney, he was the son of Sir Saul Samuel KCMG, who was member of parliament for Orange and Wellington (1854–80) and Agent General in London for New South Wales (1880–97). Louis Samuel studied at the University of Sydney and was articled to Moriarty at the Harbours and Rivers Department to become an engineer. After further study in Europe he returned to Sydney and set up his own business as a civil engineer and contractor.

Even the simplest dockyard buildings had style in the nineteenth century. This toilet block stood between the docks until the early years of this century, and can be seen in the photograph opposite. It was presumably for officers and management. The facilities provided for the workmen were much more basic.

This contract was extended to include the erection and installation of a sliding iron caisson, and the construction of an engine and boiler house for the pumping machinery. Easton and Anderson built the caisson. The pumping machinery was built by James Watt and Company and installed by their agent, Mr G Smale.

The caisson was built of wrought iron. It was 90 feet long, 14 feet 9 inches wide and 39 feet 1.5 inches deep from deck to keel. It was fitted with a falling deck and rested on delta metal rollers, 18 inches in diameter. Whilst the caisson could be floated in or out of position, in normal operation it was drawn into a caisson chamber at the side of the dock. The movement of the caisson was controlled so that its first movement on opening or last on closing was away from or towards the dock fit to prevent damage to the granite face of the dock entrance.

The new dock pumping station was connected to the Fitzroy Dock by a culvert about 3 feet in diameter. It was formed in the cement backing of the altar on the north side of the dock and by tunnels, one driven through the rock which separated the Fitzroy Dock from the new dock and the other connecting the western end of the culvert with the pump wells.

Samuel contracted acute peritonitis and died on 29 November 1887, at the age of 26, and his younger brother, Edward, completed the work. The new dock, named Sutherland Dock after a Minister of Works in a previous New South Wales Government, was completed in March 1890, at a total final cost of £267,825.

Cockatoo Island from Birchgrove on a weekend around the turn of the century. The large dredger alongside the island on the far right is probably the *Glaucus,* built in 1903. (Tyrrell collection)

For a little while the new dock fulfilled the parliamentary ambitions that it should be the largest in the world. As built the Sutherland Dock had a maximum length of 638 feet with the caisson in the outer fit, or 608 feet with it in the inner fit. The width at the entrance was 84 feet, and the maximum depth of water over the sill at high water was 32 feet. In about 1911 the floor of the dock was widened to accommodate the new flagship of the Australian Navy HMAS *Australia* by cutting away the lower altars for most of the length of the dock.[24] The dock was lengthened in 1928 to its final length of 680 feet from the inner fit, and the width at the entrance was increased to 88 feet. The original wrought iron caisson was replaced in 1975. The old caisson was towed to sea and sunk off Dee Why.

The original design of the Sutherland Dock also provided for the construction of a dredger dock between the head of the two docks, accessible from either the Fitzroy or Sutherland Dock, but it was never built.

The cruiser *Encounter* in the Sutherland Dock in about 1911. Work on the widening of the floor to accommodate the battle cruiser *Australia* is underway. Timber ways have been rigged up to remove a length of the starboard propeller shaft from the dock. After the floating crane *Titan* was completed in 1919 this task was made easier, and the ship would be positioned as far aft in the dock as possible to allow *Titan* to lift the shaft out of the dock. (RAN photograph)

THE EARLY DOCKYARD 1857–1913

In 1855, the administration of Cockatoo Island became the responsibility of the Chief Secretary's Department of the Government of New South Wales, and in 1864 the prison administration was taken over by the Department of Prisons. In 1870 the dockyard was placed under the control of the engineer in chief of the New South Wales Public Works Department, Harbours and Rivers Branch. The island was then used for the construction and maintenance of government vessels and plant in addition to the docking of warships and other ships in the Fitzroy Dock.

By the end of 1864, 148 ships had been docked in the Fitzroy Dock. They included HM Ships *Iris*, *Elk*, *Cordelia*, *Pelorus* and *Niger*. HMS *Herald* was docked for a second time in March 1859 before leaving the Australia Station to return to Britain. The first foreign warship to use the dock was the Austrian frigate HIMS *Novara*.

Apart from Colonial Government vessels, the first merchant ship to dock at Cockatoo Island was the Peninsular and Oriental Company's (P&O) *Benares*, which docked in May 1859. She came to the island because Mort's Dock was occupied. Nevertheless this first commercial use of the Fitzroy Dock soon raised concerns amongst the operators of the other docks and slips in Sydney.

In petitions to the Legislative Assembly in early 1860, Captain Thomas Rowntree (the lessee of the Mort's Dry Dock in Waterview Bay) and Mr John Cuthbert (a shipbuilder and lessee of the ASN Company's patent slip at Pyrmont) complained about the use of the Fitzroy Dock in competition with their facilities. A Select Committee chaired by Mr Henry Parkes was appointed by the Assembly in April 1860 to examine the complaints.[25]

Opposite top:
HMS *Galatea* in the Fitzroy Dock in October 1870. (Government Printing Office Collection: State Library of New South Wales)

Opposite bottom:
This photograph of a French armoured corvette in the Fitzroy Dock appears to have been taken in the 1870s. The ship is probably the *Alma*. Her sister ship *Atalante* docked at Cockatoo Island in 1884. With their five sister ships they were the first ironclads fitted with guns in barbettes. (J C Jeremy Collection)

The petitioners claimed that the Governor Sir Charles Fitz Roy had given assurances that the dock would be used for government vessels only. John Cuthbert suggested that, if the dock was to be used for non-government work then it should be leased to a private operator. Another petitioner, Mr H Drake of Hely, Drake and Harper, expressed his satisfaction with the arrangements at the Fitzroy Dock. His firm had hired it to dock the ships *Granite City*, *Eli Whitney* and *Susan*, as well as the schooner *Adolphus Yates* and the barque *Woodlark*. During questioning by the Committee he drew attention to the fact that Captain Rowntree was a sub-tenant of P&O and leased the Waterview Bay dock only on occasions when that company did not need the dock for its own ships. He agreed that a similar arrangement at the Fitzroy Dock would be equitable.

The Committee found no evidence:

> that a pledge was given, as alleged, by the late Governor, Sir Charles Fitz Roy that the Fitz Roy Dock should not be brought into competition with private establishments of a similar character.[26]

Because of the complication imposed by the prison establishment, the committee was unable to recommend the leasing of the dock by public competition, and did not recommend any change to the management arrangements.[27]

There are few records setting out the details of dockings at Cockatoo Island for the period 1865 to 1891. A New South Wales official publication dated about 1886 says:

> Some large ships-of-war and other first class vessels have been taken in the dock. Amongst the former may be mentioned HMS *Galatea*, commanded at the time by HRH the Duke of Edinburgh, and the French ironclad *Atalanta* (sic); and amongst the latter the steamships *Whampoa* and *Chimborazo*.

> The dock is in almost constant occupation, HM war-ships, foreign men-of-war, and the mail-ships of the PMS Company being regularly accommodated there, together with the numerous fleet of tugs, dredges, &c., belonging to the Colonial Government. Dredges, tugs, and punts for the Dredge Service are built at the island, a large staff of mechanics being constantly employed for this purpose, and for keeping in repair the large fleet of dredges, tugs, &c., belonging to the Department.[28]

Cockatoo Island in the 1880s.
(J C Jeremy Collection)

The document also states:

It should be mentioned that the Government do not undertake the repairs of any vessels docked there except their own, to avoid, as much as possible, competition with private enterpise (sic).[29]

In addition to the ships named in this publication, surviving photographs help identify other ships that occupied the Fitzroy Dock during the period. These include the famous cruiser HMS *Calliope*, which earned fame at Apia on the night of 16 March 1889 when the ship survived a severe hurricane which sank four German and United States ships with the loss of 146 lives. *Calliope* was docked at Cockatoo Island for repairs.

The construction of the Fitzroy Dock had provided the Royal Navy with a much-needed capability to dock ships, which had not before been possible in the Pacific. Previously, underwater repairs were carried out by hauling over the ship on a suitable hard slip, or between 1838 and 1846 on a patent slipway in Sydney.[30] Despite some reluctance the Admiralty had contributed to the cost of the Fitzroy Dock, on the condition that Royal Navy ships had preference for its use. Most Royal Navy ships on the Australia Station were based in Sydney and whilst by 1864 other docking facilities were available at Bombay, Singapore, Whampoa and Shanghai, they would most probably have docked in Sydney, at least until the Alfred Graving Dock was opened in Melbourne in 1874, and the Calliope Dock opened in Auckland in 1888.[31]

Some significant ship repairs were carried out at the Fitzroy Dock during the nineteenth century. For example, in November 1882 the Orient passenger liner *Austral* (5524 tons gross) sank in Neutral Bay whilst coal was being taken on board. Five lives were lost. After 122 days on the bottom of the harbour, the ship was raised on 12 March 1883. After that length of time on the bottom the task of cleaning the *Austral* must have been considerable. Several hundred men were employed on the job, which included the removal of 1500 tons of coal before the ship could enter dock. She was at Cockatoo Island for about three weeks whilst temporary repairs were carried out. These repairs, which must have been extensive, were sufficient for the ship to steam to the Clyde for a major refit.[32]

Records of the number of ships docked at Cockatoo Island are included in most of the Annual Reports of the Public Works Department for the years 1891 to 1910.[33] They provide a basis for estimating the total number of ships docked between 1857 (when the

The British cruiser HMS *Calliope* in the Fitzroy Dock.

Fitzroy Dock opened) and 1911. These records suggest that some 3400 dockings may have been carried out at the dockyard in that period (see Appendix 12).

Shipbuilding began at Cockatoo Island about 1870, and many ships, mostly small, were built before the Commonwealth took over the island in 1913. They included dredgers, hopper barges, tugs and other small craft that were built for the Government.

There is a list of vessels built at Cockatoo between 1870 and 1912 in Appendix 2. This list has been prepared from surviving records and suggests that nearly 150 vessels were built there in that period.[34] Amongst these vessels the 56-ton tug *Hinton*, which was imported in parts from England and assembled at Cockatoo Island in 1886, was the first steel ship built in Australia.

The type of work carried out can be judged from the Annual Report for the year 1892:

> Hitherto iron has been almost exclusively used for dredge, steamer, and punt building, at the Fitzroy Dock works; but, during 1892, an experiment in wood construction has been tried with gratifying results, the dredge *Groper*, 115 ft. x 50 ft. x 9 ft. for the Von Schmidt suction machinery, having been expeditiously built by the Dock shipwrights. One of the boilers for the *Groper* was made at the works, the engines were fitted on board, and the vessel was completed at the Dock after Mr Higgins' pumping and cutting mechanism was fixed. Eight pontoons for the *Groper* were built at the island, and much shipwrights' work done at HMS *Curacoa* and *Cordelia*, and HMCS *Wolverine*, and at the *Jupiter*, *Orestes*, *Rhea*, *Ceres*, *Dawn*, and to several punts attached to the various dredges.

> Large anchor boats were built for the suction dredges, and much of the woodwork for the *Dictys* was prepared during 1892. The *Thetis* was fitted with additional passenger and bridge accommodation.

> In the shipbuilding, boiler making, and fitting branches much activity was displayed. An iron hopper barge to carry 330 tons was built for the dredge *Hunter*, and two smaller iron ones for grab dredges.

> The dredge *Archimedes'* well was widened, to suit larger buckets, the vessel was cut and lengthened, a new boiler was fitted, new buckets made, and the engine and machinery overhauled.

> Important alterations were made to the dredge *Samson*. The hull was strengthened by having new plates and frames substituted for defective ones, and the whole forward part of the vessel was increased in beam by 8 feet, to ensure stability and carry more weight. New boilers were made, and the ladders were repaired and hung independently of the shafts.

> Extensive renewals were carried out with two of the oldest hopper barges, and others were strengthened and adapted for carrying more silt. More than the usual number of ladder dredge buckets were made during the year, many of them with steel backs.

> The work of building the rock-breaker, *Poseidon*, begun in 1891, was completed

in 1892, and the machinery was fitted on board.

New large grab buckets were made for the 15-ton crane, and the ordinary grabs for the various Priestman cranes were repaired. Repairs were effected to the machinery, hull, and boilers of the *Rhea*, *Orestes*, *Ceres*, and *Ajax*, and new centrifugal pumps made for *Neptune* and *Juno*.

Considerable progress was made with the *Dictys*, and much work done for Garden Island and country towns water supply.[35]

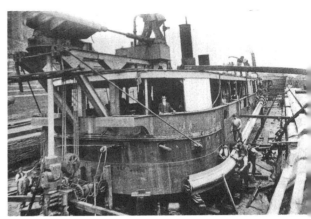

The sand pump dredger *Dictys* in the Fitzroy Dock in about 1892. (PWD)

In that year 90 vessels were docked — 41 in the Sutherland Dock and 49 in the Fitzroy Dock.

Despite the policy of the government not to compete with private industry much of the machinery fitted in vessels built on the island was also built there. The scope of work for the yard increased when the Sutherland Dock was opened, but the opening of a new dock at Woolwich by Mort's Dock and Engineering Company in November 1901 meant that large ships (other than naval ships) which formerly docked in the Sutherland Dock, were lost to Cockatoo.

The number of men on the island, under the general superintendent, Mr E J H Broad, varied considerably. Only 110 men were employed at one time in 1893. By 1900 the number had risen to 603, but the extent of the work carried out suggests that these figures represent permanent employees only.

Between 1900 and 1903, the dockyard completed a 200-ton suction dredger, *Richmond*, which had an overall length of 122 feet and a beam of 20 feet, and two tugs, *Mayfield* and *Burrunda*. The latter, 132 tons gross, 108 feet 4 inches long and 20 feet 2 inches beam, was later renamed *Waratah*, and remained in service until 1968. Given to the Sydney Maritime Museum, the tug was restored to a very high standard, and is today the oldest known Cockatoo built ship. It regularly steams on Sydney Harbour.

The steam tug *Phoenix*, built at the Government Dockyard, Biloela in 1900. (PWD)

During these years the management of the dockyard came in for much criticism, with allegations of political interference and inefficiency. By 1903 the number of people employed had fallen to 318, and on 5 January 1903 the government appointed a Royal Commission to examine the claims. After examining 47 witnesses their report was completed on 16 April.[36] The Commission found that there had been extensive political interference in the management of the yard by the Minister for Public Works, the Honourable E W O'Sullivan, making the manager of the yard, Broad, ineffective. It was found to be common for employees with grievances to approach the Minister directly, and the management of the yard was often directed by the Minister to reinstate dismissed employees, or to employ particular persons, sometimes as old as 70 or 80.

The superintendent of the Government Dockyard, Mr A E Cutler (left) with a member of his staff, Mr Boreland, in 1910. (Town & Country Journal)

The Commission also found that the facilities at Cockatoo were inadequate, and that recommendations made by a previous enquiry (in 1899) had not been implemented. They recommended radical change in the administration of the dockyard, removing it completely from political influence. It urged that Broad be allowed to retire and that Mr A E Cutler, then principal assistant engineer, Water Supply and Sewerage Branch, be appointed as superintendent.

Cutler had joined the New South Wales public service in 1885 as a draughtsman in the Harbours and Rivers Department. In 1889 he was promoted to assistant engineer, and later was appointed principal assistant engineer to the Water Supply and Sewerage Branch. He came to Cockatoo in 1903 as acting superintendent, and was confirmed in the position the following year. Later he held a number of positions in the New South Wales public service, finally becoming general manager of the State Government's Walsh Island Dockyard in Newcastle, in June 1920. He retired in May 1924.

The Commission's report also recommended that the facilities on the island be im-proved by the installation of machinery previously bought, but still in store, the re-modeling of the boiler shop, and by enlarging of the engine erecting shop.

In 1903 the facilities on Cockatoo Island comprised 'a boilermaker's shop, machine shop for large tools, erecting shop, foundry, blacksmiths' shop, pattern shop, shipwrights' shop'.[37] Most of these buildings were on the eastern and south-eastern part of the island. The

The fisheries investigation trawler *Endeavour* at a buoy off Cockatoo Island in 1909. The ship was lost in the Southern Ocean in 1914. (PWD)

The sand pump dredger *Glaucus*, completed at Cockatoo Island in 1903. (PWD)

Above left:
The wooden steam tug
Hydra, built in 1912.
(J C Jeremy Collection)

Above right:
The dredger *Latona*.
Built in 1911, it sur-
vived until the 1960s.
(Tyrrell Collection)

foundries were capable of non-ferrous and ferrous castings, the latter up to 12 tons. At that time brass founding had been carried out 'for many years', but the iron foundry was recent. Most of the shipbuilding was carried out on slipways built on the shore in front of the machine shop.

In 1904, the government began a modernisation programme, and further work was done after 1908. In addition to the extension of the machine and fitting shops, a new patent slipway (which had previous-ly been recommended by the 1899 enquiry) was built on the eastern shore on part of the area occupied by the shipbuilding slips. It was completed in 1909.

Shipbuilding facilities were improved by the construction of two new slipways on the reclaimed land south of the Fitzroy Dock, complete with cantilever cranes and steel working machinery, mostly made on the island. This area became known as the 'southern ship-yard' and the slipways were referred to as No. 2 and No. 3 after the cruiser slipway (No. 1) was built. No. 2 slipway was the first to be completed, some time before 1907, with No. 3 coming later. This work was finished by 1910.

These new slipways were supplemented by the small slipway on the eastern shore in front of the dockyard machine shop, and another in the southern shipyard (south of No. 3 slipway), which was known as No. 4. A further slipway, No. 5, was built south of the Sutherland Dock in 1912 for the construction of dredgers and other small craft.

Ships built after 1904 included 10 dredgers, five hopper barges and several tugs, together with much of their machinery, boilers and auxiliaries.

In 1908 Cockatoo built a fisheries investigation trawler for the Commonwealth Government. The keel of the *Endeavour* was laid on the eastern shore slipway on 1 June 1908 and the ship was completed at the end of January 1909. Its main machinery was built on the island. The construction contract provided for a six months' maintenance (warranty) period, and in its report for the year ended 30 June 1909 the managing committee was 'happy to state that during the period men-tioned we were not called upon to spend a single penny on repairs'.[38]

The dredger *Latona* was designed and built at Cockatoo for service on the harbour bars of New South Wales. Completed in 1911, it was a

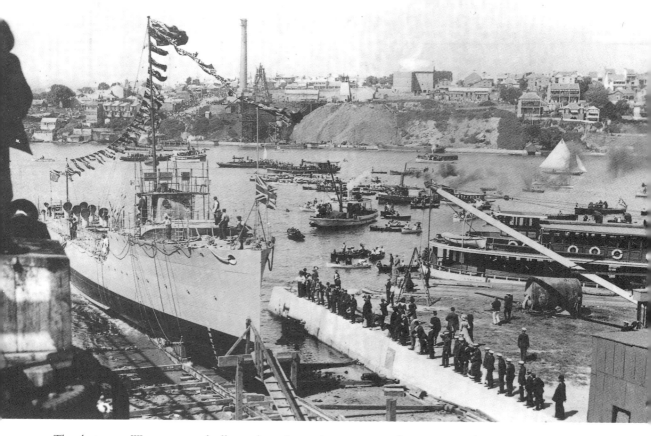

shallow draught twin screw trailing suction hopper dredger, 166 feet long and 35 feet in beam. The *Latona* was still operating in 1960.

Cockatoo also designed and built a single screw barge loading bucket dredger with a capacity of 1300 tons per hour for the Melbourne Harbor Trust. Completed in September 1912, the *John Stewart* was 152 feet long and had a beam of 32 feet.

Other work in 1912 included a new steel hull for the dredger *Groper*, and the modification of another large dredger, which was cut in half in dock and lengthened about 20 feet. The freeboard of a large tug was also increased by extending the side frames, raising the topsides about two and a half feet and fitting a new deck and superstructure.

The expansion of shipbuilding facilities at Cockatoo in 1908 was also prompted by the Commonwealth Government's plans for the new Australian Navy. The Australian Government had begun to examine the purchase of torpedo boat destroyers for the Australian Navy in July 1907, and proposals were invited from British shipbuilders. On 5 February 1909, the government approved the purchase of three torpedo boat destroyers of the River class, two to be built in Britain, and a third which was to

The destroyer *Warrego* entering the water at her launching on 4 April 1911.
(J C Jeremy Collection)

The Melbourne Harbor Trust bucket dredger *John Stewart* in the Fitzroy Dock shortly before completion in 1913.
(J C Jeremy Collection)

be supplied as prepared material for assembly in Australia. This ship was intended to provide experience for the construction of further ships of the type in Australia.[39]

Money was also allocated to establish a government shipyard in Australia for the purpose.

Shortly after the government's plans were announced, the superintendent of Cockatoo, Cutler, approached the Minister for Defence to express the New South Wales Government's interest in building the ships. As it was agreed that it would be some 12 to 15 months before Cockatoo could be ready, the original plans were not changed, and the first two ships, *Parramatta* and *Yarra* were wholly built in Britain. The job of reassembling the third ship was given to Cockatoo. In 1909 nine men were sent 'home' from Australia to gain experience in the construction of these ships. Six were employees of the Government Dockyard at Cockatoo Island.

The order for the preparation of material for *Warrego* was placed with the London and Glasgow Engineering Company (later Fairfields Shipbuilding & Engineering Company), Govan, Scotland. *Warrego* was laid down on 29 May 1909 as their Ship No. 470. Work was complete by mid-1910 and the ship was dismantled and shipped to Sydney, where the keel was laid for a second time at Cockatoo on 1 December 1910.

Warrego was launched on 4 April 1911, and completed for service on 1 June 1912. The job had taken six months longer than planned and had not been without its problems. It was essential experience for the yard in warship construction.

In March 1911, the Prime Minister asked the New South Wales Government if it would be prepared to build a second class cruiser and three further torpedo boat destroyers. Although the response was prompt, negotiations over price and contract conditions were not completed until 18 June 1912. The contract to build the ships at cost plus 8 per cent had effect from 1 August 1912, but the dockyard had begun ordering materials on 10 October 1911.

In May 1909 the Commonwealth had sought the New South Wales Government's assistance to obtain a suitable site for a Naval Dockyard. By 1912 the need was pressing, and with naval construction already underway at Cockatoo, negotiations began for the transfer of the island to the Commonwealth.

Many of the ships built at Cockatoo Island before 1912 were built on slipways on the eastern shore of the island. These slipways can be seen in front of the machine shop in this photograph taken in about 1893. (PWD)

The actual transfer of the island, together with the neighbouring Spectacle Island, was made on 31 January 1913. The total purchase price was £867,716 19s, made up as follows:

	£
Cockatoo Island, freehold land, 36.5 acres	96 500
Fee-simple of bed of harbour with rights to reclaim 15.75 acres	9 000
Schnapper Island, freehold land, 0.4 acre	1 300
Fee-simple of bed of harbour, with right to reclaim 6.25 acres	3 375
Exclusive right to establish buoys and	
construct wharves and jetties inside certain areas	10 000
Workshops, buildings, houses and furniture	173 923
Sutherland and Fitzroy Docks, with all plant connected therewith	350 000
Other equipment, tools, and miscellaneous	223 618

The buildings on the eastern shore of the island in 1893. The building on the left is a boat house associated with the training ship *Sobraon*. (PWD)

The agreement to transfer the island was made between the Premier of New South Wales, William Holman and the Prime Minister Andrew Fisher and signed on 26 October 1915. It was ratified by the *Naval Properties Transfer Act 1925*.

With the transfer to the Commonwealth, a new era began for Cockatoo Island, as the first Naval Dockyard for the Royal Australian Navy.

Chapter Four

ADMINISTRATION UNDER COMMONWEALTH OWNERSHIP 1913–92

THE COMMONWEALTH NAVAL DOCKYARD, COCKATOO ISLAND

The transfer of Cockatoo Island to the Commonwealth was not universally popular. Whilst he strongly supported the construction of ships in Australia, Captain Clarkson (later Rear Admiral Sir William Clarkson, RN) Third Naval Member of the Naval Board and chief of construction, had earlier expressed the view that:

> In my opinion Cockatoo Island Dockyard has neither the staff organisation nor the facilities for building vessels for the Royal Australian Navy with either efficiency, economy or dispatch. I consider that if the proposal to build vessels there is carried out the result will be disastrous.[40]

Captain Clarkson's concerns were certainly valid in some respects, as evidenced by the major problems arising from inadequate power supplies which were to hinder the dockyard throughout World War I. He had urged the construction of a new shipyard on another site. Had this recommendation been followed, the administrative difficulties that also occurred during the war would probably still have caused major problems.

The superintendent of the New South Wales Government Dockyard, Mr A E Cutler, continued as acting general manager of the Commonwealth Naval Dockyard until a new general manager was appointed.

A committee was set up in the United Kingdom to find a new general manager with warship training and experience. It selected Mr John King Salter, one of the three principal officers on the staff of the constructive manager of Chatham Dockyard, for the position.

John King Salter, general manager of the Commonwealth Naval Dockyard from 1914 to 1920.

King Salter, a graduate of Trinity College, Cambridge and a member of the Royal Corps of Naval Constructors was an experienced shipbuilder. He arrived at Cockatoo in 1914 and found that the dockyard lacked sufficient trained shipbuilders for the considerable warship building programme then in hand. Over the next few years he recruited a number of experienced people from Britain to supplement the Australian workforce.

The need to develop the island as a naval dockyard was to give him much greater difficulty.

As general manager he reported to the Naval Board, which dealt with matters of policy. There was no individual member of the Naval Board with total responsibility for the dockyard. The First Naval Member controlled the civil engineering at the island, with actual work being carried out by the Naval Works Branch. The Second Naval Member was largely responsible for personnel, and the Third Naval Member was in charge of stores and construction, including shipbuilding and mechanical engineering.[41]

With the approach of war, the Naval Board directed that the dockyard be under the control of the senior naval officer in Sydney, a practical approach for the management of the shipbuilding and repair work.[42] The Naval Board was still, however, to heavily influence the affairs of Cockatoo.

Shortly after the Commonwealth took over the yard, it became clear that the island's existing power supplies were inadequate. In April 1913, a consulting engineer, Mr George Julius (later Sir George) was engaged to report on the power supply system generally. He found that, not only was the system inadequate, but the generating plant consisted of a number of obsolete units in very bad condition, which would wear out soon.

In his report, submitted on 29 July 1913, he recommended that the existing steam equipment be replaced by a diesel plant, located inside the existing dock pump house, for a capital cost of £35,400. Other improvements to the system would increase the total cost to £41,950. Whilst the diesel plant would be more expensive to install, Julius pointed out that it would be much cheaper to run than a coal fired steam plant.[43]

This report on the condition of the boilers on the island prompted the Naval Board to order the plant to be shut down pending a detailed survey by a committee appointed for the purpose. Some of the boilers were condemned, and working around the clock, the dockyard installed two locomotive boilers to enable operations to resume.

Progress on a new power plant was slow, and hindered by differences of opinion between the acting general manager, Cutler, and the Naval Board. Plans and specifications were almost complete by late March 1914, when the newly arrived general manager, King Salter, reviewed the proposals. He did not like the reliance on imported fuel imposed by the selection of diesel engines, but more importantly, decided that the capacity of the plant should be doubled to provide for the additional workshop machinery that was needed throughout the dockyard. Six alternative schemes were then prepared, and finally, in September 1914, plans were approved for a steam plant to be installed in a new power station on the site of the existing dock pump house. Tenders for the new equipment closed in October 1915, but the new power station was not completed until after the war.

As a result of these delays, problems with power were so acute that, at one stage, the generators intended for HMAS *Brisbane* were used to supply electricity to the workshops.

The acquisition of new workshop machinery was no better. Whilst some progress had been made by the time he arrived, King Salter found that some equipment was urgently needed, and in April 1914 he advertised for tenders for machine tools in the Sydney newspapers. He also tried to advertise in the Commonwealth Government *Gazette*, and submitted a proof to Navy Office (in Melbourne) for approval. The advertisement was not allowed, and the Naval Board told King Salter that his action in advertising in the newspapers was irregular. Tenders had to be invited through Navy Office by advertisement in all states.

Despite the urgent need for at least some of the equipment, particularly a hydraulic press needed to make the boilers for the torpedo boat destroyers, little progress was made for many months. At the insistence of Navy Office, the dockyard prepared detailed specifications for the new machinery. This job took some five months, resulting in a pile of paper eight or nine feet high, for the 180 machines required. Tenders were finally invited by Navy Office, closing on 27 October 1915.

The Joint Committee of Public Accounts examined the administrative difficulties faced by the dockyard in detail. The Committee reported to the Commonwealth Parliament in October 1915. The report stated:

Top: The new power station under construction in February 1918. It was constructed around the old power station, which can be seen behind the chimney on the right.

Centre: The power station as completed. The generators (on the left) were removed in the 1960s but the air compressors and switchboard (right) were used until 1991, and are still there.

Making ample allowance for all extenuating circumstances, the Committee is unable to arrive at any other conclusion than that there has been undue delay in equipping the Dockyard with the necessary plant to enable the building of warships to be carried on expeditiously and economically. It is impossible to specify, even approximately, the loss to the Commonwealth on this account, but there is no doubt whatever that the lack of proper equipment at Cockatoo Island has been a prime factor — perhaps the principal one — in increasing beyond all reason, as will be shown later, the cost of the work executed at this Dockyard. Besides the direct loss in this respect, the handling of defective appliances and frequent breakdowns cannot but have had a demoralising effect on the workmen in still further reducing the output.

The efforts of Mr King Salter to remedy shortcomings when he took charge were not, in our opinion, adequately supported by the Naval Board. Some of the much wanted equipment was immediately within reach, and we consider the position was sufficiently serious to have justified without any hesitation the suspension of ordinary routine and regulation in favour of the most direct way to its acquisition. There was no question of an immediate lack of funds.[44]

The Committee also examined the store keeping practices in the dockyard, and found a number of serious shortcomings. There was a lack of proper storage space on the island, and King Salter told the Committee 'everything is so jumbled that we have to buy things from hand to mouth'.[45] Record keeping was poor, and there were a number of deficiencies, including over 900 tons of pig iron.

Before the Commonwealth took over, materials and equipment for the destroyers and the cruiser *Brisbane* had been purchased by the dockyard through the New South Wales Agent General in London. Following the transfer to the Commonwealth, all material requirements were processed by Navy Office, with orders for imported items being sent on to the Admiralty through the High Commissioner, a process that introduced much delay. Moreover, invoices and shipping documents did not come directly to the island, but through Navy Office, often arriving at Cockatoo a month or six weeks after the goods.

The Public Accounts Committee's report also stated:

Objection was taken to the present system of obtaining stores in small quantities. The quality also in many cases was very poor. Even some of the State contract supplies were not up to the Dockyard requirements, which were 'for the best of everything'. It was stated 'as quite possible' as the result of purchasing from hand to mouth as was done at Cockatoo Island, that some of the stores thus procured consisted of material which had been rejected by the Admiralty.[46]

Despite these difficulties, the Commonwealth Naval Dockyard achieved much during the war years, a tribute to the leadership of John King Salter and the skills of the Cockatoo people. The cost of the ships built during the war was, however, considerably higher than equivalent constructions in Britain, although their quality was at least as good.

HMAS *Brisbane* cost about twice as much as each of her sister ships *Sydney* and *Melbourne*. The destroyers were almost as expensive. This high cost was subject to much criticism, but the critics rarely took into account the actual circumstances faced by the builder.

By the end of World War I, Cockatoo had grown to a considerable size, and at the end of December 1919 employment reached its highest level ever, with 4085 people on the books. When King Salter left in 1920 to become constructive manager of the Royal Naval Dockyard at Simonstown, South Africa, the yard was building another cruiser, *Adelaide,* and several merchant ships for the Australian Commonwealth Line.

At the end of the war, the Admiralty sent Admiral of the Fleet Viscount Jellicoe of Scapa on a world tour of the Dominions and India to advise on naval defence requirements. In his report of 1919 he recommended that the Commodore in Charge, Sydney, should be responsible for the control of Cockatoo Island. This view differed from the findings of the Royal Commission into Naval and Defence Administration of 1918, which had proposed that control of ship construction and ship repair should be given to the general manager who would be responsible directly to the Naval Board.

On 25 October 1919 the Minister for the Navy, Sir Joseph Cook set up a committee to consider the administration of both Cockatoo Dockyard and Garden Island. The committee consisted of the First Naval Member, Rear Admiral Sir Percy Grant RN, the Second Naval Member, Commodore H L Cochrane RN, and Engineer Commander L Howell RN. Their report was submitted on 3 January 1920. In it they complained of a general lack of understanding of the principles of running dockyards, but expressed the view that no further expansion was possible at Cockatoo Island. They recommended that another site be selected for the dockyard, and were 'at a loss to understand how Cockatoo Island Dockyard came to be acquired from the New South Wales Government'. Their main recommendation was that 'since the government must, therefore, abandon the Yard as a Naval concern we suggest that it be handed over forthwith to the Ship Construction Branch of the Prime Minister's Department'.[47] The Ship Construction Branch had been established during the war with responsibility for the construction of merchant ships.

The government approved the change of administration that had been recommended, although the dockyard was not transferred until 28 June 1921. Throughout the period of administration by the Naval Board, it was clear that those responsible had little understanding of the needs of the dockyard, and the Naval Board was not in a position to manage shipbuilding and repair to the standard that would be expected by officers used to the resources and experience of the Admiralty. With impending transfer of responsibility to the Prime

Minister's Department, the events of early 1921 suggest that control of the dockyard was completely lost.

When the cruiser *Brisbane* and the torpedo boat destroyers were ordered from the State Government in 1912, payment was to be on the basis of cost plus 8 per cent profit. After transfer of the dockyard to the Commonwealth, the government paid the actual cost from the new construction budget allocation. The Joint Committee of Public Accounts in their 1915 report was critical of the accounting system used for the shipbuilding at Cockatoo, commenting:

> In trying to ascertain the value of the output of the Dock, or the cost of any particular undertaking, such as the construction of the cruiser *Brisbane* we are unable to arrive at anything like accuracy. The regular records of cost of materials imported for the warships are not available at Cockatoo, and further inquiry at the Navy Office and elsewhere does not enable us to lay our hands on the necessary documents.[48]

By mid-1920 the work on the refitting of transports and re-conversion for commercial service had been largely completed. The dockyard was building the cruiser HMAS *Adelaide* and the coal storage vessel *Mombah* for the RAN, and had orders for two 12,500-ton refrigerated cargo ships for the Commonwealth Line. Work on the cargo ships was 'in abeyance', and the acting general manager, James Clark, was reluctant to lose the men only then becoming available from the refit work. In August 1920 he sought an increase in funds allocated for navy construction for the 1920/21 financial year from £197,000 to £306,000. The estimates for the year had been closed for submission to Parliament by then, and the request could not be met.

Nevertheless Clark proceeded to transfer men to the naval work, and in January 1921 he was warned that the expenditure on the ships would exceed the total allocation. He was asked what additional funds would be required, and the reasons why it would not be possible to avoid the extra expenditure. He simply advised the Naval Board that it would not be possible to keep within the amount budgeted.

It became clear that the funds would be exhausted by the end of February 1921, and on the 21st of that month Clark asked for directions whether he should stop work and discharge 1800 of the 2500 employees at the dockyard. The Naval Board failed to take positive action, and the indecision continued until 9 March when the Naval Board instructed the Commodore Superintendent Sydney to inform the acting general manager that all work on the *Adelaide* and *Mombah* should cease. Work on both ships was suspended the following day, and the bulk of the workforce dismissed.

In early 1921 there had also been reports of the disappearance of stores and material from the island, and even gambling during working hours. On 21 March an inter-departmental committee was set up to examine these accusations, and the over-expenditure of funds. It consisted of Engineer Commander J L Deacon RN, Mr A Bolle from the Department of the Treasury, and Mr R Ford, from the Ship Construction Branch of the Prime Minister's Department. They reported on 1 and 5 April, very critical of the dockyard management for the over-expenditure, but finding a need only for improved procedures to deal with the other matters.

Parliament was not satisfied, and under pressure from the opposition, the Prime Minister set up a Royal Commission consisting of members of Parliament, which reported on 7 July 1921.[49] The Commission found no evidence of theft of stores, and felt that the rumours of gambling had been 'greatly magnified'. The report was very critical of the divided control of the dockyard, where the acting general manager was under the direction of the Commodore Superintendent, responsible to the Naval Board, but was also receiving conflicting instructions from the Minister in charge of shipbuilding. As an example, it referred to the instructions of the Minister that the yard should obtain as much private work as possible, whereas the Naval Board directed that the policy of the government was opposed to the dockyard entering into open competition with outside firms.

The report also addressed the importance of Cockatoo Dockyard to the naval defence of Australia:

> Cockatoo Dockyard is the only naval establishment of its kind in the Commonwealth, and in spite of certain limitations as regards size and docking facilities, we are of the opinion that it should be maintained in its efficiency for the purpose of effecting what ever repairs and fittings may be necessary for ships of war. It may be mentioned that the present docking facilities at Cockatoo Island cannot accommodate a ship larger than HMAS *Australia*.

> Evidence is before us that Cockatoo Dockyard compares most favourably with the best equipped Dockyards in the British Empire as regards machinery and appliances. Notwithstanding this fact, we are of the opinion that the Dockyard is handicapped by the want of a dock capable of taking the largest capital ship at present in the Royal Navy or such a ship as is likely to be built and may visit these shores.[50]

The Commission recommended that a permanent naval base be established under the complete control of the Navy Department. They also noted that there was insufficient work, naval and commercial, to keep both Cockatoo Island and Garden Island fully employed. They recommended that, until such time as a permanent naval base was established, all navy work (with the exception of minor repairs to be done at Garden Island) should be carried out by the Ship Construction Branch Board of Control at Cockatoo Dockyard on a mutually agreed basis under the direct supervision of naval officers selected by the Navy Department.

Two docks larger than the Sutherland Dock were built in Australia during World War II. The Cairncross Dock in Brisbane was completed in June 1944. It was 830 feet long and 110 feet wide. The need for a capital ship dock (capable of docking the largest battle ships and aircraft carriers) was not satisfied until the completion of the Captain Cook Dock at Garden Island in 1945.

Surprisingly, the Commission made no comment about the over-spending or the dismissals, although two members of the Commission did so in an Addendum. They said:

> The manner of the dismissal of the workmen at Cockatoo Dock seems to have been heartless and unjustifiable, the reason being that the Annual Vote for Naval Construction had at the time of the stoppage of work become exhausted ...

> In our opinion there has been unnecessary delay in recommencing operations and undue hardship inflicted thereby on many workmen and their families. We regret that such should be the case, and we now strongly recommend that work should be resumed immediately.[51]

A minority report by W J McWilliams supported the views of Rear Admiral Sir William Clarkson, the Third Naval Member of the Naval Board. McWilliams said that Cockatoo Island 'can never be an eco-nomically worked dockyard' and:

> To continue to combine naval work per se with the building of mercantile ships can only perpetuate the past blunders, extravagance, and absurdly high cost in construction and repairs.[52]

Highly critical of the dual control of affairs at Cockatoo Island, he sup-ported the construction of a proper naval dock, with Cockatoo and Garden Island being retained only until such time as an up-to-date dockyard was completed.

> As a naval dockyard Cockatoo Island is an impossibility. To quote Rear Admiral Sir William Clarkson, it can only be regarded as a stop-gap; and every pound spent on that site is so much money wasted. There is not one redeem-ing feature in Cockatoo Island as a modern dockyard.[53]

So ended a most unhappy period in the dockyard's history. There is no doubt that the acting general manager exceeded his authority by incur-ring the over-expenditure. However, the Naval Board did not give him adequate support, and the subsequent inquiries did little to address the real problems of management of the dockyard or the poor treatment of the people of Cockatoo.

COCKATOO ISLAND DOCKYARD

In May 1921, a Shipbuilding Board of Control had been created to man-age the Commonwealth's programme of merchant shipbuilding. It con-sisted of Mr Robert Farquhar, who was appointed Director of Commonwealth Shipbuilding, as chairman, and Mr H C Brown, then secretary of the Ship Construction Branch of the Prime Minister's

Department, as finance member. Farquhar, a naval architect, had previously been general manager of the Walkers shipyard, in Maryborough, Queensland.

The functions of the Shipbuilding Board of Control included the control and supervision of the government shipbuilding yards at Cockatoo Island and Williamstown in Victoria, and the placing of both yards on a sound business footing. The control of Cockatoo Island was taken over from the Navy on 29 June 1921, and work on the *Adelaide* and *Mombah* was resumed on 18 July.

In March 1923, rumours circulated that the government intended to sell Cockatoo Island, however the Prime Minister, Mr Bruce, stated in mid-April that the dockyard was to be retained. On 1 September 1923, in accordance with the provisions of the Commonwealth *Shipping Act 1923*, Cockatoo Island (along with nearby Schnapper Island) was transferred to and vested in the Australian Commonwealth Shipping Board for its management and control. The Commonwealth Line was also taken over by the Shipping Board.

Mr Farquhar was appointed a member of the Shipping Board, and as director of shipbuilding was responsible for the management and operations of Cockatoo Dockyard.

The value of Cockatoo Dockyard was assessed at £400,000 at the time of transfer, written down from an original cost of £2,275,000. Under Section 14 (4) of the Shipping Act, the Board was empowered to carry on the business of manufacturer, engineer, dock owner, shipbuilder and repairer. The intention was to put the dockyard on a commercial basis: it was to pay taxes and interest, and was to use every possible legitimate endeavour to obtain private work, recovering overhead charges and a reasonable profit.

The docking and repair of the Commonwealth Line steamers provided the yard with a base load of work, and a number of contracts were obtained for forgings, castings, boilers and general engineering work. Navy work was generally limited to dockings, with most refits being carried out by the Navy at Garden Island.

As a general rule, the yard quoted fixed prices for private work. For work for the Navy and the Commonwealth Line it was usual to charge the actual cost of labour and material plus 42.5 per cent for overhead and 10 per cent profit. The yard completed the construction of the refrigerated cargo steamers *Fordsdale* and *Ferndale* at cost, however fixed prices were quoted for other ships, which included the Commonwealth Lighthouse Service steamers *Cape Leeuwin*, *Cape York*, and *Cape Otway*, and the seaplane carrier HMAS *Albatross* for the RAN. All returned a small profit, less than two per cent on sales.

By the middle of the 1920s, the amount of government work available was insufficient to fully utilise the dockyard's resources and commercial orders were a valuable part of the yard's business. Private industry complained at times that Cockatoo Dockyard quoted intentionally low prices in order to obtain work, and that losses on private work had been made up from undue profits on government work, although surviving records do not support this contention.

The most controversial issue was the winning of an order from the Sydney Municipal Council for the Bunnerong Power Station. The dockyard and 11 other firms had tendered for the supply, erection and maintenance of six turbo-alternator sets for the Council's Bunnerong Power Station at Botany Bay. The dockyard's tender in association with Metropolitan Vickers Limited and the New South Wales Government Dockyard at Walsh Island in Newcastle was successful, however the New South Wales Chamber of Manufacturers objected on the grounds that Cockatoo Island was not independent of government control.

On 27 April 1926, the Prime Minister referred the matter to the Parliamentary Joint Committee of Public Accounts in the following terms:

> With reference to the investigations of your Committee into the activities of the Commonwealth Shipping Board, I desire to inform you that complaints have been made to this government in connection with a contract recently secured by the Board from the Sydney Municipal Council for the manufacture of heavy electrical machinery.
>
> It is contended that the manufacture of heavy electrical machinery for land purposes is outside the legitimate functions of a Government Dockyard, and constitutes an unwarranted and unreasonable incursion into the field of private enterprise.
>
> It is further contended that considerations other than ordinary commercial principles were responsible for the placing of the order, inasmuch as the Dockyard quoted £661,224 for a job which included only 55 per cent of Australian work, whilst a competing Australian firm quoted £619,173 with 96 per cent of Australian work.
>
> The Government would be glad if you could make it convenient for your Committee to immediately investigate the circumstances surrounding this particular contract, and advise whether the foregoing statements are correct. The Government is particularly anxious to know at as early date as possible whether in accepting this contract, the Dockyard is responsible for the placing of orders abroad which would otherwise have gone to Australian firms and Australian workmen.[54]

Whilst the Committee was not unanimous in its views, it reported to Parliament in November 1927 that an incursion into the field of private enterprise had occurred, for the following reasons:

> (a) the Dockyard and the plant have been handed over to the Board at greatly reduced capital value;
>
> (b) although the Shipping Act provides that the debentures shall bear interest payable half-yearly, and the Board makes provision therefor in its books, no

interest has been paid to the Treasury, and the Board consequently enjoys the use of such money without cost;

(c) whilst provision has to be made by the Board for rates and taxes, no payments on these accounts have been demanded;

(d) any losses incurred by the Dockyard will have to be made good at the expense of the taxpayers of Australia.[55]

The Committee recognised the importance of Cockatoo Dockyard to the defence of Australia, and the obligation on the management of the yard to secure such work as would enable it to keep the dockyard in active and profitable operation. It suggested that if certain naval work then being carried out at Garden Island were sent to Cockatoo there would be less need to seek outside work. This suggestion was resisted by the Navy, who sought to justify the retention of the work at Garden Island because of (in part) its 'secret and confidential nature'.

Meanwhile, the Attorney General approved an action to be brought by the Commonwealth in the High Court of Australia on behalf of Mr Frank Edwards, secretary of the Chamber of Manufacturers in New South Wales, against the Australian Commonwealth Shipping Board and the Municipal Council of Sydney. In relation to the agreement entered into between the Shipping Board and the Council on 1 April 1926 for the construction of the generating plant, he sought:

(1) A declaration that the said agreement is beyond the powers of the said Shipping Board;

(2) A declaration that the said Shipping Board is not entitled to utilize or expend its properties, assets or funds in furtherance of such agreement;

(3) An injunction restraining the defendants and each of them from further proceeding with the agreement.[56]

The High Court heard the matter in Sydney in August 1927, and in its written reasons handed down on 1 November 1927 stated:

The Parliament has only such power as is expressly or by necessary implication vested in it by the Constitution. There is no power which enables the Parliament or the Executive Government to set up manufacturing or engineering businesses for general commercial purposes. The trade and commerce power was referred to, but that is a power to regulate trade and commerce with other countries and among the States. The naval and defence power coupled with the incidental power conferred by sec. 51 (XXXIX.) was also relied upon. Extensive as is that power, still it does not authorize the establishment of businesses for the purpose of trade and wholly unconnected with any purpose of naval or military defence. It was suggested, however, that the dockyard and workshops on Cockatoo Island were required for the purposes of the naval defence of the Commonwealth, and that it was impracticable to maintain them efficiently for that purpose unless the managing body — the Shipping Board — was authorized to enter upon general manufacturing and engineering activities, because the cost of maintenance of the works would be excessive and the working staff would be unable to obtain proper experience. Despite the practical difficulties facing the Commonwealth in the maintenance of its dockyard and works, the power of naval and military defence does not warrant these activities in the ordinary conditions of peace, whatever be the position in time of war or in conditions arising out of or connected with war.

The executive power of the Commonwealth was also touched upon; but it is impossible to say that an activity unwarranted in express terms by the Constitution is nevertheless vested in the Executive, and can therefore be conferred as an executive function upon such a body as the Shipping Board.[57]

On 17 March 1927 the Attorney General reported to Parliament:

The view of the High Court substantially was, that there are no powers in the Constitution which enable the Commonwealth Parliament by statute to authorise a corporation created by it to carry on business of a general kind unconnected with the specific legislative powers of the Commonwealth.[58]

The loss of this contract and the wider implications of the High Court decision were a serious blow for Cockatoo Dockyard. The loss to Britain of the contract for the construction of a new cruiser for the RAN was only partly compensated for by the order for HMAS *Albatross*, and the workload of the yard continued to decline. Employment fell steadily from 1290 in 1928 to 560 by 1932.

In April 1928, Prime Minister Bruce, announced the sale of the Commonwealth Line of steamers, and the government's intention to seek tenders for the leasing of Cockatoo Island Dockyard. Tenders were invited on 22 January 1929, closing on 30 March that year, for the lease of the Island for a period of 20 years, with the option for renewal for a further term, not exceeding 10 years. The closing date for tenders was later extended to 5 November, but no tenders were received.

Following the sale of the Commonwealth Line, the administration of Cockatoo Dockyard became the main remaining duty of the

The dockyard management in the 1920s. In the front row are Jack Payne, Robert Farquahar and John Wilson.

Commonwealth Shipping Board. Robert Farquhar retired in 1928, and was succeeded by Mr Jack Payne, who became chairman of the Shipping Board and general manager of Cockatoo Dockyard.

Jack Payne came to Sydney from England in 1912 under contract to the New South Wales Government, having accepted the position of engineering manager at Cockatoo. He was responsible for all the engineering work of the yard until 1921, when he became manager, responsible to the director (Farquhar) for all the dockyard's operations. He was also chairman of the Institution of Engineers Australia in 1924-25.

In the 1929 to 1932 period the dockyard found it hard to obtain sufficient work to cover the cost of maintaining the yard. The Bunnerong decision greatly restricted the opportunities, although the dockyard continued to tender for major work when the opportunity arose. For example, in 1930 the yard submitted a £250,000 tender for the supply of steel water pipes to the Metropolitan Water Supply and Sewerage Board. The Board acknowledged that the dockyard's price was the lowest, but eliminated the tender because of possible complications from the Bunnerong decision.

The dockyard had made a small profit for a number of years (£5096 in 1924/25, falling to £2261 in 1926/27), but by 1931 was struggling to recover costs and was eating into reserves. In February 1931 Jack Payne wrote a long letter to the secretary of the Prime Minister's Department setting out the problems facing the yard. He urged for the provision of £50,000 in the estimates for the Prime Minister's Department for the financial year 1931/32 as the minimum expenditure to maintain the dockyard in an operational condition. In its last year of operation by the Commonwealth, Cockatoo Dockyard lost about £70,000, without allowing for interest and depreciation.

Jack Payne did not live to see the resolution of the dockyard's problems. He died suddenly in his office on the island on 13 July 1932.

INTO PRIVATE HANDS

Whilst no formal tenders had been received for the lease of the dockyard, some interest had been expressed by Australian business. In January 1933, the Prime Minister, Mr Lyons, announced that, following long negotiations, Cockatoo Island would be leased to an Australian company.

On 3 February 1933 an agreement was signed between the Australian Commonwealth Shipping Board and Cockatoo Docks and Engineering Company Limited to lease Cockatoo Island for a period of 21 years, from 1 March 1933. The Company had been founded in January specifically for the purpose.

The lease was authorised by the *Cockatoo Island Dockyard Agreement Act 1933*. The rent to be paid by the Company was based on a percentage of turnover, with a minimum of £1000 and a maximum of

3/9/34

Cockatoo Dock & Eng. Co.
Cockatoo.

To   Umbrella,   12/6
 "   1 Doz. Eggs.   1/4
                       13/10..

broken by sheep.
While on my way home from shopping on Friday night, laden with parcels and thereby unable to protect myself, this sheep started butting me from just a little beyond Mr Morgan's right up to our gate. I do consider it is just beyond a joke as it is unnecessary for me to say that, seldom do we women

on the Island come on without carrying parcels.

                    Mrs Izatt

The sheep altered life on Cockatoo Island in subtle ways, as illustrated by this letter. (J C Jeremy Collection)

£50,000 per year. In the event that the government did not place government work at the dockyard to the value of £40,000 each year for any of the first three years, the Commonwealth would contribute towards the loss (if any) sustained by the Company in that year up to £16,666 on a pound for pound basis.

The Company was obliged to do nothing that would impair the efficiency of the island as a dockyard for naval purposes. Priority had to be given to Defence work, but the Company was also to receive preference for naval work usually carried out at the dockyard.

The chairman of the Company was George Davis (later Sir George, and founder of the Davis Gelatine Company). The managing director was Norman Frazer. Whilst he was new to shipbuilding, Frazer was an experienced industrialist having run his own large timber and saw-milling company, Bell & Frazer, of Balmain. He introduced many economies at the dockyard, and the company remained very lean during the 1930s. Frazer also introduced sheep to Cockatoo Island to control the grass, and sheep remained part of the dockyard environment thereafter.

At last Cockatoo was able to undertake work for any customer free from the restrictions which had so limited it during the previous decade. The Company reported a net profit of £510 at the end of its first year (equivalent to 0.4 per cent of sales). The workload gradually grew with a modest programme of naval shipbuilding, ship repair, and a wide range of commercial work, from heavy engineering to the manufacture of equipment for the dairy industry.

By the time World War II was approaching Cockatoo Dockyard was the only shipyard of any size in Australia actively building ships, and it was ready to help resuscitate an Australian shipbuilding industry, as described in Chapter 6.

During the 1930s, contracts for the construction of the sloops and other ships for the RAN were placed on a fixed price incentive basis, which worked very well. The contract price was a maximum price, with any savings being shared two-thirds by the Navy, and one third by the Company. Payment for Navy refit and repair work was charged at actual cost for labour and materials plus 42.5 per cent overhead and 10 per cent profit.

The 1933 lease gave the Commonwealth the right to resume control of all or part of the dockyard in the event of war. However following the outbreak of World War II, it was agreed that resumption would not occur, but that a change in the trading arrangements was appropriate to limit the profit that might be earned by the Company.

Discussions began September 1940, led for the Navy by Mr H G Brain OBE MSM, the business member of the Naval Board, and in November 1941 the Wartime Agreement was signed. It operated from 1 March 1940, but included a special clause to deal with the period from September 1939 to February 1940. The agreement was intended to terminate six months after hostilities ended. This was later changed to provide for termination after six months notice by either party, and the agreement with modification remained in effect until 1954. The signatories to the agreement were the Company, the Secretary of the Department of the Navy, and the Australian Shipbuilding Board, which had been constituted in accordance with the National Security (Shipbuilding) Regulations under the *National Security Act 1940*. The landlord, the Australian Commonwealth Shipping Board, was not consulted and was not a party to the agreement.

The Wartime Agreement provided for the Commonwealth to pay the full cost of operations, except for taxation and special company expenses. The Company was paid a management fee based upon turnover plus 50 per cent of the net revenue from ship docking. The management fee reduced from a maximum of 2.0 per cent at a turnover of £1,325,000 (or less) to a minimum of 1.5 per cent at a turnover of £2,000,000 (or more). Wage rates paid in the dockyard were not to be varied without Commonwealth approval, and commercial work, other than work of a minor nature, was not to be accepted without the approval of the Commonwealth. In effect, the Company became the manager of the dockyard for the Commonwealth.

Throughout the period of the Wartime Agreement, the Company was not called upon to meet any charges of a capital nature: the Commonwealth paid all costs of improvements and new plant and machinery. The effect of the Wartime Agreement was to reduce net profit on sales, before tax, from 6.8 per cent in 1938 to an average of 2.7 per cent for the war years.

THE VICKERS YEARS

Cockatoo had enjoyed a working relationship with Vickers, the large British shipbuilding and engineering company, for many years. Some of the workmen and managers had been trained at the Vickers shipyard at

Sir Keith Smith
escorting Mrs
R G Menzies at the
launching of
HMAS *Voyager* on
1 March 1952.
(J C Jeremy Collection)

Captain G I D
Hutcheson CBE RAN
(Retd), managing
director 1947 to 1962;
chairman 1962 to 1965.

Barrow in Furness before coming to Australia. Others had been sent there for training from Sydney. In 1937, Vickers Armstrongs Limited obtained a small nominee share holding in Cockatoo Docks & Engineering Company Pty. Limited, and the Vickers representative in Australia, Sir Keith Smith, joined the Board in 1938.

With his brother Ross, Keith Smith had flown the Vimy bomber that had been entered by Vickers for the 1919 Commonwealth of Australia prize for the first flight by Australians from Britain to Australia in a British aircraft. The flight took 28 days, and the brothers were knighted for their efforts. Sir Ross Smith was killed in a flying accident in 1920.

In 1947 Vickers Limited bought the majority of the shares in the Company as part of the expansion of Vickers' engineering interests in Australia.[59] Norman Frazer became chairman, and Engineer Captain G I D Hutcheson, RAN (Retired) became managing director. Hutcheson was an engineering graduate of Adelaide University, who had joined the RAN in 1918. Highly regarded in the Navy and in industry, he had been the first principal naval overseer at Cockatoo between June 1939 and August 1942, and later general manager of the Garden Island Naval Dockyard.

Sir Keith Smith succeeded Norman Frazer as chairman when Frazer retired in 1949. Sir Keith died in late 1955, and in early 1956 Mr A R L Wiltshire, of Melbourne was appointed to replace him as chairman of the Company.

In 1949 the government decided to repeal the Commonwealth *Shipping Act 1923*, and to abolish the Australian Commonwealth Shipping Board, whose only remaining task was the administration of the Cockatoo Island and Schnapper Island leases. Both the Company and the Board argued unsuccessfully against the change, and the *Cockatoo & Schnapper Islands Act 1949*, transferred all right, title and interest of the Australian Commonwealth Shipping Board to the Commonwealth Government. The control of the management of the Island became the responsibility of the Minister for the Navy, and the Cockatoo Island Lease Supervisory Board was formed to administer the lease and the facilities.

In February 1954, the lease was renewed for a further 20 years and 8 months,. and the trading arrangements were reviewed. Inflation was eroding the value of the Company's reward (the management fee), and the Australian Shipbuilding Board no longer wanted to be involved with the operation of the dockyard. With the termination of the Wartime Agreement, contracts would have been managed under the terms of the 1933 lease. However the parties recognised that it would have been quite impractical for the Company to give fixed prices for the naval work then in hand, as information was being provided by the Navy on a progressive basis, and the scope of work was subject to constant change.

Therefore a new Trading Agreement, signed on 16 May 1956 (with effect from 1 July 1954), increased the management fee payable to the Company by altering the levels of turnover at which the 2.0 and 1.5 per cent fees applied. These levels were changed again in July 1963 by a new Trading Agreement. This agreement also provided for the profit from trading, rather than being credited to the Commonwealth, as had been the case previously, to be shared between the Company and the Commonwealth, based on the relative value of Commonwealth and non-Commonwealth turnover.

Some changes were then made to the constitution of the Cockatoo Island Lease Supervisory Board, which became the Cockatoo Island Lease Supervisory Committee in 1957. At that time the Chairman became the Navy's General Overseer and Superintendent of Inspection, East Australia Area, with a representative of the Department of Works as Member, and the Area Finance representative, Department of the Navy, as Member and Secretary.

Since the start of the lease in 1933, the Company had consistently traded profitably. After the war, the profit made from non-government work was sufficient to provide for the management fee, together with a substantial payment into consolidated revenue. For example, in the five years ending in 1960, the total turnover of the Company was £14,500,000, comprising £9,500,000 Navy work and £5,000,000 commercial work. The trading profit was £607,000 of which £263,000 was paid into consolidated revenue after deducting the management fee of £344,000. The Company also paid the Commonwealth £115,000 in company tax in the period. The dividend paid to Vickers Limited was only £94,000, however this return was considered adequate as the Commonwealth paid all capital equipment and major maintenance costs and the trading risk was low.

Captain R G Parker OBE RAN (Retd) (centre), managing director 1962 to 1971, on board *Stuart* during sea trials in October 1962, with assistant shipyard superintendents Alan Mitchell (left) and George McGoogan (right).
(RAN photograph)

The loss made by the Company on the construction of the passenger vehicle ship *Empress of Australia* in 1964–65 highlighted the fact that the Trading Agreement provided for the Commonwealth to share the losses as well as the profits from the dockyard's trading. The total loss on the contract was £487,259 of which the Commonwealth's share amounted to £168,386.

This loss also drew attention to the need for change in the management arrangements for the dockyard. There was little incentive for the Company to improve efficiency and none to invest capital in the facilities to improve productivity. Further impetus was given by a Navy review of naval shipbuilding and repair requirements. This review redefined the role of the three Commonwealth owned dockyards at Garden Island, Williamstown and Cockatoo Island. The role of Cockatoo Dockyard was defined as:

(a) The construction, modernisation and conversion of warships up to approximately 4000 tons standard displacement and complexity equivalent to a Type 12 Destroyer Escort (1964 programme), and auxiliary ships up to the maximum capacity of the slipways.

(b) Major structural repair of damaged naval ships in an emergency.

(c) The refit of naval surface ships beyond the capacity of Garden Island and Williamstown: auxiliaries from 1967 and some warships from 1973.

(d) The main refitting base for RAN submarines.

(e) The main refitting base for RAN patrol craft.

(f) The manufacture and repair of stores, spares and equipment for RAN logistic authorities, as required.[60]

In addition, the dockyard was expected to undertake as much commercial work as possible, particularly to fill the gaps in the naval programme.

To fulfil this expectation it was clear that the management systems of the Company would need to be improved, and the dockyard modernised to provide the specialised facilities needed to enable the introduction of modern shipbuilding methods.

In 1965, the Company engaged the P-E Consulting Group (Australia) to review the management structure. In 1966 the Department of the Navy and the Company jointly commissioned the same company to prepare an overall plan for the development of the dockyard. The plan included the design of facilities for the refit of Oberon class submarines (that were then under construction in Scotland), and plans for the modernisation of the shipyard.

The report on the management structure was completed in January 1967. It emphasised the need for considerable change to the organisation of the company and the culture of the management if the dockyard was to adequately fulfil its role. The company partly implemented the consultant's recommendations, but perhaps the greatest need was for new trading arrangements to provide the incentive for change.

The proposed plans for the development of the dockyard were finished in September 1967, and resulted in extensive improvements, as described in Chapter 3.

In 1962, Captain Hutcheson had retired as managing director of the Company, remaining as chairman. He then became the managing director of Vickers Australia Limited, which had been formed in 1956 as the holding company for the Vickers' engineering operations in Australia, other than Cockatoo. He died in 1965.

At Cockatoo, he was succeeded as managing director by another retired RAN engineering officer, Captain R G Parker OBE. Roger Parker had been principal naval overseer at Cockatoo between September 1948 and March 1949, and had been general manager of both the

Williamstown and Garden Island dockyards before coming to Cockatoo in March 1959 as assistant managing director.

With Parker due to retire in 1971, the lease expiring in 1974, and a demanding naval role for the dockyard, there was a need for an early review of the lease and trading arrangements to provide security of tenure, better reward for Vickers, and proper incentive for improved productivity. In July 1969, the Company submitted a proposal to the Navy for major changes to the relationship with the Commonwealth.

Negotiations continued for two years, and were led for the Company by Parker and the Managing Director of Vickers Australia (and Vickers Holdings Limited) Peter Scott Maxwell. The First Assistant Secretary, Finance and Materiel (Department of the Navy), Mat Hyland OBE led the Commonwealth negotiating team.

Richard (Dick) Humbley, managing director 1971 to 1981.

Scott Maxwell had come to Australia in 1967 from Barrow. A submarine Engineering Officer during World War II, he had become involved in the development of HTP (high test peroxide) propulsion for submarines, and later the Royal Navy nuclear submarine programme.[61] He was also a director of Cockatoo, and until he retired in 1986 was a driving force and inspiration for all involved in the dockyard's affairs.

The new Trading Agreement and Lease took effect from 1 January 1972, for a period of 21 years. It provided for a much more commercial relationship between the Company and the Commonwealth, with the Company assuming full responsibility for any profit or loss. Commonwealth work was to be undertaken as far as practical on fixed or firm prices, and when this was not possible, on an incentive basis, or actual cost plus 5.0 per cent. The Company became responsible, with some exceptions, for the provision of replacement plant and machinery, and for regular maintenance, for which a sum of at least 5.0 per cent of the cost of turnover was to be set aside each year, to be recovered through the dockyard overhead. The Commonwealth remained responsible for buildings, wharves, cranes and services, although the Company could invest in these facilities if it wished.

Priority was to be given to submarines at all times. Other scheduled naval work and major commercial work taken on with the specific approval of the Navy was given priority over unscheduled Commonwealth requirements. The Company was given no preference for Commonwealth work, other than submarines. Rent was established at $500,000 for 1972, to be varied each year in accordance with movements in the consumer price index, and there was provision for review of the rent in the event that there was less than one submarine under refit at the dockyard.

Roger Parker retired in October 1971, and was succeeded by Captain R R W Humbley, RAN (Retired). Dick Humbley had joined the RAN volunteer reserve in 1941 after graduating from the University of Sydney with a Bachelor of Economics degree. He later transferred to the RAN and from 1961 to 1964 he had been closely involved with Cockatoo affairs when, as the general overseer and superintendent of inspection he had been chairman of the Cockatoo Island Lease Supervisory Committee. His last RAN post was director general naval production at Navy Office in Canberra.

In 1972, the name of the Company was changed to Vickers Cockatoo Dockyard Pty Limited to reflect the links with Vickers. The dockyard was looking forward to a major project for the Navy, the construction of a fast combat support ship (AOE) of 20,000 tons, in addition to the refit of the Oberon class submarines, which had begun the previous year. In December 1972 the government changed, and the AOE project and the light destroyer (DDL) project (for which Cockatoo had tendered for the detailed design in association with Gibbs & Cox, and Canadian Vickers) were reviewed. The new Whitlam Labor Government cancelled both projects in August 1973.

As early as June 1973 it was clear to the Company that the new Trading Agreement was not working as well as planned, and in October 1973 it proposed that the new agreement be reviewed. The Company contended that the assumptions on which the rent and reward formula had been based were no longer valid, and the formula for the recovery of overheads set out in the agreement placed the Company at a disability in obtaining commercial work in the circumstances of greatly reduced workload. Other problems had arisen with the arrangements for maintenance, insurance and indemnity, and the replacement of plant.

In July 1975 these matters were referred to a Defence (Industrial) Committee panel. Mr N F Stevens OBE, a partner of Robertson, Darling & Wolfenden (Chartered Accountants), and vice-chairman of the Defence (Industrial) Committee was appointed chairman of the panel.

In September of that year the panel made a number of recommendations, not all of which were accepted by the Commonwealth. A number of changes were agreed, in particular to the overhead recovery formula, and to rent. Rent became the sum of $550,000 plus 15 per cent of profit before tax, after deducting the base figure, and maintenance expenditure was linked to the cost of direct labour rather than total turnover. These changes were approved by the Minister for Defence and took effect in September 1976.

A number of issues remained unresolved, in particular uncertainties regarding insurance of Commonwealth assets on Cockatoo Island and the provision of a permanent shore depot and car park for dockyard employees.

Meanwhile, the group relationship with the Vickers in Britain continued to be of great value to

The directors of Vickers Cockatoo Dockyard Pty Limited in June 1977. Standing (l to r) J C Jeremy (technical director), P J Pannell, P D Scott Maxwell DSC, R F Jones (commercial director), C J Harper. Seated (l to r) J Coleman (production director), R Humbley (managing director), E P M Harty (chairman), Sir Gregory Kater. Inset (l to r) W Richardson CBE DL, G M Bunning and Sir John Wilson. (Douglass Baglin)

Cockatoo, as a means of training staff and keeping in touch with current technology, particularly relating to submarines. After 1972, the close link was maintained by the presence of the chairman of the Vickers Shipbuilding Group at Barrow in Furness on the Cockatoo board. Appointed in January 1972, Sir Leonard Redshaw retired in 1976 and was replaced by William ('Bill') Richardson.

In 1977 the aircraft and shipbuilding interests of Vickers in Britain were nationalised. A technical aid agreement had been set in place before nationalisation took effect, but the links weakened rapidly after 1980. Bill Richardson remained a director of Cockatoo until he retired in 1984. His calm, friendly advice based on his long practical shipbuilding experience was greatly appreciated by the management team at Cockatoo during the difficult contract for the construction of HMAS *Success*.

By 1977, the changes to the trading arrangements were beginning to show results, with net profit before tax rising from only one per cent in 1972 to nearly three per cent, although profits had been affected by losses on some commercial contracts.

With the dockyard operating on a more commercial basis, Vickers considered it appropriate for Vickers Cockatoo Dockyard Pty Limited to be owned by their Australian subsidiary Vickers Australia Limited rather than directly through their holding company Vickers Holdings Pty Limited. Accordingly in June 1978, Vickers Holdings sold Cockatoo to Vickers Australia by the allocation of 937,728 ordinary $1.00 shares in Vickers Australia to Vickers Holdings. This valued Cockatoo at about $1,687,100, and although some analysts questioned the valuation in view of the low profits of Cockatoo, particularly in 1973 and 1974, the purchase was approved by the Vickers Australia shareholders.

John Jeremy, managing director 1981 to 1986, chief executive 1986 to 1991.

There was a general reduction in the amount of commercial work at Cockatoo in the 1970s. This was partly a result of a general decline in ship repair in the Port of Sydney, but also the growth in heavy engineering capability throughout Australia that had occurred in the years after the war. The facilities at Cockatoo Island were no longer unique, and the island and shipyard location became a disadvantage in tendering for work, except that which was unusual and difficult, or which needed the specialised skills of Cockatoo.

By 1978, most of the work at Cockatoo was for the RAN, and the majority was undertaken on a cost-plus basis. On a number of occasions the Company suggested that there should be a move towards fixed price or incentive contracting for the submarine refits. The RAN was reluctant to change because of the difficulty in accurately defining the task and a lack of resources to fully specify the work in advance.

The Trading Agreement called up the Commonwealth's Standard Conditions for the Determination of Cost of Cost-plus Contracts as the standard for the calculation of the admissible overheads for cost-plus work at Cockatoo. Perfectly suitable for application by a contractor where the cost-plus work was a small part of the total turnover, they proved inadequate at Cockatoo and a number of disputes arose over admissibility of costs, which remained unresolved for nearly ten years.

By 1983, the Navy's project for the acquisition of a new class of submarines to replace the Oberon class was well underway. The Company believed that there was a need for early planning for a review of the Trading Agreement and Lease if Cockatoo was to have any opportunity to participate in this project, which was to run well beyond the end of the lease. Proposals for an early review were made in 1984, and again in December 1985, when changes in the submarine refit contracts to some form of fixed price were again proposed. Despite many discussions, no progress was made.

Meanwhile, there had been a number of changes in the Company. In 1981, the post-war custom of having a retired naval officer at the helm of Cockatoo was broken by the appointment of John Jeremy to succeed Dick Humbley as managing director on the latter's retirement in September. Jeremy had started at Cockatoo in 1960 as an apprentice ship draughtsman. He graduated in naval architecture from the University of New South Wales in 1967, and spent some time in Britain on a Vickers scholarship, the first awarded to an Australian. On his return, he held positions in the planning and technical areas before being appointed to the board as technical director in 1976.

At the corporate level, Vickers Australia Limited merged with the Commonwealth Steel Company Limited in 1984 to form Comsteel Vickers Limited. The new company was 38 per cent owned by Vickers Limited and 38 per cent by BHP, with the remaining shares held by various institutions and the Australian public. The name of Vickers Cockatoo Dockyard Pty Limited was changed to Cockatoo Dockyard Pty Limited the same year. In February 1986, Comsteel Vickers was acquired by Australian National Industries Limited, and Cockatoo's long association with Vickers ended.

The change of ownership brought with it a change in management style. Vickers' overseas subsidiaries were usually managed by boards with a strong representation of capable local non-executive directors.[62] Whilst most of the Australian subsidiaries became divisions of Vickers Australia during the 1970s, Cockatoo retained its board of directors and continued to operate as a distinct entity within the Vickers Australia group. This was considered necessary at the time because of the Company's special relationship with the Commonwealth.

When ANI took over the Company in 1986, all the non-executive directors resigned. In keeping with the usual ANI management style, the executive directors — John Jeremy (managing director), Ron Jones (commercial director), Charles Yandell (production director), Roger Seymour (technical director) and John Hines (personnel director) — also resigned from the board later in the year. The board of Cockatoo then comprised the managing director of ANI, Neil Jones, the finance director of ANI, John Maher, and Bob Cox, an executive director of ANI.

THE FINAL PERIOD

There had also been changes in the Commonwealth's administrative arrangements for Cockatoo Dockyard. In 1982, the Cockatoo Island Lease Supervisory Committee, which had worked well for many years, was abolished and the responsibility for Cockatoo Dockyard was transferred to the Defence Shipbuilding Division of the recently formed Department of Defence Support. This department was disbanded in December 1984, and the responsibility for the management and administration of Cockatoo Dockyard was passed to the Defence Industry Division of the Department of Defence. This role was again transferred to the Logistics Division of the Department of Defence following a departmental reorganisation in August 1987.

From the Company's point of view, these changes introduced delay and indecision into the Commonwealth's management of their obligations under the Trading Agreement and Lease, as new people took time to become familiar with the, often long, history of the current issues.

In October 1986, the Commonwealth agreed with the company that the Trading Agreement was not working in accordance with the needs of the 1980s, and expressed the view that the expectations of both parties were not fully capable of realisation. They acknowledged that there should be less Commonwealth intrusion into financial matters, were keen to see the relationship on a more commercial footing.

In the early 1980s, the Department of Defence reviewed defence shipbuilding requirements, and the likely future demand for the existing refit capacity. On 1 April 1987 the Minister for Defence, Kim Beazley announced the government's intention to sell the Williamstown Naval Dockyard in Victoria, and not to renew the lease of Cockatoo Island Dockyard beyond the end of the refit work on the Oberon class submarines. In his statement he said:

> The Commonwealth owned dockyard on Cockatoo Island, Sydney, NSW, has also had a long history in shipbuilding and ship repair. The yard recently produced HMAS *Success* and has an on-going role as the refit yard for Oberon class submarines. The yard is operated under a Lease and Trading Agreement by Cockatoo Island Dockyard Pty Ltd (sic), which is now owned by Australian National Industries.
>
> The on-going submarine work is substantial and demanding. I have just

approved a further major refit in the on-going programme for HMAS *Ovens* at a cost of some $50 million. Over $45 million of this will be undertaken by Cockatoo Island Dockyard. A further three such refits are planned to be completed by the early 1990s.

The yard has, from time to time, undertaken substantial repair and refit work on surface ships and opportunities can be expected to further arise.

The Oberon class submarines are due to go out of service from 1992. Many of the facilities on the island are old and substantial investment would be required for the yard to take on a major new program, such as the New Surface Combatants. The Lease and Trading Agreement, under which the yard is operated, is not well suited to current requirements. Recognising the capabilities and capacity elsewhere in the industry and the nature of the yard, the Government does not intend to renew the Lease and Trading Agreement after the completion of the Oberon work.

Options for the long term future use of the Island, including use of its dock facilities as an annex to Garden Island Dockyard, the relocation to it of service establishments now occupying foreshore land in Sydney, or early partial sale will now be examined and decisions made as soon as possible.

This decision on the future of the yard is being announced at this time, rather than nearer to 1992, the current termination date for the Lease and Trading Agreement, to enable those associated with the yard to make decisions as to their future participation in the industry at a time when all of the alternatives are open.[63]

In May 1987, the Treasurer announced the government's decision to sell Cockatoo Island. Both announcements were made without any prior consultation with the Company, despite an obligation in the Lease for the parties to consult about the future of the lease in January 1990 regarding its possible extension. The effect on the Company's business was immediate. Negotiations for some significant commercial work were immediately broken off and an impression was created in the market place that the Company was about to cease trading. This impression was to greatly limit opportunities for the Company to benefit from its considerable expertise in another location.

The announcements did, however, prompt early resolution of a number of long outstanding financial issues. Overhead recovery arrangements were also modified, resulting in a cost penalty for commercial work, but the obligation in the Trading Agreement for the Company to seek commercial work to the maximum practicable extend was waived. The revised procedures (known as the Advance Agreement) took effect in September 1987 and proved to be the most workable financial arrangement achieved since 1972.

In his statement of 1 April 1987, the Minister for Defence had said:

Should the company wish, and satisfactory arrangements can be made for continuation of the Oberon submarine work, the Commonwealth would consider either an earlier termination or an extension to complete the Oberon work. Renegotiation of the Lease and Trading Agreement is needed in the interim.[64]

The Advance Agreement of September 1987 provided for revised trading arrangements but the company had not sought, and nor had there been any discussions about, an early termination of the lease.

The uncertainty about the future of the dockyard continued during 1988. At a meeting in September that year the Minister for Defence told the Company that the Commonwealth had appointed Schroders Australia to advise the Commonwealth on the possibility of early termination of the lease and the terms of a possible commercial settlement with the Company.

The company made two submissions to Schroders setting out possible terms for such a settlement, which included substantial financial compensation for the loss of remaining submarine and other Commonwealth and commercial work. No progress was made towards such a settlement.

In late 1988, the Navy was becoming concerned that an early termination of the lease, were it to happen, could leave it without proper support for the submarines. In early 1989 expressions of interest in taking over the submarine work were sought from industry, on the basis that the work might be carried out at Garden Island in Sydney, or in Western Australia.

The public uncertainty surrounding the future of Cockatoo also prompted two major industrial disputes. The first, in 1987, was over a claim for increased redundancy pay. The second, in 1989, followed the Navy's decision to seek alternative locations for the last two Oberon refits. This time the claim was for the last refits to remain at Cockatoo, but the dispute was resolved after 14 weeks by the Commonwealth offering further improvements in redundancy pay and a financial incentive tied to performance on the two submarine refits that were then in hand.

Industrial disputation of this kind rarely changes governmental decisions, but this final strike had considerable influence on the government's decision in June 1990 to place the last refits at Garden Island, despite cost and time penalties and notwithstanding Defence recommendations for the work to remain at Cockatoo.[65]

When this decision was made, Cockatoo was completing a refit of the submarine HMAS *Ovens*, and was in the middle of the refit of HMAS *Orion*. The dockyard was also completing several hundred minor stores orders for the Navy and some steam turbine repairs for the New South Wales Electricity Commission.

In the late 1980s there had been speculation that the sale of Cockatoo Island would realise a substantial sum for the Commonwealth. After June 1990, in discussions relating to the plans for the run down and closure of the dockyard, the Department of

Defence expressed a wish to obtain vacant possession of the island by the end of 1991 to enable an early sale. Accordingly, the run down of dockyard's activities began in early 1991. It was finished by the time the last submarine refit, the second for HMAS *Orion*, was completed on 4 June 1991.

In the event, the lease was allowed to run its course until 31 December 1992, but the only work done on the Island after June 1991 was the decommissioning of facilities and the sale of plant and machinery. (This work is described in Chapter 5.)

Meanwhile, no progress had been made towards any commercial settlement with the Commonwealth. In late 1991 the Company submitted a formal claim for compensation for loss of profits and setting out other matters relating to the continuing administration of the dockyard's affairs. Included was the need for procedures for the Commonwealth to continue to pay uninsured worker's compensation and common law personal injury claim costs. These costs were normally recovered through the dockyard's overhead.

At a meeting in late November 1991, the Commonwealth countered with a claim that, in its view, the Company owed the Commonwealth a substantial sum of money for cleaning up alleged pollution arising from the operation of the dockyard. Nevertheless, the meeting ended with a proposal by the Commonwealth that the Company be paid $4,550,000 as compensation for the loss of the submarine work and that a release be given to the Company on the environmental condition of the island.

This offer was conditional on the Company accepting liability for future worker's compensation and common law costs. The Commonwealth denied liability for these costs, claiming that its earlier acceptance into overhead of costs arising from common law claims had been 'a mistake'.

In early 1992 the Company accepted the main terms of the offer, but rejected the Commonwealth's position on the overhead costs, suggesting resolution of that matter by arbitration. The Commonwealth responded by withdrawing the offer in its entirety.

The High Court case of 1926 had laid the foundation for the lease of Cockatoo Dockyard to a private company, which was one of the early 'privatisations'. Now the operation of the dockyard by the Company was also to end in litigation — litigation that lasted nearly four and a half years.

The 1972 Lease and Trading Agreement provided for disputes between the parties to be referred to a single arbitrator agreed by the parties. On 23 December 1992, one week before the lease expired, both parties exchanged Notices of Dispute. Mr John West QC was appointed arbitrator.[66]

There were in effect two cases. The first involved claims by the

Company against the Commonwealth for damages relating to the termination of the submarine refitting programme at the Dockyard together with several matters raised by both parties relating to recovery of overheads, which became known as the 'Commercial Case'. The second claim, by the Commonwealth against the Company for alleged pollution of Cockatoo Island, became known as the 'Pollution Case'.

Hearings began in February 1993, and with the expectation that the disputes might be heard quickly, the arbitrator decided to hear both cases before handing down a final award dealing with both matters. However, progress in the arbitration did not live up to the initial expectations. In October 1994 the arbitrator handed down an interim award relating to some of the overhead issues, ordering the Commonwealth to pay Cockatoo $565,649. In an action before the Supreme Court of New South Wales the Company sought to have this award enforced.[67]

The Company succeeded in this action, which was to prove to be only one of several appearances by the parties before the Supreme Court or the Court of Appeal.

Progress with the arbitration continued to be slow, particularly with the Pollution Case. The Commonwealth's case was extensively modified over time, and by mid-1995 there had been many changes to the Commonwealth's statement of particulars. In late 1995 the arbitrator decided to depart from his original intention to hear all the major issues before handing down a final award. With the agreement of the parties, he handed down an interim award dealing with the Commercial Case on 8 December 1995.

The arbitrator found that the Commonwealth was in breach of contract by placing the refits of the submarines *Onslow* and *Otama* with others, and awarded the Company $16.2 million for loss of profits and disputed overhead costs, including interest up to the date of the award.

The Commonwealth unsuccessfully sought leave to appeal against this decision in the Supreme Court, and was also unsuccessful in an application to the Court of Appeal seeking to overturn the Supreme Court's decision. As it had done the previous year, the Commonwealth also unsuccessfully sought in the Supreme Court and the Court of Appeal to have the award suspended. Finally (in August 1996) the Commonwealth paid Cockatoo nearly $17.3 million (including additional interest) arising from the Commercial Case award.

Frustrated by its inability to propound an acceptable case before the arbitrator in its pollution claim, the Commonwealth sought to have the arbitrator disqualify himself from further hearings. The arbitrator rejected the Commonwealth's application in March 1996, and the matter moved to the Supreme Court. The Commonwealth presented its arguments to the Court over two weeks in June 1996, with the case then being adjourned until February 1997.

Regardless of the outcome of this action, the Commonwealth and the Company were facing protracted and expensive proceedings if the Pollution Case was ever to be brought to a final award. In late 1996 the dispute began to move towards settlement, which was finally achieved in early 1997. ANI reported to its shareholders:

> A negotiated settlement, subject to final legal documentation, has now been reached with the Commonwealth whereby a payment of $4.9 million will be made by the Commonwealth to ANI. All outstanding disputes between the Commonwealth and ANI in the Arbitration relating to the closure of Cockatoo Dockyard have now been settled.[68]

The Commonwealth's decision in early 1992 to withdraw its offer of $4.55 million in compensation for the loss of the submarine refits proved expensive. In addition to the approximately $22 million paid to the Company, by June 1996 the Commonwealth's legal costs had reached $13.6 million and a further $3.6 million had been spent with consultants on environmental studies.[69] The Company's costs were over $11 million.

After 179 days of hearings the arbitration was finally concluded when the arbitrator handed down his final award dismissing the remaining matters on 15 May 1997.

DOCKYARD
DEVELOPMENT

WORLD WAR I

The period from 1913 to 1918 saw the greatest expansion of the facilities on Cockatoo Island, apart from the construction of the docks. Most of the buildings and many of the cranes and machine tools built or installed then were to remain in use for the rest of the dockyard's life.

Shortly before the island was transferred to the Commonwealth, a new slipway for the construction of the cruiser *Brisbane* had been laid out on the northern shore. Construction began in October 1912, and the new slipway was sited partly on solid rock and partly on fill composed of boulders and sand.[70]

A small plate shop was built by the New South Wales Government on the northern shore as part of the preparations for the construction of the cruiser *Brisbane*. It was erected in about 1912. (D J Mitchell Collection)

Work in the dockyard electrical workshop built on the upper part of the island during World War I.

It had originally been intended to be a simple, open slipway, with the launch ways carried into the water on piles. When he arrived at Cockatoo Island the new general manager, King Salter was unhappy with this arrangement and obtained Naval Board approval to extend the concrete of the slipway into deep water to provide more support for the launch ways. A caisson was also fitted to enable work on the lower end of the ways to proceed in the dry.

By the time work was begun on these extensions, the *Brisbane* was well advanced, and her launching was considerably delayed. Further work was done after the *Brisbane* had been launched. The completed slipway, designated No. 1, was a very substantial and permanent structure, built of concrete for its full length and most of its width. The concrete was poured over 40 feet thick in places. The wooden caisson for the slipway was built on Cockatoo Island and completed in August 1915, shortly before the *Brisbane* was launched.

The slipway was widened in the early 1920s to accommodate the refrigerated cargo ships *Fordsdale* and *Ferndale*. It then remained largely unaltered until 1963, when it was widened to enable the passenger ship *Empress of Australia* to be launched in January 1964. A steel bulkhead replaced the wooden caisson, again replaced by a larger structure after the launching of HMAS *Stalwart* in 1966. The design of at least one ship (the fast combat support ship *Protector*, cancelled in 1973), was influenced by the maximum width of No. 1 slipway, as its substantial construction would have made any major widening a costly exercise.

The new Commonwealth Naval Dockyard needed many other facilities, and the building programme affected most parts of the island. The Cruiser Wharf on the north-eastern shore of the island was completed by 1914. It was presumably so named because it was intended to be the fitting out wharf for the *Brisbane*. During World War I either the dockyard itself or the Naval Works Department built:

◆ a new bolt shop

◆ a new brass foundry

◆ two pontoon ferry wharves (the Parramatta and Camber Wharves)

◆ a tunnel under the rock of the island from the head of the Sutherland Dock for access to the northern shipyard

◆ a 25-ton gantry crane and track beside No. 1 slipway to ship machinery into the *Brisbane*

◆ a gantry for a travelling crane in the fitting shop

◆ police and muster stations

- a ship fitting shop
- a coppersmith's shop
- a timber store
- a surgery
- two houses and four cottages
- an electrical workshop (on the top of the island)
- a tool room and store, on the site of the eastern shipbuilding slipway
- a three storey general store south of the Sutherland Dock
- a 10-ton furnace in the brass foundry
- a new annealing furnace
- a new forge
- small administrative offices
- latrines for workmen
- a three storey drawing office building on the top of the island
- a new platers' shed in the northern shipyard
- two 5-ton jib cranes for the shipyard
- a new power station including boilers and fittings for three 1000-kilowatt turbo generators, and three 1500 cubic feet air compressors, and installation of new dock pumps
- a new Sutherland Wharf
- extensions to the Fitzroy Wharf, Cruiser Wharf, plumbers', blacksmiths', boilermakers' and sheet iron shops, brass foundry, turbine shop and slipways
- new roads
- a new sail loft
- new mess rooms for workmen.

Extensive rock excavation was needed to accommodate the new workshops, and the spoil was used to reclaim further land for dockyard use, particularly in the northern shipyard. New electric power distribution systems, water, hydraulic and compressed air systems and sewerage systems were also installed.

Cockatoo Island in January 1934. The cruiser in the Sutherland Dock (far left) is HMAS *Canberra*. Note the barren area on the Hunters Hill peninsular in the background that is now Kelly's Bush.

The new cruiser HMAS *Australia* entering the Sutherland Dock for the first time in January 1929.

The general store building burning down in September 1937.

Much equipment for the new workshops was also designed and made on Cockatoo Island. It included many machine tools, a 15-ton overhead crane for the new power station, two 50-ton overhead cranes for the turbine shop, a 5-ton steel converter, plant for testing and annealing air bottles for submarines, and a balancing machine for turbine rotors. Fourteen other cranes were built or assembled for workshops and wharves, with capacities from 2.5 to 25 tons.

By the end of the war, Cockatoo was a very well equipped naval dockyard, built on the pattern of a British Royal dockyard. Almost every part and fitting needed for a warship, apart from the armament, could be built on the island, ranging from fine joiner work to turbines, boilers and propellers.

No attempt was made to connect the island to the mainland, and all material, equipment and workmen continued to be brought in by water.

There was little change to the island in the 1920s, apart from the extension of the Sutherland Dock in 1928 to accommodate the new cruisers *Australia* and *Canberra*. HMAS *Australia* made first use of the extension on 29 January 1929. The material excavated from the dock was used to fill in the No. 5 slipway west of the boatshed and launch slipway, and an area to the east of the boatshed. Some may also have been placed in the northern shipyard area.

Between 1920 and 1933 several vessels were built for dockyard use, including a workshop punt and a hopper barge. The workshop punt later became the oxygen barge, its role until it was replaced and sold in the 1970s. The hopper barge had a 100-ton capacity and was used for transporting yard rubbish out to sea until this practice was suspended during World War II. Towards the end of this period, a new caisson was built for the Fitzroy Dock. It was launched by the floating crane *Titan* on 19 July 1932. The old caisson was retained at the dockyard for a number of years.

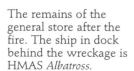

The remains of the general store after the fire. The ship in dock behind the wreckage is HMAS *Albatross*.

The prominent general store building by the Sutherland Dock was destroyed by fire in September 1937. In December of that year the island was connected to shore electrical power for the first time by a single 6600 Volt cable laid from Balmain to the power house. This change had been foreshadowed by the report of a Cabinet Committee as early as 1932. This AC supply was passed to the island's low voltage DC supply system through two transformers and two banks of Hewittic mercury arc rectifiers.[71]

The Commonwealth also provided some new machine tools for the manufacture of machinery for the RAN sloops. However there was little other major change to the island before World War II.

WORLD WAR II

Over £400,000 was spent between 1939 and 1945 on new buildings plant and facilities on the island. Most of the work was funded by the Australian Shipbuilding Board to meet the needs of the merchant shipbuilding programme. The work included:

◆ the new No. 2 slipway adjacent to No. 1 in the northern shipyard for the construction of the second of the Tribal class destroyer *Warramunga*. (The first ship built on this slipway was actually *Warrego*.)
◆ a new turbine shop, complete with 10- and 70-ton overhead cranes for the assembly of marine propulsion engines
◆ a new platers' shop, built on reclaimed ground in the northern shipyard
◆ a new non-ferrous foundry (with 5- and 30-ton cranes)
◆ the new 250-ton patent slipway in Timber Bay
◆ the new Bolt Shop Wharf, built in concrete as an extension of the Cruiser Wharf
◆ a new plate yard wharf with 5-ton crane
◆ the new Fitzroy Wharf with 5-ton crane
◆ the new Destroyer Wharf
◆ extension of the iron foundry
◆ extension of the boiler shop
◆ conversion of the old turbine shop into a heavy machine shop
◆ new marking off and progress departments
◆ erection of canteens and general amenities for dockyard personnel.

The construction of the new turbine shop and the new brass foundry required the excavation of a large volume of sandstone from the

The first launching from the new No. 2 slipway. The sloop *Warrego* was named by Mrs R G Menzies on 10 February 1940.

central core of the island, in the order of 100,000 cubic yards.[72] This material was used as fill, mainly on the northern side of the island, and the new platers' shop was built on the land that was created.

In addition to the buildings mentioned above, a number of new stores and amenities were built south of the Sutherland Dock. These included a new timber mill that was built in 1942 on the site of the No. 5 slipway. Other changes during the war years included modifications to several workshops, the erection of new toilet blocks at various locations around the island, further rock excavation for a new sub-station at the power station, and the construction of a road to the top of the island, which became known as the 'Burma Road'.

A number of air raid shelters were also built at various locations around the island early in the war. This work included major changes to some of the convict built buildings. One shelter comprised a tunnel through the centre of the island, and included a first aid station. The material excavated from this tunnel was used as fill in the northern shipyard.

POST-WAR DEVELOPMENT

After the war, development of the island was linked to specific projects for some 20 years, until the preparation of the master plan for the modernisation of the dockyard in 1967.

In 1946 the docking capacity was increased by the arrival of the Admiralty floating dock *AFD 17*, which was berthed at the Fitzroy Wharf.

AFD 17 was built by the Devonport Dockyard in England in 1942. After service in Iceland, the dock was towed to Australia in 1945. It was slightly damaged during the voyage, and after repairs by Mort's Dock and at Cockatoo Dockyard, the dock was moored at Cockatoo Island.

The British Admiralty tried to sell *AFD 17* in 1946, initially for £205,000, although the asking price was later reduced to £150,000. All state governments were approached, but none were interested in acquiring the dock. Even though the RAN had no peacetime need for it, and could see only limited wartime use, the Commonwealth bought the dock in 1948 for £75,000 as part of an overall settlement for Royal Navy wartime assets remaining in Australia.

AFD 17 had a lifting capacity of 2750 tons, a pontoon length of 350 feet, and a width between fenders of 50 feet. The RAN considered it too small for the newer combat ships then being built. Nevertheless, during its

Excavation for the new turbine shop underway in December 1943. Most of the material from this excavation was used as fill to extend the northern shipyard.
(J C Jeremy Collection)

22-year life, *AFD 17* was quite active. Its first docking was the tug *Lindfield* on 17 December 1946. By 24 March 1964, when the last docking (of the Royal Navy submarine HMS *Taciturn*) was completed, *AFD 17* had docked 641 vessels. Most were of small ships like tugs and ferries, but the dock also served ships of the RAN and RN including the frigates *Swan, Hawkesbury, Murchison, Warrego, Shoalhaven, Culgoa, Queenborough, Parramatta* and *Stuart,* and the submarines *Tactician, Telemachus, Thorough, Aurochs, Andrew, Anchorite, Tabard, Trump* and *Taciturn.*

The Company was responsible for general maintenance of *AFD 17,* but the Commonwealth was reluctant to see any large sums spent on it. It was periodically surveyed afloat and docked in the Captain Cook Dock at Garden Island in 1952. By 1956 it had deteriorated to the point that the cost of repairs (£250,000) was not considered justified, and in 1957 the Navy decided to dispose of it as scrap. Following representations from the Company, the Navy agreed that it should be retained, subject to minimum maintenance, recognising that it had a limited life.

The Type 12 frigate *Stuart* in the floating dock *AFD 17* during fitting out in March 1962.
(J C Jeremy)

Despite its condition, the dock continued to be useful; indeed 1959 was the busiest year for the dock with 58 dockings. By 1964, however, it was clearly in very poor condition, and it was docked at Garden Island for a further survey. *AFD 17* had come to the end of its useful life and was condemned. It was subsequently sold and broken up for scrap in Sydney.

Parts of *AFD 17* continued to serve for many years — its two 5-ton electric travelling cranes were refitted with longer jibs and were used at the Fitzroy Dock until the dockyard closed in 1991.

The order for the construction of Daring class destroyers in 1946 resulted in some changes to the northern shipyard to enable the construction of these all-welded ships in pre-fabricated units.

A welding bay was added to the new platers' shed, and a 40-ton Whirley crane was bought from the United States and installed between Nos. 1 and 2 slipways. The old cantilever cranes which had previously been in this position were moved seaward north of a concrete slab which was laid for pre-fabrication of units. More room was needed in the shipyard for the construction of units and reclamation of the northern shipyard continued until the early to mid-1960s.

The old iron foundry was converted into a marker's off and progress shop in 1947. New machine tools were also installed in the machine shops during the early 1950s for the manufacture of the English Electric steam turbines for the Type 12 frigates. A new administrative building and a new standards room were also completed in the early 1950s.

The facilities for the refit of the Oberon class submarines were completed in 1971. Telemotor and high pressure air components were refitted in this clean room.

The platers' shop was extended to the east in 1962, and a cold frame bending machine was installed in the old platers' shop in the early 1960s to enable ships' frames to be bent cold, rather than heating to a red heat in a furnace and bending on a cast iron slab.

In the early 1960s the Sutherland Wharf was improved by the construction of two concrete structures, to support cranes and enable ships to use the wharf, which by then was in poor condition. This work was completed in late 1965 and the structures were incorporated in the new Sutherland Wharf, which was finished in 1971.

To meet the needs of the Oberon class submarine refitting programme due to start in about 1970, and to enable the yard to carry out its intended shipbuilding role, a survey of physical facilities was carried out during 1966 and 1967.[73] This survey resulted in the subsequent approval of an extensive modernisation of the dockyard, although ultimately not all of the recommended works were approved or completed.

The work that was completed included facilities for the refit of the submarines (apart from the reconstruction and extension of the Fitzroy Wharf, which fell victim to financial economy) and some of the improvements that had been proposed for the modernisation of the shipyard.

The submarine refit facilities were concentrated in the south-east corner of the island, in two buildings, one next to the Bolt Wharf, and the other on the site of the disused southern shipyard.

The first building, next to the Bolt Wharf, housed the principal mechanical and electrical workshops, together with amenities for 1000 workmen. The building included:

◆ a dirty transit store, the first stop for equipment removed from a submarine
◆ a mechanical assembly shop, with local workshops and stores
◆ a telemotor and high pressure air room; a clean room, air conditioned and supplied with filtered air
◆ functional test rooms, for full functional, noise and vibration trials of submarine equipment
◆ an electrical production shop, and electrical assembly shop, with cleaning bays, machine tools and testing facilities
◆ an electroplating shop.

The other building, on the site of the disused southern shipyard contained:

◆ secure transit stores and lay apart stores
◆ stripping and cleaning areas, with ultrasonic cleaning facilities for electronic equipment

◆ an electronics workshop

◆ test rooms for sonar and torpedo fire control systems to allow complete functional testing

◆ a sonar directing gear workshop

◆ a battery connector shop

◆ a clean transit store

◆ a radio and radar workshop

◆ an instrument workshop

◆ accommodation for stand-by ships' crews, including sleeping and mess spaces for officers and sailors

◆ offices and amenities for dockyard staff.

The mechanical assembly shop in the submarine refit facilities.

Other areas modernised at the same time included the boiler and pipe shops, with extensive improvements to power, air, water and sewerage services. The Bolt and Destroyer wharves were also rehabilitated in the mid-1970s. New 5-ton travelling cranes were fitted on both.

When completed these facilities were amongst the most modern in the world for the refit of conventional (non-nuclear) submarines. They served the submarine refit programme well for 20 years.

In addition to modern workshops and services, docking facilities were also augmented.

During the 1966 survey, it became clear that additional docking facilities would be needed if the existing docks were not to be overloaded with submarines. The Fitzroy Dock had been almost fully committed to the refits of the Royal Navy T class submarines in the early 1960s. *AFD 17* had also been used for submarine dockings. With *AFD 17* scrapped, the Sutherland Dock was also used. On 2 April 1966 both docks were full when all three submarines of the Royal Navy Fourth Submarine Squadron were in dock at Cockatoo together.

At that time, the Fitzroy and Sutherland docks were the only docks available for commercial work in Sydney and the start of 'two stream' submarine refitting (that is, two submarines in hand at any time) in the late 1970s was expected to require two docks fully committed to submarines.

Five potential solutions were considered: a new graving dock; a floating dock; a ship lift; a slipway; and a slave dock. The slave dock option was selected as the cheapest and simplest.

The slave dock was designed by Cockatoo Dockyard specifically for the needs of the Oberon class submarines.[74] It is basically a simple pontoon, with no pumping or flooding arrangements of its own, which depends on another dock for its operation.

At Cockatoo, the slave dock was first docked down in the Sutherland Dock. Flooding plates in the bottom of the dock and in bulkheads in the pontoon were opened to allow the slave dock to free flood when the Sutherland Dock was flooded. A submarine was then brought into the dock, positioned over the slave dock, and docked down as the Sutherland Dock was pumped dry. After the flooding plates were closed, the slave dock was floated out carrying the submarine, and berthed at a wharf.

The new dock, *SD 3201*, was built by Cockatoo Dockyard on the No. 1 slipway (as Ship No. 237), and launched on 8 March 1974. It was completed shortly thereafter, but had to wait for its trials for an available submarine. Over four days in October 1974, the trials were completed with the Royal Navy submarine HMS *Odin*, which was then attached to the RAN Submarine Squadron.

The first RAN submarine to use the slave dock was HMAS *Onslow*, which docked on 5 May 1975 at the start of her 1975–77 refit. The Commonwealth formally accepted *SD 3201* on 8 May 1975.

Over the next 15 years the slave dock was able to provide the refit docking capacity needed, with the other docks mainly being used for intermediate and survey dockings. On occasions it was necessary to dock a submarine at the start of its refit in one of the graving docks (usually Fitzroy) for some weeks whilst the previous submarine was readied for undocking from the slave dock.

The last submarine to use the slave dock at Cockatoo was HMAS *Orion*, which undocked in November 1990. The slave dock was then transferred to Australian Defence Industries at Garden Island for use for the much delayed refit of HMAS *Onslow*.

The 50-ton Butters crane, bought from BHP's Whyalla shipyard to help build HMAS *Success*, dominated the western Sydney skyline.

The 1967 plans for the modernisation of the shipyard included:

♦ widening and lengthening No. 1 slipway
♦ consolidation of No. 2 slipway
♦ the installation of two new 50-ton berth cranes
♦ a new stockyard for storing, handling and preparing steel plates and sections
♦ a new complex of shops for working steel plates and building prefabricated units up to 100 tons weight under cover
♦ new materials handling facilities throughout the shipyard
♦ improved outfitting facilities
♦ a new amenities building for shipyard workers.

Plans were also prepared for improvements to roads and services throughout the island. Little progress was made with the shipyard modernisation. In late 1968 the Company was asked by the Navy to identify the minimum work which might be required to enable the Dockyard to build a fast combat support ship and three light destroyers as part of a new construction programme intended to stretch into the 1970s. Various works were nominated, which were completed by the Commonwealth by about 1973.

These works included a new Plate Wharf just to the north of No. 2 slipway and a new plate yard in the area between the pre-fabrication area and the shoreline north of No. 2 slipway. A new plate preparation line, comprising a conveyor, plate leveling machine, shot blasting and paint spraying plant was installed and the platers' shop was extended to the west to accommodate the plate line conveyor and a new plate cutting machine. The 40-ton Whirley crane was converted to hydraulic operation.[75]

Other major works completed by 1973 included:

◆ the construction of a sewage treatment plant on the site of the old boiler house
◆ the erection of two water tanks on the top of the island
◆ replacement of the floor of the Fitzroy Dock in concrete and the provision of concrete dock blocks
◆ replacement of part of the floor of the Sutherland Dock in concrete
◆ construction of a pit in the floor of the Sutherland Dock to accommodate the sonar domes of the guided missile destroyers *Perth*, *Hobart* and *Brisbane*.

The fast combat support ship (AOE) and light destroyer (DDL) projects were cancelled in 1973,[76] and the Commonwealth did no further work on the shipyard modernisation. When the Company won the order for the fleet underway replenishment ship, HMAS *Success*, in 1979–80, some additional im-provements were completed at Company expense. They included the purchase of a 50-ton Butters shipyard crane from the closed BHP shipyard at Whyalla and the conversion of the brass and iron foundries (which had been closed in the 1960s) into

Success under construction on No. 1 slipway in 1983.

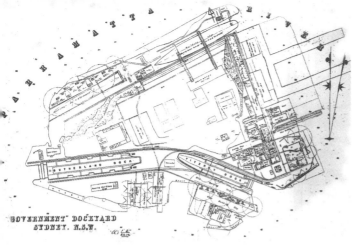

GOVERNMENT DOCKYARD
SYDNEY. N.S.W.

This 1912 plan of the island shows some ambitious plans for battle cruiser construction on the north-east corner of the island.

fabrication shops. Additional power supplies were provided and the flame-cutting machine converted to numerical control.

The last major Commonwealth project for the modernisation of facilities at Cockatoo was the replacement of the cranes at the Sutherland Dock, and the modernisation of the dock pumping system. By the 1970s, the existing cranes were obsolete and inefficient. The original 1890 steam cranes were still in service, and the more modern 10-ton electric crane (installed in 1924) was unreliable and did not meet current safety standards. The Commonwealth had fitted this crane with a trailing cable electrical supply in the 1970s, but the cable reel did not work and the crane had to be attended by an electrician whenever it was used to prevent it from running over its own cable.

In 1980 the government approved the installation of a 30- and a 5-tonne portal crane on the south side of the dock, with a 3-tonne portal crane on the other. The work included modification to existing buildings to accommodate the much larger 30-tonne crane, and the whole project was to be completed by mid-1982, at a cost of $4.2 million. The dock pumps, which had been installed in 1920, were also to be replaced and the valves overhauled.

The work took much longer than planned, and funding constraints caused further delay. The dock pumping system was completed, and the 30-tonne crane installed on a short section of track by December 1984, but despite some seven years work the rest of the project was never finished.

The unusual combination of cranes proposed for the Sutherland Dock arose partly from the constraints of the site, and partly from heritage considerations. The Australian Heritage Commission listed of the whole island on the Register of the National Estate in 1981, which limited the extent of rock trimming that could take place on the northern side of the dock. The new cranes had to be designed around this restriction.

The Commonwealth completed some other works on the island after 1972, but these were mainly limited to the rehabilitation and repair of existing facilities.

PLANS UNFULFILLED

The incomplete shipyard modernisation and dock crane replacement were only some of the stillborn development plans for Cockatoo Island. Many schemes were proposed over the years, some of which were mere feasibility studies. Others were serious proposals, which if carried out might have changed the history of Australian shipbuilding.

Included in the World War I plans was a 600 feet long, 60 feet wide wharf known as the 'Australia Pier'. It was to have been built perpendicular to the Cruiser Wharf on the eastern shore and fitted with a 5-ton travelling gantry crane that had 50 feet outreach on each side. The wharf was never approved.

The demands of World War II resulted in many changes, but amongst the unfulfilled plans was an access road to the island that was proposed in 1944. The plan envisaged an 800 feet long concrete pier extending to the south-west from the Sutherland Wharf, joined to the mainland at Roseby Street, Drummoyne by a 60 feet wide pontoon road and causeway at Schnapper Island.

Various schemes were prepared in 1944 for enlarging the No. 1 slipway, or building a new slipway, to enable the yard to build an aircraft carrier up to the size of the British Centaur class light fleet carrier. The most ambitious scheme would have needed the excavation of the whole of the raised part of the island for a new slipway 1000 feet long and 140 feet wide. More practical was the scheme to enlarge the existing No. 1 slipway to 750 feet by 90 feet, retaining a No. 2 slipway at destroyer size of 450 feet by 60 feet.

After the war, the Naval Board prepared plans for the development of an improved naval shipbuilding capability in Australia. This work coincided with an examination by the British Admiralty of the means for the rapid production of warships in British Commonwealth yards in the event of a future war with the Soviet Union. The Admiralty considered that the best locations for a special naval shipyard in Australia were either Whyalla in South Australia, or an extended Cockatoo Dockyard in Sydney.

In 1947, the RAN had prepared a long range plan for an extension of Cockatoo for building large naval ships when circumstances demanded it. This plan was

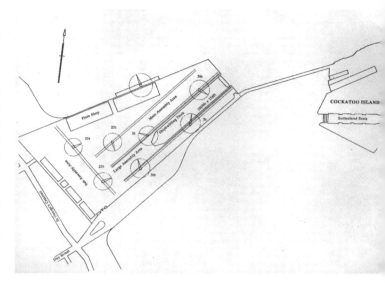

The proposed Drummoyne shipyard of 1947.
(J C Jeremy)

The proposed causeway of 1944 to connect the island to the mainland.

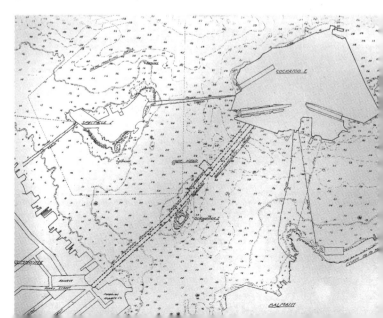

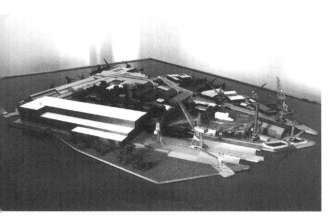

A model showing the proposed facilities for the construction of submarines at Cockatoo Island. Had it ever been built, the construction hall would have been one of the largest industrial buildings in Sydney.

favoured by the Admiralty in view of the previous naval work of Cockatoo, its proximity to other industry, and the government's financial interest in it.

The RAN plan involved the leveling of Spectacle Island and the reclamation of the harbour between that island and the mainland at Drummoyne for the construction of a shipyard with a shipbuilding dock 1000 feet long and 156 feet wide. The new yard was to be connected to Cockatoo Island by a piered causeway to the northern shipyard, providing Cockatoo with direct road access to the mainland. The capacity of this yard, had it been built, would have been considerable.

The 1967 Master Plan for Cockatoo Dockyard was the most complete plan for the yard since World War I. Unfortunately, only that part relating to the submarine refitting facilities was properly implemented, and even then the new Fitzroy Wharf, which was central to the logic of the equipment flow during a refit, fell victim to government financial limitations. Although some work was done on the shipyard, almost nothing was done to rectify other deficiencies in wharves, cranes, and offices, workshops and services, which predominantly dated from before 1918.

By the early 1980s, it was clear that much needed to be done if Cockatoo was to continue to operate in the long term, as much equipment that had been condemned as obsolete 20 years before was still being used. Expenditure by the Commonwealth of over $10 million on major repairs to buildings, cranes, wharves and services between 1975 and 1983 had been supplemented by normal Company maintenance (recovered from revenue) of over $15 million. The Company had also invested about $4.3 million in capital improvements in the same period. Despite this expenditure, the Company estimated in 1984 that about $22 million more was needed just to maintain essential facilities and services.

The Company argued that this expenditure was justified if Cockatoo was to be involved in a major project like the construction of the RAN's new submarines, then being planned. The Company prepared several plans for a major modernisation of the shipyard, one of which included a prefabrication and assembly building 200 metres long and 39.65 metres wide, large enough to build submarines or frigates completely under cover. It would have been one of the largest industrial buildings in Australia. Together with the construction of a ship lift and side transfer areas in the Timber Bay for future refit work, the total cost was estimated to be about $30 million, considerably less than the construction of a new facility on a new site.

Had these plans materialised, the problem of access to the yard, on an island in the middle of Sydney Harbour, would have remained. Changes to the method of funding and implementation of capital works on the island would also have been needed, as the Commonwealth processes were far too slow and cumbersome. The acquisition by the Company of the 50-ton crane for the shipyard in 1979–80 (including a new crane track and power supplies) had taken about one year from idea to reality. The Sutherland Dock crane project, funded and carried out by the Commonwealth, took seven years and was never finished.

The problems and costs associated with the development of Cockatoo, with all its location and heritage constraints, influenced the government thinking which led to the 1987 decision to draw the history of the remarkable dockyard to a close.

DECOMMISSIONING AND DEMOLITION

The operation of Cockatoo Island as a dockyard ceased at the end of 1991. During 1991 and 1992 the dockyard was 'decommissioned', with stores and equipment removed and sold.

In late 1991, an auction sale was conducted on the island, at which most of the machine tools and equipment were sold. Removal of equipment by the purchasers began soon after. A further auction was conducted in April 1992, when the remaining equipment, cranes and a number of buildings were sold. The buildings and most of the cranes were demolished by the purchasers during 1992.

The purchasers of equipment and scrap materials stripped all the remaining buildings, with the exception of parts of the machine shop. Here heavy machine tools that had been installed before World War II were retained for heritage reasons, together with some similar machinery salvaged form other parts of the island. Steam generating plant removed from the floating crane *Titan* was also stored there.

For heritage reasons the boatshed and the power house were left completely untouched at the request of the Commonwealth. They were left as if the workers had simply gone home at the end of the day.

Finally, in the last few days of 1992, the two docks were flooded.

The site of the coppersmiths' shop, plumbers' shop and boiler shop in September 1992 near the end of demolition. (J C Jeremy)

Chapter Six

SHIPBUILDING

January 25th 1913 was a busy day at Cockatoo Island, and a notable day in the history of Australian shipbuilding. On that day the Minister for Defence, Senator Pearce, came to the dockyard for the laying of the keels of the cruiser *Brisbane* and the destroyers *Derwent* and *Torrens*, events which marked the start of the first major naval shipbuilding programme in Australia.

The two destroyers were sister ships of the *Warrego*, completed at Cockatoo in 1912. They had a displacement of 688 tons (full load), an overall length of 250 feet 9 inches, and were propelled by Parsons steam turbines, driving three screws. Their armament was one 4-inch and three 12-pounder guns, one 303 Maxim gun, and three 18-inch torpedo tubes. They had a designed speed of 26 knots.

Derwent was the first ship launched, on 19 December 1914. She was soon renamed *Huon* to avoid confusion with a Royal Navy destroyer of the same name. *Torrens* was launched in August 1915, and a third destroyer *Swan* in December 1915. *Huon* was completed on 4 February 1916: the first modern warship wholly built in Australia. Whilst based on contemporary British designs, the Australian River class ships were unique to the RAN. The specification for the ships required that: 'all material entering into the construction of the vessel or her fitments are to be obtained only from the makers on the British Admiralty aft (sic: list)'.[77] Whilst the possibility of using Australian made equipment and materials was considered to speed construction, most was

The torpedo boat destroyers *Derwent* (left) and *Torrens* (right) in frame on 22 April 1913.
(Mitchell Library, State Library of New South Wales)

imported. Cockatoo built the turbines for all three ships and the Yarrow boilers for the third ship were built by the Eveleigh Railway Workshops in Sydney.[78] The ships were built of galvanised steel, with an average cost of £158,300, substantially more than their British-built sisters, which cost £81,500 each.

Workmen trimming a plate with a guillotine in the plate shop in about 1920.

The methods used for the construction of these destroyers were typical of the time. The shape of the ship and its parts were defined in the mould loft, where the lines of the ship were laid off full size, and wood patterns and tapes were made for marking off the plates and sections. Plates were cut by shearing or burning, and rivet holes were punched, in the plate shop. Sections (frames and deck beams) which required shaping were heated to a red heat in furnaces then bent to shape on cast iron bend-ing slabs. The shape was checked on a scrieve board next to the bending slab, where the loftsmen had scribed the frame sections of the ship into the wooden floor. Plates which needed to be formed were rolled cold to templates supplied by the loft. Complex shapes were sometimes formed by heating and pressing.

The first act in building a riveted ship on the slipway was to lay the keel, a thicker than average plate upon which the frames were erected, one by one. Bulkheads were often built on the ground before erection, as this was easier and they helped to maintain the ship's form on the building berth. The plating was then offered up to the frames, plate by plate, and bolted in place before riveting. It was often possible to erect a ship very quickly by this means.

Most connections in ships built in Australia before 1945 were riveted.[79] The rivets were heated in small fires of coal or coke, supplied with air from the yard's compressed air system immediately adjacent to the work site.

The torpedo boat destroyer *Torrens* entering the water on 28 August 1915. The ship was named by Lady Helen Munro-Ferguson, wife of the Governor-General.

The rivets were driven with hydraulic riveting machines slung from cranes, or by hand-held air-driven hammers. Seams were caulked with air-driven caulking tools, which was generally a very noisy process. (Electric welding was introduced at Cockatoo by the early 1920s for some small parts.)

The second class protected cruiser *Brisbane* was of the second Town (Chatham) class. Her overall length was 457 feet, and full load displacement 5408 tons. She was propelled by Parsons reaction steam turbines (built by Vickers in Britain), and 12 coal-fired Yarrow small tube boilers, all made at Cockatoo Island. The ship had four screws and a designed speed of 25 knots at 25,000 shaft horsepower (SHP). She was armed with eight 6-inch and four 3-pounder guns and two submerged 21-inch torpedo tubes.

HMAS *Huon* leaving Cockatoo Dockyard in December 1915. This destroyer was the first steel warship fully built in Australia, rather than assembled from imported parts like her sister ship *Warrego*.

The launching of *Brisbane* was delayed by the reconstruction of the slipway on which she was being built. Because each part of a riveted ship's hull is erected separately (apart from some bulkheads and other small fabrications) the shipyard cranes did not need to lift much more than 5 tons. This limited the amount of equipment that could be shipped before launching, and machinery was usually shipped later during fitting out at a wharf. To cope with the delays imposed by the slipway problems, the dockyard designed and built a 25-ton gantry crane which was erected on the south side of No. 1 slipway to enable machinery and other equipment to be shipped into *Brisbane* before launching.

Brisbane was therefore much more advanced than originally planned when Mrs Fisher (wife of the Prime Minister) launched the ship at noon on 30 September 1915, with main engines and boilers shipped and fitting out well underway. Thousands watched the

The first cruiser built in the Commonwealth for the RAN, *Brisbane* was launched on 30 September 1915. There does not seem to have been any particularly strict control of spectator vessels.

Brisbane aground on Spectacle Island after launching.

launching of *Brisbane*, including a surprisingly large number who took advantage of the view from the top of the gantry crane, and small boats surrounded the ship as it entered the water. One boatman tried to rescue the remains of the champagne bottle which prevented an anchor from being dropped to slow the ship. *Brisbane* gently ran aground on Spectacle Island, but was soon taken in charge by tugs and berthed at the newly built Cruiser Wharf for fitting out.

HMAS *Brisbane* was commissioned on 30 October 1916, and completed on 12 December 1916. The original contract had specified completion by 1 December 1914, but the problems with the slipway, difficulties with the concurrent development of the dockyard, shortages of skilled labour, and the late delivery of machinery and equipment caused many delays. Nevertheless, the quality of the ship was stated to be very high, and in some respects better than similar work done in Britain.

The British Admiralty had designed the destroyers and the cruiser, but some detailed work was done at Cockatoo. This was made easier for *Brisbane* as the ship was essentially a repeat of the British-built *Melbourne* and *Sydney*, and the destroyers repeats of the earlier *Yarra*, *Parramatta* and *Warrego*. A much greater technical challenge was given

The new cruiser HMAS *Brisbane* leaving the dockyard on 12 December 1916. The ship appears to have circled Cockatoo Island after departure, as Hunters Hill is in the background of this photograph.
(J C Jeremy Collection)

The dredger *Hercules* fitting out at the Fitzroy Wharf watched over by an armed guard. The *Hercules* was completed in April 1915 and was a familiar sight around Sydney harbour until 1972, when it was scuttled of the coast with the tug *Bustler*. *Bustler* was also built at Cockatoo and was completed in 1917.

Preparing HMAS *Brisbane* for hand over to the RAN in December 1916. The ship is already flying the white ensign having bee n commissioned on 30 October. (J C Jeremy Collection)

The dredger *CND 2* was built for the Commonwealth Navigation Department and completed in August 1915. It was assembled on No. 5 slipway from parts shipped to Sydney from Britain.

to the dockyard in August 1915 with the order for a second cruiser. This ship was to be based on the third Town (Birmingham) class.

The dockyard received the first drawings for the *Adelaide* in September 1916. The ship was 4 feet longer than *Brisbane* and quite different, particularly in the propulsion plant. This meant the dockyard needed larger machine tools, bigger cranes and more workshop space. The ship was unique, and a new drawing office was built to accommodate the increased draughting staff needed for the job.

Adelaide was laid down on No. 1 slipway on 20 November 1917, and launched only eight months later on 27 July 1918. She was not to completed, however, until 31 July 1922, earning the nickname 'HMAS Long Delayed', a title that was not entirely fair to her builders.

HMAS *Adelaide* had an overall length of 462 feet 8 inches, and a full load displacement of 5557 tons. She was propelled by Parsons reaction steam turbines driving two shafts (instead of four as in *Brisbane*), with a maximum speed of 25 knots at 25,000 SHP. Twelve Yarrow boilers, capable of burning either coal or oil supplied steam. All the boilers and turbines were built at Cockatoo. Her armament comprised nine 6-inch, one 3-inch, one 12-pounder and four 3-pounder guns, and two submerged 21-inch torpedo tubes.

The construction of *Adelaide* was severely delayed by the late delivery of material and equipment from Britain. Although she had been launched in 1918, much of the equipment did not arrive until 1920 or 1921, including steel plates, pipes, ventilation fans and refrigeration equipment. Forgings for the impulse wheels for the main turbines did not arrive until December 1919, after which the rotors had to be built up and completed.[80]

The wartime shipbuilding programme was also disrupted by the administrative problems described earlier in Chapter 4, and the construction of *Adelaide* was completely suspended between 10 March and 14 July 1921.

The heavy demand on machine tool manufacturers in Britain during the war meant that some of the machine tools ordered for Cockatoo were diverted elsewhere, and the dockyard was forced to make replacements on the island. Particularly significant were the delays to the construction of the floating crane *Titan*, as the turbines for *Adelaide* were too heavy for the dockyard's other cranes and could not be shipped until *Titan* was fully completed.

Titan had been ordered from Gowans Sheldon & Company, Carlisle, for assembly at Cockatoo. The pontoon for the 150-ton floating crane was built at Cockatoo in 1917. Unfortunately the lead screws, which weighed about 40 tons each, were lost when the cargo ship *Afric* was torpedoed and sunk on the way to Australia. Although *Titan* could be used in a limited way with the jib fixed in position, replacement of the missing parts was vital. The first replacement screws were condemned as unfit for service and an alternative contractor had to be found. *Titan* was finally completed in December 1919, well in time to ship *Adelaide's* turbines in November 1920.

Cockatoo Dockyard was particularly busy in

The steam launch *Greswell* under construction in 1914 on the eastern shore of the island. Much of the shipbuilding between 1870 and 1914 was done here, but after *Greswell* was launched a tool room was built on the site.

Progress on No. 1 slipway on 20 November 1917, the day the keel for the new cruiser *Adelaide* was laid.

the period immediately following World War I, not only with new construction, but also a heavy load of refitting work, and the employment in the yard reached an all-time peak of 4085 people at the end of December 1919.

As well as the second cruiser, the yard was also completing a collier for the RAN. *Biloela* (named after the Queensland town, not Cockatoo Island) had been designed by Navy Office in Melbourne, but all the working drawings were prepared at Cockatoo. This was the first ship to be built with steel plates rolled in Australia. The plates and sections

Rapid progress on the erection of *Adelaide*, 1 February 1918.

were produced by BHP at their new steel works at Newcastle, and they were smaller than would have been supplied from Britain or the United States. Almost all of the equipment for *Biloela* was manufactured in Australia, with the exception of chain cable and steel wire rope.[81]

Biloela had a full load displacement of 10,040 tons, and a length between perpendiculars of 370 feet. She was powered by a triple expansion steam engine, made at Cockatoo, and had a maximum speed of 11 knots. She was launched by Mrs King Salter, wife of the dockyard's general manager, on 10 April 1919, and was completed on 10 July 1920.

In addition to these major ships, Cockatoo built many smaller vessels during the war years. They included four non-propelled lightships for the Commonwealth Lighthouse Service, one of which, *Carpentaria No. 2*, completed in 1918, is now on permanent display at the Australian National Maritime Museum in Sydney. Other ships included oil lighters, barges, pontoons and workboats.

The yard also built the hull and machinery for a 35-foot steam cutter for HMAS *Brisbane*, six 21-foot motor launches for the RAN torpedo boat destroyers, 15 lifeboats, 18 cutters, 18 gigs, 10 whalers, 30 dinghies, eight balsa rafts, 665 life rafts, seven punts, 60 bipartite bridging pontoons and one 35-foot motor boat for HMAS *Adelaide*.

As well as the naval construction programme, the dockyard was also building merchant ships for the Commonwealth shipping line.

The Commonwealth Government Line of Steamers was formed in June 1916, when Prime Minister W M ('Billy') Hughes arranged the purchase of 15 second-hand cargo steamers, subsequently known as the 'Australs'. In addition to buying ships, the government embarked on a shipbuilding programme to acquire 50 steel cargo ships, all to be built in Australia, and five passenger-cargo ships.[82]

Cockatoo built four of these ships; two of the 19 Isherwood cargo ships that were completed, and the only two refrigerated cargo ships. Much of the design work for the ships was done at Cockatoo under the supervision of the General Manager, King Salter.[83]

The two Isherwood ships built at Cockatoo were No. 6, *Dundula*, and No. 35, *Eudunda*. They were 331 feet long (between perpendiculars) with a beam of 47 feet 9 inches, and had a deadweight capacity of 5608 and 6170 tons respectively. They were propelled by triple expansion steam engines of 1565 and 2424 IHP giving trial speeds of 10 and 12.5 knots.

The Isherwood system of construction was introduced in 1906, and led to a renewed interest in longitudinal framing in merchant ships. In this system, the usual closely spaced transverse frames are replaced by widely spaced deep frames and closely spaced longitudinal frames, which are continuous between bulkheads. Despite the saving in weight, and generally lower construction cost, this method of construction was seldom used for cargo ships because of the intrusion of the deep web frames into the space available for cargo. Longitudinal framing was widely adopted for tankers, and later for warships, where it provided considerable improvements in longitudinal strength.

The keel of *Dundula*, the first commercial cargo ship to be built at Cockatoo, was laid on 8 July 1918 and the ship was launched by Lady Helen Munro Ferguson, wife of the Governor General, on 9 July the following year. The ship left Cockatoo on 3 November 1919 under tow for Melbourne, where the main engine, which had been built by Thompson's of Castlemaine, was fitted at the Williamstown Dockyard. After trials, *Dundula* entered service in May 1920.

The launching of *Adelaide* on 27 July 1918. The gantry crane supporting a large number of spectators in the background was built on the island during World War I to enable the machinery to be shipped into *Brisbane* before launching.
(J C Jeremy Collection)

The naval collier *Biloela* leaving the dockyard completion in July 1920.
(J C Jeremy Collection)

The second ship, *Eudunda*, was ordered in June 1919, and left Cockatoo in December 1920, also to have the main engine installed in Melbourne. She ran trials in August 1921, but did not enter service until April 1922.

The D and E class cargo ships were never a success. They were expensive to operate, and too small and slow for overseas trade. By September 1923 many had already been laid up, two immediately on completion. Nevertheless some were to have long lives: *Eudunda* served Burns Philp & Company as the *Mangola* until May 1957, finally reaching the shipbreakers in 1959.[84] Of the four planned refrigerated cargo ships, only the two built by Cockatoo, Nos 47 and 48, were completed. Nos 49 and 50, which were to have been built by the New South Wales Government yard at Walsh Island in Newcastle, were cancelled.

Work on the *Fordsdale* began in the drawing office at Cockatoo in October 1919, but was stopped for a time the following year. The ship was not laid down until 1922, and was completed in March 1924. Her sister ship *Ferndale* was laid down in June 1923 and completed in October 1924.

These ships were the largest merchant ships ever built in Sydney. They had an overall length of 520 feet, and a beam of 63 feet. Their deadweight capacity was 12,500 tons on a displacement of 20,100 tons. They were twin screw ships, propelled by quadruple expansion steam engines of 6700 IHP, which were built at Cockatoo. Each ship had six oil-fired Scotch boilers, also of Cockatoo manufacture. They were then the biggest engines and boilers yet built in Australia. But by the time these ships were completed, the construction of merchant ships in Australia had almost come to an end. The launching of *Ferndale* on 12 June 1924 was the last launching of any ship built for the Commonwealth Line.

The E class cargo steamer *Eudunda* fitting out alongside the Destroyer Wharf in 1920.

Both ships received high praise for the quality of their construction, but their high cost (£828,469 and £752,065) was the subject of much criticism. The cost of Australian-built ships, and particularly Cockatoo-built ships, was constantly under political scrutiny during the 1920s, and especially in connection with the naval construction programme of 1924–25.

There was little shipbuilding at Cockatoo in the years immediately after the completion of the *Fordsdale* and *Ferndale*. The coal storage vessel *Mombah* was built for the RAN between 1920 and 1923, but after 1925 the only significant shipbuilding work was the building of two lighthouse service steamers for the Commonwealth. Completed in June and November 1925, the *Cape Leeuwin* and *Cape York* had an overall length of 235 feet, and were powered by a triple expansion steam engine driving a single screw.

The refrigerated cargo steamer *Fordsdale* nearly ready for launching on No. 1 slipway in March 1923.

The possibility of building a modern cruiser at Cockatoo was first discussed in 1923, and initial studies were based on the British Effingham class.[85] On 27 June 1924 the Prime Minister announced a naval construction programme that provided for the acquisition of two 10,000-ton cruisers, at least one to be built in Britain, and two modern submarines. On 3 July 1924, the Department of Defence asked the dockyard to help the Naval Board respond to a request from the Prime Minister for an estimate of the time and cost for building a cruiser at Cockatoo Island.[86]

The ship would be unlike previous ships built by Cockatoo, being designed to the tonnage limitations of the Washington Treaty, with the consequent need to limit weight by the use of modern materials such as high tensile steel and non-ferrous alloys. The dockyard promptly completed a very comprehensive estimate and responded at the beginning of August.

Ferndale, the second of the two refrigerated cargo ships built for the Commonwealth Line, on trials in 1924.

The drawing of the proposed 10,000-ton cruiser, upon which the dockyard's first estimate for the RAN cruisers in 1924 was based. This sketch design on the British Effingham class: when finally built in Britain later in the decade the *Australia* and *Canberra* were built to the Kent class design.

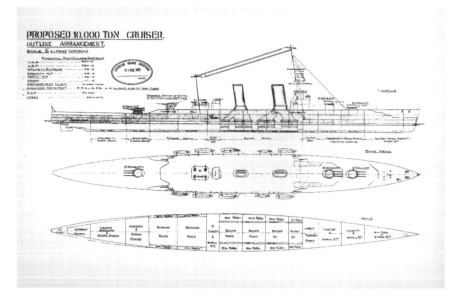

The dockyard's estimate was £2,898,000. The Naval Board's own estimate was substantially higher at £3,356,935. In view of the wide difference in these two prices, on 5 August the Prime Minister asked Sir John Monash to chair a conference between the Commonwealth Shipping Board and the Naval Board to try to arrive at an agreed estimate. Monash reported on 19 August that the conference had been unable to reach any unanimity on the cost of building the cruiser in Australia.

Whilst he felt that the Commonwealth Shipping Board's estimate was the most reliable, Sir John Monash concluded:

> There has emerged from this inquiry the certainty that, upon any set of assumptions, the cost of building a 10,000-ton cruiser at Cockatoo Dock would be, roundly, £1,000,000 more than the sum for which such a cruiser could be purchased from a British dockyard, and delivered in an Australian port.[87]

He went on to advocate the building of the ship in Britain.

On 22 December 1924, the Department of Defence invited the Australian Commonwealth Shipping Board (Cockatoo Dockyard), the New South Wales Government shipyard at Walsh Island, Newcastle, and British yards to tender for the construction of a heavy cruiser of the Kent class.[88] Tenders closed on 25 January 1925. The British yards were also asked to quote on the basis of construction, by them, in Australia.

On 24 March 1925, the Prime Minister told Parliament:

> These tenders have now been received, and included 10 tenders from shipbuilders in Great Britain for the construction of one or two cruisers in Great Britain. One tender was also received from a British shipbuilder for the construction of one vessel at their works in Great Britain and one in Australia.

Tenders were also received from the Commonwealth Shipping Board and from the New South Wales Government Dockyard for the construction of one cruiser at Cockatoo Island dockyard and Walsh Island dockyard respectively.

The tenders received from Great Britain from the 10 shipbuilders competing show a very narrow margin of difference, but the three tenders for construction in Australia show very substantial variations. The difference between the cost of construction in Great Britain and Australia, based on the lowest Australian tender is approximately £818,000. The percentage increase for the construction of one of these cruisers in Australia is as follows:

	Percentage of increase over lowest British tender
Commonwealth Shipping Board:	
British Built machinery	68 per cent
Australian built machinery	73 per cent
Walsh Island Dockyard:	
British built machinery	96.8 per cent
British Shipbuilder:	
Building in Australia	over 100 per cent

The tender received from the British shipbuilder contemplated that Cockatoo Island dockyard should be handed over for the purpose of construction, subject to the following conditions: 'The use of the dockyard, workshops, and offices be afforded free of cost or depreciation or maintenance.' This factor has been taken into account in calculating the cost of a cruiser constructed in Australia by a British shipbuilder.

After careful consideration the Government has decided to place the order for the construction of the two cruisers with Messrs John Brown and Company, Limited, Clydebank, at a total cost, fully equipped and ready for sea, with necessary spare parts, of approximately £4,250,000 and to employ the £800,000 saved by the placing of the order in Great Britain in building a modern 6000 tons seaplane carrier in Australia, at the approximate cost of the £800,000 saved.[89]

In his speech at the opening of Parliament on 10 June 1925, the Governor-General announced the government's intention that the seaplane carrier be built at Cockatoo Island Dockyard.

Cockatoo had submitted a rough estimate of £835,000 for the construction of a seaplane carrier in February 1925. At that time, the ship had not been designed, and much remained to be done at the time of the government's announcement.[90]

Shipping the boilers into the seaplane carrier *Albatross*. The boilers were landed on the elevated track by the floating crane *Titan*, then lowered into the ship by the temporary crane.

Australia's first aircraft carrier HMAS *Albatross*. The ship was transferred to the Royal Navy in 1938 as part payment for the cruiser *Hobart*.
(The Fairfax Photo Library)

The British Admiralty designed *Albatross* specifically for the RAN. There had been no previous *ab initio* design of a seaplane carrier, and *Albatross* was unique. Her designer, Stephen Payne, commented: 'You can say the hull was designed around three holds, three cranes, and 21 knots'.[91]

Cockatoo was formally invited to tender on 15 October 1925.[92] By this time the design was much more developed, and the fixed price offered in the tender, that was submitted on 27 November, was much more accurate. The price had increased to £941,127, principally due to the application of British Admiralty standards rather than the commercial standards first assumed. The order was placed on 2 February 1926.

HMAS *Albatross* was a rather ugly ship of 4800 tons standard displacement, 437 feet long overall, armed with four 4.7-inch and several smaller guns, and propelled by Parsons geared turbines with twin

screws for a designed speed of 21 knots at 12,000 SHP. She achieved 22.3 knots at 13,400 SHP on trials. There were three hangars, and nine aircraft could be carried, which were handled over the side by crane. The complement was about 450 officers and men.

The ship was laid down on 5 May 1926, and was launched by Lady Stonehaven, wife of the Governor General on 23 February 1928. HMAS *Albatross* was completed on 21 December 1928, at a final contract price, including extras, of £1,018,925, yielding a small profit for the shipbuilder.

Following the completion of *Albatross*, the only significant ship built at Cockatoo in the remaining years of Commonwealth administration was the lighthouse steamer *Cape Otway*. A small ship of 208 feet 7 inches overall length, she was powered by a triple expansion steam engine, and was completed in October 1931. By that time employment at the dockyard was at a very low level and in an effort to keep some shipbuilding skills alive, and to train apprentices, the dockyard started to build a small 75-foot steam tug. It was still under construction when Cockatoo Docks & Engineering Company took over the dockyard, and it was launched as *Codeco* by *Titan* on 27 June 1933. On completion in February 1934, the tug was taken over by the RAN for use at the Garden Island dockyard, and renamed *Wattle*.[93]

It was not long before the outlook for shipbuilding at Cockatoo began to improve. Discussions between the Company and the Department of Defence about the possibility of building a sloop at Cockatoo began in May 1933. An order for the ship was placed on 22 December 1933, and Ship 114 was launched as *Yarra* in March 1935, and completed on 12 December that year. *Yarra* was a modified

The lighthouse ship *Cape Otway* was completed in October 1931.

Grimsby class sloop, and working drawings had been obtained from the Admiralty for guidance. The design had been modified for RAN service as a patrol vessel, convoy escort and minesweeper.

As completed HMAS *Yarra* had a full load displacement of 1366 tons, an overall length of 265 feet, and was fitted with three 4-inch anti-aircraft guns, four 3-pounders and some machine guns. The machinery, which was built at Cockatoo, comprised two sets of Parsons geared turbines and Yarrow small tube, three drum boilers, driving twin screws for a trial speed of 17 knots at 2131 SHP.

Parramatta, the third Grimsby class sloop, was launched on 10 June 1939. She was sunk off Tobruk on 27 November 1941. (Phil Bushell)

A second ship, HMAS *Swan*, was ordered in 1934 and completed in December 1936. There was some debate at the time about the need for these ships, but they proved to be useful in RAN service. *Yarra* was lost south of Java on 4 March 1942, but *Swan* remained in service for 28 years and was finally broken up at Woolwich near Cockatoo Island in 1965–66.

In the mid-1930s, Cockatoo tendered for many commercial vessels of all sizes in competition with overseas builders. There was no subsidy or bounty for Australian shipbuilders in those days and most of the tenders were

HMAS *Yarra* was the first of four sloops of the Grimsby class built at Cockatoo Island. Completed in December 1935, she was sunk south of Java on 4 March 1942. (RAN photograph)

unsuccessful. Several tugs were built, including the *Warang* and *Waree* for the Waratah Tug Company. An oil lighter, *Shell 23*, and a small tug were completed for the Shell Company.

A small ship was designed and built at Cockatoo in 1937–38 for the Department of Trade and Customs. The patrol vessel *Vigilant* was intended to patrol northern

Australian waters, and was 102 feet long with a displacement of about 100 tons. She was the first Australian-built ship in which aluminium was used as a structural material; the wheelhouse being so built to save weight. *Vigilant* was taken over by the RAN during World War II and served first as HMAS *Vigilant*, later being renamed *Sleuth* and finally *Hawk*.

A number of small craft were also produced, including a series of fast launches for the Civil Aviation Board for the Empire Flying Boat Service. These boats were built to Thornycroft designs, and six were based on a design that the Company had selected for a small fast Company launch, *Codock Jnr*. The relationship with Thornycroft continued for the construction of two target towing launches *Koree* and *Wadjemup* that were built for the Department of Defence in 1939.

A boom defence vessel, HMAS *Kookaburra*, was ordered in February 1938 and in March 1938 the Company received an order for two more sloops of the Yarra class. *Parramatta* and *Warrego* were both laid down before the war, in November 1938 and March 1939. Another boom defence vessel, *Koala*, which was based on the British Barricade class, was ordered in December 1938. Two more, *Kangaroo* and *Karangi* were built in 1939–40.

The increased pace of naval shipbuilding continued when the Company was asked on 22 December 1938 to submit a tender for the construction of two modern destroyers of the Tribal class. On 24 January 1939 Department of Defence wrote advising that the Naval Board wanted the ships to be completed as early as possible, and authorising preliminary work in advance of the tender. The Company was to proceed with working drawing preparation, material ordering, loft work and slipway preparation.

The Company's tender was submitted on 10 July 1939, on a fixed price incentive basis, with a maximum price of £720,000 each. The order was placed on 6 October 1939, and the first ship, *Arunta* was laid down on No. 1 slipway on 15 November 1939. The keel of *Warramunga* was laid on the new No. 2 slipway on 10 February 1940, the day HMAS *Warrego* was launched by Mrs Menzies, wife of the Prime Minister.

Almost, but not quite. *Arunta* stuck part way to the water on 30 November 1940. The first LDV, *Bathurst*, lies at the shipyard wharf shortly before her completion. The second Tribal class destroyer, *Warramunga*, is under construction on No. 2 slipway.

On board *Arunta*
during sea trials in
early 1942.
(RAN photograph)

Progress with *Arunta* was rapid, and she was to be launched by Lady Gowrie, wife of the Governor-General on 30 November 1940. That day was very wet, and the rain had held up the official party, delaying the launching past the high tide. *Arunta* moved part of the way down the slip, in the pouring rain, and stopped. She was successfully launched the following day after more grease had been applied under the fore poppets.

The launching hitch was not a bad omen, and *Arunta* was completed on 30 April 1942 in good time to make a substantial contribution to the war in the Pacific. Her sister ship *Warramunga* was delayed a little by changing priorities for labour, and late delivery of materials, but was completed on 22 December 1942.

The Tribal class destroyers were handsome and powerfully armed ships. They differed from the 16 British ships of the class, with a smaller after funnel and a modified armament. They were 377 feet long overall, with a full load displacement of about 2550 tons. They were armed with six 4.7-inch guns in three twin turrets, one twin 4-inch mounting, one four-barrel 2-pounder pom-pom, six 20-millimetre Oerlikons, four 21-inch torpedo tubes, and two depth charge throwers.

The main machinery, which was built at Cockatoo, comprised Parsons impulse reaction steam turbines, three Admiralty 3-drum watertube boilers with superheaters, driving two 10-foot 3-inch propellers. On trials *Arunta* made 35 knots at 47,410 SHP, and *Warramunga* 36.65 knots at 46,380 SHP (on a low displacement). They were the fastest ships ever built at Cockatoo.

On 2 February 1940 the Company was asked to proceed with a third ship, and the keel of *Kurnai* was laid on No. 1 slipway on 30 November 1940. This act must have been largely ceremonial as little work was done on the ship due to demands of much higher priority. To make way for the first of the A class standard merchant ships the keel was removed from No. 1 slipway and re-laid on No. 2 on 18 February 1942. *Kurnai* was further delayed by late delivery of equipment and defective rivet material. She was named *Bataan* and launched by Mrs

Douglas MacArthur on 15 January 1944. She was completed on 26 June 1945, too late to play a significant part in the war.

As war approached in 1939, the RAN prepared plans for a class of small, simple escort/minesweeping ships, which could be readily built in Australia in some numbers. On 21 September 1939, the Department of Defence wrote to the Company advising that a number of these ships, known as local defence vessels (LDV), were urgently required for naval service. The letter went on to say:

> Several firms in various States have been invited to submit offers for these, but as your Company is the only one in Australia possessing a complete ship-building organisation, it is under consideration that, subject to a satisfactory financial arrangement, one of the vessels be built by you, and that you proceed with all possible speed with the mould loft work, so as to be in a position to supply other builders such information as will reduce their loft work to a minimum, observing that this will be of material assistance to them. It is clear that it will be necessary to use all building facilities throughout Australia to the utmost during the War.

Other firms invited to tender have been advised that:

> 'In order to ensure the greatest economy of effort in their production, interchange and circulation of plans between the builders will be arranged to the fullest extent practicable, so as to reduce drawing office and mould loft work to a minimum. Such parts as steel castings for the hull will be produced by one firm for all vessels. The boilers, being of naval design, will be built at Cockatoo Island or Garden Island, and the auxiliary engines, it is proposed, will be ordered independently by the Naval Board in numbers sufficient for all ships.

Warramunga at full power. The ship achieved over 36 knots during trials.

HMAS *Goulburn* was the second of eight local defence vessels (later known as Australian minesweepers) built at Cockatoo Dockyard. She was completed in February 1941.
(RAN photograph)

The general standard of construction of the vessels and their machinery, except where otherwise specified, is to be in accordance with approved mercantile practice. All equipment of specially naval character will be supplied by the Naval Board and fitted by the builder.' [94]

Cockatoo submitted a tender on 6 October 1939, and following some negotiation over the price, LDV No. 1 was formally ordered on 9 December 1939. HMAS *Bathurst*, the lead ship of what was to become a class of 60 ships, was laid down on 10 February 1940 and completed on 5 December.

Two more were ordered from Cockatoo in April 1940 (*Goulburn* and *Bendigo*), and a further two in July 1940 (*Wollongong* and *Cessnock*), all paid for by the British Admiralty. A further three were ordered in September 1940 for the Indian Navy (*Madras*, *Bengal* and *Bombay*). The last was reallocated to the RAN in June 1941 and completed in November 1942 as HMAS *Glenelg*.[95]

The LDVs were redesignated Australian minesweepers (AMS), Bathurst class in 1940. Although similar to the Royal Navy minesweepers of the Bangor class, the Bathurst class was designed for the RAN in Australia. They were 186 feet long overall, 31 feet in the beam, and about 950 tons full load displacement. They were armed with one 4-inch gun, some smaller guns and depth charges. The main engines were triple expansion steam engines of 1750 IHP in the early ships (and 2000 IHP later), with two watertube boilers, and two shafts.

The New South Wales State Dockyard in Newcastle, Poole & Steel in Sydney, BHP Whyalla, Evans Deakin in Brisbane, Walkers in Maryborough, Mort's Dock in Sydney, and the Williamstown Naval Dockyard in Victoria built other ships of the class. This programme, and the assistance given by Cockatoo, was instrumental in re-establishing a shipbuilding industry in Australia, and preparing the yards for merchant ship construction.

Early in the war, the Commonwealth decided that a programme of merchant ship construction should also be carried out in Australia. As a first step the war cabinet directed Engineer Rear Admiral P E McNeil, Chief of Naval Construction, to review the position and report on the feasibility of such a programme.

Admiral McNeil's report of 13 January 1941 became the basis for the development of the subsequent programme.[96] The Australian Shipbuilding Board which was formed in March 1941 became responsible for its implementation. In his report, Admiral McNeil assumed that naval construction would continue throughout the war, and that any programme of merchant ship construction would have to proceed, at least for some time, concurrently with that for the construction of small naval vessels. Practical considerations suggested that a standard merchant ship of around 8000 tons deadweight would be within the capability of the Australian industry, and suitable for coastal and overseas trade.

Prior to the formation of the Shipbuilding Board, Admiral McNeil had obtained from Great Britain drawings of the *Scottish Monarch*, a cargo vessel of 9000 tons deadweight and a speed of 10.5 knots. The Board considered that the *Scottish Monarch* design, modified as necessary for a speed of 12 knots, should be adopted as the standard ship to be built under the Australian merchant shipbuilding programme.

The A class standard steamship *River Clarence* was the first of the class to be completed. (RAN photograph)

Originally a programme of 60 merchant ships had been planned, however the outbreak of war with Japan, and the very high demand for ship repair work which resulted, made the necessary rate of production impracticable. Eight ships were ordered initially, with five more ordered later, making a total of 13 A class standard merchant ships laid down during the war.

Two of these ships were allocated to Cockatoo, and the standard ships A1 and A2 were ordered on 19 May 1941. Prime Minister Menzies laid down the first of the class, *River Clarence*, on No. 1 slipway on 29 July 1941. Addressing the assembled workers, he noted the achievements of Cockatoo, saying:

> The story of this place over the last few years would, I believe, make a remarkable romance. It is, in my opinion, an astonishing thing to look back over the last four or five years and realise the development that has taken place all over Australia in the production of ships. And I want to say to all of you who are engaged in this work of shipbuilding that I want you to regard yourselves as being engaged in the true service of this country and in the true service of the British Empire.[97]

The A class ships had an overall length of 449 feet 2 inches, a beam of 56 feet 6 inches, and a deadweight of about 9000 tons.[98] The full load displacement was about 13,000 tons. They were fitted with a triple expansion steam engine with a Bauer-Wach exhaust steam turbine, of 3000 IHP, for a service speed of 11.5 to 12 knots.

The construction of *River Clarence* and *River Hunter* was severely delayed by the heavy demands placed on the dockyard for the repair of damaged ships and other work of a higher priority. The experience in other yards was similar, except at BHP in Whyalla, where there was no interference from ship repair work. The merchant ship programme did at least ensure a valuable pool of skilled labour that could be drawn upon for urgent ship repairs, but the delays to the new ships were very costly.

River Clarence was the first standard ship to be completed, on 31 May 1943. *River Hunter* was modified during construction to arrange all the accommodation above the shelter deck amidships, and was not completed until 25 June 1946.

The A class programme was curtailed in 1943 and a programme of smaller ships for the Australian coastal trade approved. Cockatoo did not build any of these ships but made a significant contribution in other ways, as described in Chapter 10.

To meet a shortage at the time, the war cabinet approved the construction of three ocean-going tugs and three harbour tugs in October 1944. The three ocean-going tugs were ordered from Cockatoo on 25 November 1944. They were to have been 145 feet 10 inches long overall, with a beam of 30 feet and a full load displacement of 897 tons. Machinery available from cancelled naval orders was to be used, with a frigate triple expansion steam engine of 1750 IHP and a watertube boiler giving a speed of 12.5 knots.

One tug, *TA1* (Ship 180) was 46 per cent erected on No. 2 slipway when they were all cancelled on 3 September 1945. Efforts to sell the tug were unsuccessful, and it was broken up in the late 1940s.

Two other ships were built at Cockatoo during the war, the frigates HMAS *Barcoo* and HMAS *Barwon*.

By May 1941 the need for frigates for ocean escort and convoy work had been clearly identified. At that time 48 Australian minesweepers had been ordered, and more were needed. Later in the year the war cabinet approved Naval Board proposals for the final 12 minesweepers and for six frigates of the River class.[99] River class frigates Nos 1 and 2 were ordered from Cockatoo on 16 August 1941.

The frigate programme was increased during 1942 to a total of 22 ships. The number that could be built was influenced by the heavy demand for labour for ship repair work, the need to minimise delays to the merchant shipbuilding programme, and the capacity to build machinery for the ships. Four more ships (Nos 16 to 19) were ordered from Cockatoo on 10 December 1942.

Barcoo was laid down in October 1942 and completed in February 1944. *Barwon* was laid down in May 1943 but not completed until January 1946. They were 301 feet 7 inches long overall, 36 feet 6 inches in the beam and had a full load displacement of about 2150 tons. Propelled by twin screws driven by four-cylinder triple-expansion engines, each of 2250 IHP, with two Admiralty three drum watertube boilers, the ships had a speed of 20 knots. They were armed with two 4-inch and a number of smaller guns, and eight depth charge throwers.

The second River class frigate built at Cockatoo Island, HMAS *Barwon*, was handed over to the RAN on 12 January 1946. She saw little service, being paid off in March 1947. She was sold for scrap in 1962. (J C Jeremy Collection)

Frigates 16 to 19 were to be of the improved River class, of which only four were finally completed.[100] Their configuration was wholly Australian. They were to mount two twin 4-inch anti-aircraft mountings, and to be propelled by steam turbines instead of reciprocating steam engines. The order for No. 19 was transferred to Walkers in October 1943 and all four were cancelled in April 1944.

In April 1946 the Naval Board queried the cost of *Barcoo* and *Barwon*, noting the low cost of those built by Walkers and the relatively high cost of the Cockatoo ships. By comparison, the actual costs of minesweepers built in each yard was almost the same. In fact, the average cost of the two Cockatoo ships, (£370,379), one of which was the lead ship of the class, compared favourably with the average cost of the 11 then completed, £368,024.

In response, the Company pointed out that the Cockatoo ships had been extensively modified within weeks of completion (*Barcoo*) or when well advanced (*Barwon*), in addition to the delay and dislocation arising from the competing demands of ship repair work. In view of the higher wage rates prevailing in Sydney, the actual costs of the ships were felt to be reasonable. This comparison did however highlight the problem of building and repairing ships in the same yard at the same time, when the new ships provided a pool of labour that could be drawn on as needed for repairs.

The cancellation of the last 10 Australian River class frigates arose from a Navy review of escort requirements in October 1943. With a pressing need for more escorts, the ordering of further frigates was considered against a preference for a series of Hunt class destroyers. The yards building frigates were heavily committed with the merchant ship programme, and it was felt that only Cockatoo was capable of building the destroyers.

In November Cockatoo examined the feasibility of building three Hunt class destroyers, and one Dido class cruiser. As the destroyers could not be completed before May and September 1946 and May 1947, and the cruiser in September 1948, so there was nothing to be gained in time to help the war effort.[101]

In October 1944, the RAN ordered two Battle class destroyers, one to be built by Cockatoo and the other by the Williamstown dockyard in Victoria. Cockatoo was to be the lead yard, and was to build the boilers and turbines for both ships. The working drawings were to be supplied by John Brown & Company, Clydebank who were then building the Royal Navy Battle class destroyers of the 1943 programme (which comprised the 3rd Flotilla of fleet destroyers of the war programme). The Australian ships were to be similar to the ships of the planned 5th and 6th Flotillas, which had increased beam (41 feet, compared to the 40 feet 6 inches of the 1943 Battles). They were also to mount the new 4.5-inch Mark VI twin gun mounting, in place of the 4.5 inch Mark IV in the earlier ships.

In September 1945, the Admiralty cancelled the 5th and 6th Flotillas, and the RAN destroyers were the only ships of the class completed with the modified armament.

Tobruk was laid down on No. 1 slipway on 5 August 1946: the last riveted destroyer to be built by Cockatoo. The ship was planned for completion in February 1949, but once more other work received a higher priority for labour, which was scarce in the immediate post-war years. She was launched on 20 December 1947, but not completed until 8 May 1950.

Tobruk, and *Anzac* built at Williamstown, were handsome ships. The large Mark VI mounting necessitated a higher bridge structure than

The Battle class destroyer *Tobruk* under construction on No. 1 slipway in January 1947. The ship on No. 2 slipway is the cancelled tug Ship 180. It was broken up later the same year. (RAN photograph)

Tobruk at speed during sea trials in December 1949.
(J C Jeremy Collection)

in the RN ships, to preserve forward vision. Weight compensation was partly achieved by the use of aluminium for the lattice foremast. They were the first RAN ships in which aluminium was widely used for ventilation trunking and furniture. Accommodation arrangements were also greatly improved.

Tobruk was 379 feet long overall, with a beam of 41 feet and a full load displacement of 3359 tons, 25 per cent more than the displacement of the Tribals. Parsons geared turbines and two Admiralty three drum boilers delivered a designed 50,000 SHP to two 11-foot 6-inch diameter propellers. She achieved 32.36 knots on trials at 51,745 SHP.

The main armament comprised four 4.5-inch guns, in the Mark VI mountings, which, for *Tobruk* were imported from Britain. The secondary armament was 12 40-millimetre guns. Six were carried by three twin 'STAAG' mountings. The Stabilised Tachymetric Anti-Aircraft Gun (STAAG) was a remarkable weapon. The mounting was hydraulically powered, and contained its own radar and fire control system. It was maintenance nightmare, and not a success. *Tobruk* also mounted a Mark 4 anti-submarine mortar known as 'Squid'.

The order for the Battle class destroyers marked the start of a postwar naval shipbuilding programme that was to keep Cockatoo and Williamstown busy for nearly twenty years. In April 1946, the government approved the construction of four destroyers of an advanced type (Daring class) in addition to the Battles. Ordered on 3 December 1946, Darings Nos 1 and 2 (*Voyager* and *Vampire*) were to be built by Cockatoo and Nos 3 and 4 (*Vendetta* and *Waterhen*) by Williamstown. Cockatoo was to be the lead yard, and a separate order was placed with Cockatoo for the manufacture of the main machinery for all ships.

The forebody of *Voyager* upside down on the prefabrication slab in June 1949. This section of the ship comprised about six units. When ready each unit was turned and placed on the slipway.
(RAN photograph)

Progress on the erection of *Voyager* in April 1951. (RAN photograph)

In giving approval for the construction of these ships, cabinet had recognised the need to maintain a naval shipbuilding capability in Australia in the interests of defence. When authorising the orders the Department of the Treasury had specified:

> The approval in principle given by Cabinet to the building of 4 additional destroyers of an advanced type may be regarded as authority to proceed with the placement of orders to ensure the maintenance of shipbuilding capacity in Australia.
>
> The main consideration involved in the maintenance of this shipbuilding capacity is its relation to:
>
> (a) the ultimate strength and composition of the post-war Australian forces
>
> (b) the balanced allocation of the post-war defence vote between service and supply departments.
>
> Until decision is reached on these matters orders to be placed under the Cabinet approval should not exceed the essential minimum necessary to maintain production capacity from time to time. The necessity to continue the work of constructing the destroyers should also be reviewed at regular intervals.[102]

The order specified that the second ship was not to be laid down until the first was launched, and the rate of annual expenditure was controlled.

The design of the Daring class destroyer arose from a Royal Navy staff requirement of June 1943 for a fleet destroyer to follow the Battle class. The basic design was approved in February 1945 and provisional orders for the first British ships were placed the following month.[103]

The Daring class were large ships, 390 feet overall length, 43 feet in the beam, and a full load displacement of about 3500 tons. The armament in the British ships was six 4.5-inch guns in three Mark VI twin mountings, two twin 40-millimetre STAAG mountings, one twin Mark 5 40-millimetre mounting, 10 torpedo tubes in two mountings and a Mark 4 Squid anti-submarine mortar. Accommodation was provided for 330 men.

The Australian ships were substantially modified during construction, and the first, HMAS *Voyager*, was completed without one set of torpedo tubes while the Squid was replaced with the Mark 10 'Limbo' mortar. Accommodation arrangements were also improved, with air conditioning of all living and most working spaces. Further improvements were incorporated in the later ships.

The machinery in the RAN ships comprised English Electric geared turbines, with two Foster Wheeler boilers driving twin screws. The designed shaft horsepower was 54,000, for a maximum speed of 33 knots.

From the shipbuilder's point of view, the most significant change in the Darings was the introduction of fully welded construction. Previous Australian-built warships had been riveted. British yards had been gradually introducing welding, but some of their Darings were still partially riveted.

Prefabrication of units was not entirely new to Cockatoo. The stern of the lighthouse ship *Cape York* had been built and erected as a pre-assembled unit in 1925. Electric welding began to be used at Cockatoo for the construction of

minor assemblies during the 1920s. Later, as part of the extensive programme for the construction of small ships during World War II small cargo vessels of about 250 tons deadweight were prefabricated in sections at many engineering works and assembled on production lines at Sydney, Newcastle and Melbourne. These ships were of welded construction. Small welded steel tugs were also built in roll-over jigs at Sydney and at Hexham on the shores of the Hunter River. This was the first use of this construction technique in Australia.[104]

The Daring class destroyers represented a complete transition for the RAN and were the first fully welded naval ships assembled from three-dimensional prefabricated units to be built in Australia. This required substantial changes in shipyard layout and construction procedures.

These destroyers were by far the most complex ships built in Australia at that time, yet a very high proportion of their armament,

Voyager, the first of three Daring class destroyers built in Australia, left Cockatoo Island on 11 February 1957.
(J C Jeremy Collection)

Vampire almost ready for launching in October 1956.
(RAN photograph)

machinery and equipment was made in Australia. The original pro-gramme provided for their completion between 1949 and 1950, but this plan was over-optimistic. Extensive delays occurred with the supply of working drawings from Britain, and by 1950 it had even been suggested that the drawings be taken over and completed in Australia. As it was, the task of modifying the drawings to incorporate RAN modifications was considerable.

The high demand for skilled labour after the war also slowed the ships and the production of their equipment, and there were considerable delays in the delivery of castings and forgings for the machinery and structural steel for the hulls.

By 1954 the way ahead was clearer, although the fourth ship, *Waterhen*, had been cancelled in March 1953. The first, HMAS *Voyager*, was handed over to the RAN on 10 February 1957, and HMAS *Vampire* was completed in June 1959.

The backlog of shipbuilding work at Cockatoo increased when in August 1950 the government approved the construction of six anti-submarine frigates, three to be built at Cockatoo and three at Williamstown. The number had been reduced to four by the time orders were placed in October 1952, for completion in 1957. Cockatoo was to be the lead yard for the Australian class.[105]

The design of the Type 12 frigate was developed by the RN after 1945 to satisfy the need for a high speed anti-submarine frigate which could be built relatively quickly in large numbers to counter the growing number of submarines with a high underwater speed. The first British ships (the Whitby class) were ordered in 1951. Whilst the design was far from simple, and not particularly easy to build, it was very successful, and 70 ships of the type were completed for seven navies between 1956 and 1981.

The RAN ships started out as copies of the Whitby class, but they were greatly modified during construction, and were quite distinct from other ships of the type. The first two, *Parramatta*, built

Smoke generator trials during *Vampire's* contractor's sea trials on 29 October 1958.
(J C Jeremy Collection)

HMAS *Vampire* ready for action.

at Cockatoo, and *Yarra*, built at Williamstown, had a full load displacement of about 2500 tons and an overall length of 370 feet. They were armed with a twin 4.5-inch Mark VI mounting, two Mark 10 Limbo anti-submarine mortars, and one twin Mark 5 Bofors 40/60 mounting. They were propelled by English Electric Y100 geared turbines with Foster Wheeler boilers and two shafts. The designed shaft horsepower was 30,000 for a maximum speed of 30 knots. Cockatoo built the turbines and boilers.

During construction, *Parramatta* and her sister ship had been modified to accommodate the Seacat anti-aircraft guided missile, which was installed in place of the Bofors mounting after completion.

The conditions that affected the Daring class also delayed the frigates, and *Parramatta* was not completed until July 1961. The second ship, *Stuart*, was laid down in March 1959. In 1960, the Navy decided to fit the second two Type 12s with the Ikara anti-submarine guided missile, then under development in Australia. *Stuart* was to be the trial ship for the system.

Construction of *Stuart* was well advanced when the extent of the necessary changes became known to the shipyard, and much of the ship's design was 'in abeyance' when she was launched by Mrs Gorton, wife of the Minister for the Navy, on 8 April 1961. Nevertheless, *Stuart* went to sea for contractors sea trials in October 1962, and fired the Ikara missile at sea for the first time in March 1963 whilst still in the builder's hands. She was completed in June 1963, in a trial's ship configuration. Her normal outfit of equipment was completed later in 1964.

To fit the Ikara missile system, *Stuart* and *Derwent* (built at Williamstown) lost one Mark 10 mortar; otherwise the armament was the same as the first two ships. The internal modifications to accommodate Ikara were however very extensive.

When HMAS *Stuart* was launched there was no ship to follow on the slips

The Type 12 frigate *Parramatta* at sea for hand over for the RAN on 4 July 1961. (RAN photograph)

HMAS *Stuart*, the second Type 12 frigate built at Cockatoo Island, and the first ship to be fitted with the Ikara anti-submarine missile and was the trials ship for the system. (RAN photograph)

Swinging to a fresh southerly wind the *Empress of Australia* waits for the tugs after launching on 18 January 1964. The ship sailed between the Australian mainland and Tasmania until 1985. She was then sold overseas and operated as *Empress* in the Mediterranean for several years, before being extensively rebuilt as a cruise ship and renamed *Royal Pacific*. She was sunk in collision with a Taiwanese fishing boat in the Malacca Strait in August 1991.

at Cockatoo, the first time since 1938, and the naval construction programme announced by the Minister for Defence at the end of June 1961 broke the long continuity in the construction of destroyer type ships in Australia.

The 1961 programme provided for the purchase of two guided missile destroyers from the United States. The Charles F. Adams (DDG 2) class was to be the first US designed combat ships for the RAN. The US Navy ordered *Perth* and *Hobart* on behalf of the RAN from the Defoe Shipbuilding Company in Bay City, Michigan. They were very capable ships, over 440 feet long, with a full load displacement of about 4600 tons, and were armed with two 5-inch guns, the Tartar anti-aircraft missile, and after arrival in Australia, Ikara. A third ship, *Brisbane*, was ordered in 1963.

Australian shipbuilders, and particularly Cockatoo, expressed disappointment at not even being asked to tender for the ships. Whilst they could unquestionably have been built in Australia, their advanced design and the lack of experience in building to US design standards could well have produced some difficulties, but the industry would have been able to respond to the challenge. The order of these ships from the United States was the first step in a series of changes in the pattern of naval shipbuilding in Australia.

With no immediate prospects of an on-going naval construction programme, Cockatoo tendered for several merchant ships in the early 1960s, in competition with the other commercial shipyards. In January 1962, Cockatoo was successful in winning the order to build a roll-on roll-off passenger vehicle ship for the Australian National Line. The ship was intended to provide a passenger and cargo service between Sydney and Tasmania, in a similar manner to the successful *Princess of Tasmania* (built by the State Dockyard in Newcastle) which operated to Tasmania from Melbourne.

The Australian Shipbuilding Board placed the order for the new ship, the first large commercial ship built by Cockatoo since the *River Hunter*, in February 1962. The basic design of the ship was done by the Board, with Cockatoo completing all the detailed design. Ship 220, laid down in September 1962, was all welded except that the frames were riveted to the shell plating. The ship was erected in pre-fabricated panels, although to save time a section of the shelter deck structure, about 60 feet long and the full width of the ship, containing crew accommodation and cold and cool rooms, was assembled on the ground and fitted out before erection at the ship. This approach was adopted to save time, and it has since become common practice as modular construction (as it is now known) has been adopted throughout the shipbuilding industry.

During construction, Ship 220 was known around the yard as the 'Duchess of Woolloomooloo', a title replaced by the much more appropriate name *Empress of Australia* when she was launched by the Honourable Catherine Sidney, daughter of the Governor-General, on 18 January 1964.

Completed in January 1965, the *Empress* was the largest ship of her type in the world. With a gross tonnage of 12,037 tons, an overall length of 445 feet and a beam of 70 feet, the *Empress* was propelled by two 10-cylinder MAN turbo charged two-stroke diesel engines, for a service speed of 18.5 knots. The vehicle deck was intended to carry some 51 cars, 33 semi-trailers and a number of containers. 250 passengers were accommodated in four, two or single berth cabins, with 18 in single or twin deluxe cabins or suites.

The *Empress* proved to be successful and reliable for her owners. However the transition from the construction of warships (which since the war had been built at cost) to commercial construction (at a fixed price) was not a happy one for the shipyard, and Cockatoo lost a substantial amount of money on the contract. The consequences of this loss have been described in Chapter 4. The yard was however soon to return to the more familiar naval work.

The decision to build an escort maintenance ship for the Navy was announced in the government's defence review of May 1963. The ship, to be built in Australia to an Australian design, was intended as a mobile workshop capable of providing support to the RAN's new destroyers and frigates in operational areas away from the dockyards

Attended by two tugs, the *Empress of Australia* about to leave Cockatoo Island for trials on 2 December 1964.

The destroyer tender *Stalwart* approaching Goat Island on the way to sea for trials on 29 November 1967. (RAN photograph)

and bases. At that time the design of the ship was not very far advanced, however it was planned to call tenders from Australian shipyards before the end of 1963.

It became apparent that the design could not be completed quickly enough to enable a complete specification to be issued for tender purposes. In September the government approved the construction of the ship at Cockatoo Dockyard, which was regarded as sufficiently experienced to build the ship to naval requirements from a minimum of information.

Lady Casey named and launched *Stalwart* on 7 October 1966, after a delay of about six weeks brought about by a protracted strike by shipwrights in support of higher wages.

Design of the ship continued throughout the building period, and some features were still being planned when the ship was handed over in February 1968. Later reclassified as a 'destroyer tender', HMAS *Stalwart* was 515 feet 6 inches long overall, 67 feet 6 inches in beam, and had a full load displacement of 15,500 tons. She was propelled by two Scott Sulzer six-cylinder direct drive diesel engines, with a maximum speed of 20 knots. With a complement of 415, the ship had workshops and facilities to support destroyers and frigates and a substantial generating capacity to supply ships alongside.

For many years *Stalwart* was mostly moored at Garden Island

serving operational ships, where she became known as 'Building 215', after her pennant number AD 215. Later she saw more sea time as fleet flagship and training ship. With the development of ship repair facilities in Western and northern Australia the need for the ship's special facilities was reduced, and *Stalwart* was paid off and sold in 1990.

Following the loss of the destroyer HMAS *Voyager* in collision with the aircraft carrier *Melbourne* in February 1964, the government approved the ordering of two more Type 12 frigates in June 1964 as replacements. The construction of the fifth and sixth ships of this class, originally proposed in 1950, had been considered again in 1958. The orders were placed with Cockatoo for *Torrens* and with Williamstown for *Swan*, with Williamstown the lead yard.

In view of the need to replace the *Voyager* as quickly as possible, it was intended that the ships be built in four years, as exact repeats of *Stuart* and *Derwent*. Within six months, however, the decision had been made to modernise the design to incorporate as many features as possible of the later RN Leander class Type 12s. The armament was also updated, and as completed *Torrens* and *Swan* were essentially of a new design.

The design work necessary to incorporate the changes was done by Navy Office, Cockatoo and Williamstown whilst the ships were being built, which provided some major challenges for the shipbuilders, and inevitably extended the building programme, and increased its cost.

Internally the ships were substantially rearranged. The upper deck was extended to the stern to increase hull volume, and a larger superstructure, all welded aluminium above 01 deck, was provided. Accommodation arrangements were greatly improved. The original British fire control systems for the guns (MRS 3) and Seacat missile systems (GWS 20) were replaced by Dutch equipment (HSA M22 and M44), and the communications and electronic warfare equipment were changed.

The machinery installation was also improved, updated from the Y100 to Y136 design with full remote control. Cockatoo made the turbines for both ships, the last steam turbines to be built at the dockyard, but the boilers were imported. They came from Vickers Armstrongs Engineers at Barrow in Furness. When they were received in Australia in 1967, they were not in the best of condition, with some rust and some welding rods left in tubes and drums. One of the boilers for *Swan*, received at Williamstown, even had an unopened tin of pilchards in one steam drum. The pilchards caused some amusement at Barrow and some even suggested that they should ask for the tin back![106]

The new general arrangement of the ships was not finalised until March 1965, however political pressure to see visible progress prompted the keel laying of both ships in August 1965. In the case of *Torrens* at least, this was a year too soon, and little progress was made for a year due to the workload building *Stalwart*. The overload in the shipyard resulted in Cockatoo sub-contracting structural prefabrication work for the first time, for both *Stalwart* and *Torrens*.

HMAS *Swan* was handed over by Williamstown in April 1970 (although the ship was not completed until some months later), and HMAS *Torrens* was completed in January 1971. They were very fine ships and one of the most successful of the Type 12 variants built anywhere.

The construction of two further ships of the class (DE 07 and 08) was considered by the Navy in 1969, however as equipment for the class was no longer in regular production the lead time would have been considerable. With a new class of destroyer type ships then being planned, the proposal did not proceed. In the event, *Torrens* was to be the last combat warship completed in Australia for the Navy for 21 years.

In late 1968, the Navy asked Cockatoo to examine the feasibility of building a fast combat support ship (AOE) and three light destroyers (DDL) at Cockatoo Dockyard. The light destroyers were to be follow-on ships to three to be built at Williamstown. The Company responded in November confirming that the proposed plan was possible with some minor modification. The Navy sought government approval for the ships in May 1969, which it was given on 22 July.

The Navy had identified the need for an additional major

Titan launching *CSL 01* on 12 July 1972. Cockatoo built three crane stores lighters that year for the RAN, and they have been a familiar sight around Sydney harbour ever since. They were all assembled in the plate yard from sections built in the boiler shop.

replenishment ship in June 1964. Cabinet approval to proceed with the acquisition of such a ship was given in November 1964, however the ship was removed from the programme in October 1965 to make way for higher priority projects. Two ships had been proposed in 1969, one for delivery in 1977 and the second to replace the existing Tide class fleet oiler HMAS *Supply* after 1980, when it was expected to have reached the end of its life.

The difficulties with the construction of *Swan* and *Torrens*, and the cost increases and delays which had occurred with most Australian naval shipbuilding since World War II prompted a review of the way in which major naval construction contracts were placed. The Defence (Industrial) Committee completed this review in December 1969. The committee reported that cost increases and delays had often resulted from projects being started before designs were sufficiently advanced, and that continuous design modification during construction further contributed. The committee recommended that all future contracts be placed on fixed prices with firm delivery dates.

The submission on which cabinet approval for the new programme had been based had assumed that the work would simply be allocated to Cockatoo and Williamstown as before. A two-year delay to the programme for the AOE was accepted to enable sufficient design work to be done to allow Cockatoo to submit a tender for the ship on a commercial basis. In order to prevent more delay if open tenders were to be sought, the government approved construction of the ship by Cockatoo, with delivery planned for late 1976.

With contract assistance a detailed specification for the AOE was completed by Navy Office, and Cockatoo submitted a formal tender in May 1972, on a fixed price incentive basis, for $33,000,757.

The 'ship that never was'. The fast combat support ship (AOE) that was to be HMAS *Protector*. The project was cancelled in August 1973.

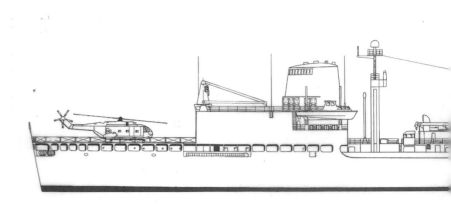

It had been intended that the AOE, which was to have been named *Protector*, be built to commercial standards like HMAS *Stalwart*. The final design, to full naval standards, was for a very capable ship of 19,600 tons full load displacement, 593 feet long overall and 72 feet in beam. The ship was to be powered by four Ruston and Hornsby 12 AO M diesels, mounted on a hydraulically positioned raft for noise reduction, driving twin controllable-pitch propellers through non-reversing gearboxes for a maximum speed of 20.6 knots.

It was to carry 9701 tons of cargo including diesel oil, AVCAT, fresh water, naval stores, ammunition and food. Six transfer stations for underway replenishment were to be provided for both solids and liquids, and two helicopters of Sea King size were to give a vertical replenishment capability. The complement was to be 335.

In order to expedite construction, Cockatoo was given preliminary orders for the preparation of structural working drawings and to order 1500 tons of steel in advance of the main construction contract. The structural drawings were prepared in Sydney. At the same time, work on system design and outfit drawings began in Montreal, Canada.

Due to the limited availability of design staff in Australia, Cockatoo had arranged for assistance from their then associated company, Canadian Vickers, who for many years had operated the Naval Central Drawing Office under contract to the Canadian Navy. In 1972 they were completing work on the detailed design and working drawings for the Canadian DDH 280 destroyer programme, and as people became available they were to undertake a high proportion of the AOE outfit working drawings.

For the first time, the fairing of the ship's lines was to be done by computer, rather than by laying out full size or tenth scale in the mould loft. An order was placed with the Danish Ship Research Association for this work.

Preparation of working drawings continued throughout 1972,

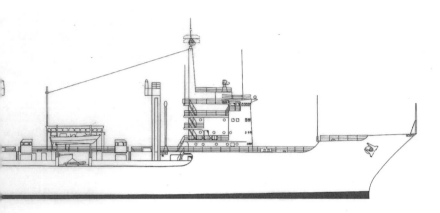

however contract negotiations were delayed by problems with the selected main propulsion diesels. The incorporation of alternative diesels had a considerable impact on the ship design. Following the change of government in December 1972, the whole project was reviewed. The new government decided that the cost was unacceptable (the total project cost was then estimated at $62 million compared to the 1969 approved figure of $42 million) and in August 1973 the ship was cancelled.

LEAN YEARS

The cancellation of the AOE left Cockatoo without any major shipbuilding work. To fill the gap between the completion of *Torrens* and the start of the proposed project, contracts had been arranged for the dockyard to build 21 flat top lighters of 60 tons and three self-propelled crane stores lighters for the Navy. These were completed in 1971 and 1972. The dockyard also designed and built the slave dock, *SD 3201* between March 1973 and May 1975.

In 1973 an opportunity arose for Cockatoo to help Vickers to respond to an interest by Indonesia in acquiring Leander class frigates. The Vickers' yard at Barrow in Furness was unable to accommodate the workload, and the possibility of building the frigates at Cockatoo, either to the Leander class design or as repeats of *Torrens*, was examined. There was no Australian objection to the proposal, and the Navy was willing to provide overseeing and trials support under sub-contract.

The Indonesian interest in frigates subsided in 1974, when they sought tenders for the supply of four corvettes of about 1000 tons. With Vickers Barrow still heavily loaded, initial proposals were developed for the construction of four Vickers Vedettes, two by Cockatoo (between 1976 and 1979) and two by Brooke Marine, at Lowestoft in England. Whilst the Navy saw advantage in Cockatoo becoming involved in this way, the cost of Australian construction was estimated to be 40 per cent higher than in Britain, in part due to the freight and insurance for the high proportion of imported equipment and material for the ships.

There was no way this cost penalty could be overcome, either by Australian government financial support or other means, and the Vickers tender was finally submitted on the basis of construction of all ships by Brooke Marine, with Cockatoo providing logistic and technical support from Australia. Three ships were finally ordered from Wilton Fijenoord in August 1975 and built in Holland between 1977 and 1980.

In 1978 Cockatoo also tendered, through de Havilland Marine, for the construction of two fisheries protection patrol boats for Burma. The offer was based on the RAN Attack class patrol boat design. Although de Havilland Marine succeeded with their proposal for six small Carpentaria class patrol boats, the order for the larger craft was placed with Swiftships in the US, who had offered a lower price and attractive finance from a West German bank.

During the early 1970s the Company tendered for many commercial ships, however the dockyard was rarely competitive with other Australian commercial shipyards for that class of work.

In September 1974 the Company did succeed in winning a contract to build a dredger for the Melbourne Harbor Trust. One of Cockatoo's early dredgers, the *John Stewart*, had been completed for the Melbourne Harbor Trust in 1912, but this one, the thirty-fourth, was the first since 1915. The *A S Mayne* (named after Arthur Stanley Mayne, chairman of the Melbourne Harbor Trust commissioners) was a non-propelled, bow well, centre ladder, barge loading, diesel-electric bucket dredger. It was 51.5 metres (169 feet) long, and 13.2 metres in the beam, with a full load displacement of about 1600 tonnes. It had a dredging capacity of 2400 tonnes per hour.

The *A S Mayne* was completed in March 1977, and whilst dredger construction had not been profitable for some Australian shipbuilders in previous years, the contract was a good one for Cockatoo.

The completion of this vessel again left Cockatoo without any shipbuilding project, although the Company was hopeful of securing some work from the naval programme first announced by the government in August 1975. The plans included the construction in Australia of a troopship and a number of patrol boats to supplement and later replace the Attack class.

Tenders for the troopship, the amphibious heavy lift ship *Tobruk*, were called at the end of 1976, and in June 1976 project definition study contracts were awarded to Brooke Marine in Britain, and to Lurssen Werft of West Germany for the patrol boats. Up to 15 boats were planned, one to be built overseas, based either on the Brooke Marine

PCF 420 or the Lurssen FPB 45 design. Cockatoo, North Queensland Engineers and Agents (NQEA) of Cairns, Carrington Slipways of Newcastle, and Dillingham of Fremantle were also invited to submit proposals for the construction of each design.

Cockatoo entered into an agreement with both competing designers to help them with the selection of Australian supplied equipment and material during the project definition study, as well as preparing a tender for the construction of the boats in competition with the other builders.

It soon became clear that Cockatoo was not going to win the order for *Tobruk*, but the dockyard was selected along with NQEA as one of the finalists for the patrol boat contract. In the final stages of the negotiations during the selection process late in 1977, both shipyards were asked to submit a proposal based on an order for seven boats only, a strong suggestion that the order might be split.

The successor to the AOE, the fleet underway replenishment ship (AOR) *Success* nearly ready for launching in early 1984.

The Prime Minister, Malcolm Fraser, announced the government's decision in his election policy speech on 21 November 1977. The contract for the *Tobruk* was awarded to Carringtons and all 14 patrol boats of the Brooke Marine design, to NQEA.

These decisions left only one opportunity for Cockatoo to participate in the then current naval shipbuilding programme. That the Company should do so was considered important for more than just commercial reasons. Since World War II, the total workload of Cockatoo Dockyard had been declining, particularly in commercial ship repair and general engineering work. The shipbuilding and ship repair industry was relatively small, and the dockyard depended heavily on training its own tradesmen, naval architects, engineers and managers. By the 1970s the main work of the dockyard had become the

Success on the way to the sea on 3 March 1984 after naming by Lady Valerie Stephen, wife of the Governor-General.

highly specialised task of submarine refitting. Not only was this class of work so specialised that it limited the scope of available experience for trainees, but the RAN was reluctant to see apprentices, in particular, used on submarine work.

A large number of Cockatoo people, who began their training during or shortly after the war, were approaching retiring age and there was a need to develop younger people with appropriate supervisory, management and technical skills. This would be easier if the dockyard had a mix of work to provide a wide range of experience. A shipbuilding contract would provide the scope the yard needed if it was to avoid becoming a 'submarine only' dockyard.

Cockatoo needed to seek conventional shipbuilding projects. However in 1976 Cockatoo had also responded to a Commonwealth request for interest in the construction in Australia of large glass reinforced plastic hulls. By February 1978 this had developed into a project definition study for the building of catamaran minehunters for the Navy.

The minehunter project became very protracted, however Cockatoo won a contract for the project definition study, which was completed in early 1980. The work included the manufacture of test pieces and the design of suitable facilities for construction of the minehunters. The Company felt that this class of work was not suited to Cockatoo Island, and a new facility was designed for the shores of the Shoalhaven River at Nowra, on the south coast of New South Wales.

In due course Cockatoo was invited to tender for the construction of two prototype minehunters, however the invitation was declined and the two ships, HMAS *Rushcutter* and HMAS *Shoalwater* were built by Carrington Slipways at Tomago. By that time Cockatoo was busy again with something much bigger.

THE AOR PROJECT

After the cancellation of the AOE, the Navy developed a set of requirements for a replenishment ship of lesser capability that could be built for a lower price. This work was completed at the end of 1974, and in early 1975, government approval was given for the release of an invitation to register interest. The government approval was conditional on the selection of a proven design, which had recently entered service with another navy, or was about to enter service, in order to reduce technical risk.

Four organisations were selected to tender for the project definition phase of the project: Direction Techniques des Construction Navales (DTCN) in France, Rijn Schelde Verolme in the Netherlands, Cockatoo, and Evans Deakin Industries in Australia. Evans Deakin withdrew, however the requirement for a proven design had effectively ruled out both Australian companies. The DTCN proposal was accepted and a project definition contract signed in February 1977.

DTCN had proposed an export version of the Durance class replenishment ship then being built for the French Navy. The project definition task was to introduce a number of RAN design changes, and to maximise the use of Australian materials and equipment in the design. A shipbuilder's estimating package was also to be prepared to enable the RAN to call tenders from Australian shipyards. Cockatoo helped DTCN during the project definition with the development of an Australian industry participation and support package.

In August 1977 cabinet gave approval for the Navy to build a fleet underway replenishment ship (AOR) to the French design, and in September 1977 the Department of Defence decided that no further consideration should be given to Australian construction.[107] Negotiations began for construction in France.

Following the loss of the *Tobruk* and patrol boat contracts, Cockatoo wrote to the Prime Minister seeking the opportunity to tender for the AOR, pointing out that the Company had asked to be given that opportunity as early as 1975. Ministerial approval was announced in April 1978, on the condition that a tender from Cockatoo was received by the end of 1978.

Unfortunately, with the move towards construction in France, the shipbuilder's estimating package had not been completed. It was subsequently prepared by Navy Office, but not finished until the end of September 1978, when it was issued to Cockatoo with a formal invitation to tender by 15 December 1978, less than three months later. On 23 August 1979, the government announced the intention to place the order for the ship with Cockatoo, and following contract negotiations the contract for AOR 01 was signed on 26 October 1979.

It was during this phase that the seeds were sown for the problems that were to emerge with the contract in coming months. To help build the ship, the Navy bought a set of working drawings from DTCN, as used for the second French ship of the class, *Meuse*. These drawings were to be used by Cockatoo, and they were applicable in so far as they represented the ship described in the contract.

It soon became evident that there were many differences in detail between the working drawings and the ship as defined in the contract documents. The effect of these differences was to considerably increase the cost and time required to build the ship, which resulted in a major contractual dispute between Cockatoo and the Navy.

The dispute was finally resolved by a re-definition of the ship in the terms of the production drawings supplied from France, and re-negotiation of the shipbuilding contract. This process took nearly three years. Finally the contract was changed from a fixed price basis, to a fixed price incentive basis, and the price increased from $68.4 million to $94.25 million.

In retrospect, a fixed price contract had been inappropriate for the

AOR. The fixed price incentive formula shared the risk between the company and the Commonwealth by setting a target price as the contract price. If the actual price exceeded the target price, the excess cost was to be borne 70 per cent by the Commonwealth and 30 per cent by the Company. If the actual cost was less than the target, the saving was to be shared in the same proportion. A ceiling price was set above which all costs were to be the Company's responsibility. The actual cost of the ship exceeded the target price set during the re-negotiation (as further amended by later changes) by about 0.03 per cent.

Contracts of this type had been commonly used for naval shipbuilding contracts in the United States and the United Kingdom. Between 1933 and 1941, all shipbuilding contracts placed by the Department of Defence with Cockatoo were on this basis, except that the contract price was the ceiling price.

The problems with this project were examined in detail by the Joint Committee of Public Accounts, during their review of Defence Project Management in 1985. In their report they stated:

> The dispute remained unresolved for an unacceptable time and reflected differences between Cockatoo Dockyard and the Commonwealth over matters fundamental to the management of any project. These matters should have been more thoroughly addressed in early project planning, definition and management.[108]

The AOR project came at the end of a more than thirty-year period of major naval construction on a loose contractual basis where the priority was technical excellence, not time and cost. The experience of this project, and some others of the period, resulted in much improved project management within Defence. The next major naval construction project, the building of the guided missile frigates *Melbourne* and *Newcastle*, avoided many of the mistakes of the AOR project.

The pre-wetting (washdown) system, designed to protect the ship from nuclear, bacteriological and chemical contamination, being tested during sea trials of *Success*.

The Minister for Defence, Sir James Killen, laid the keel for the new AOR on No. 1 slipway on 9 August 1980. Early progress was slow, due partly to difficulty in getting experienced tradesmen, notwithstanding the economic recession of 1981–82. A number of tradesmen and draughtsmen were recruited from Britain, but the dockyard's own apprentice training scheme contributed most to the workforce that built the ship.

By far the greatest delaying factors were the technical difficulties and the contractual dispute with the Commonwealth. Once the contractual problems had been overcome, the construction of AOR 01 became a more straightforward if complex task. Lady Valerie Stephen, wife of the Governor-General named and launched HMAS *Success* on 3 March 1984.

The ship was the largest naval vessel built in Australia, and the first ever to a French design. The cargo capacity was over 10,000 tonnes, on a full load displacement of 17,933 tonnes. The ship's overall length was 157.2 metres, and beam 21.2 metres.

HMAS *Success* was designed to supply cargo underway to two ships simultaneously, one on each beam. Four diesel fuelling stations were fitted, with two replenishment stations for fresh water and two for AVCAT. For dry cargo (stores, food and ammunition), there were two heavy and two light transfer positions, and a Wessex helicopter for vertical replenishment. All replenishment-at-sea equipment and liquid cargo pumping systems were controlled from a central cargo control station. The cargo pumping and control systems were hydraulically driven.

Accommodation was provided for a crew of 209, and medical facilities included an operating theatre and dental surgery. Two 16-cylinder Pielstick PC 2.5V diesel engines, each developing 7640 kilowatts drove two controllable pitch propellers through single reduction gearboxes for a maximum speed of about 20 knots.

Contractor's sea trials were carried out in early December 1985, and the ship was handed over to the Navy on 15 April 1986. Commissioned on 23 April 1986, HMAS *Success* completed an extensive series of sea acceptance and ship qualification trials before returning to Cockatoo late in 1986 for a 'post-delivery availability'. During this time a large number of minor modifications were incorporated as a result of trials experience, and some major changes, which had been deferred during construction, completed. The ship was finally accepted for operational service in early 1987.

The AOR project was unlike previous naval construction projects at Cockatoo in many ways. As it progressed new procedures for trials and acceptance were introduced, both by the shipbuilder and the Navy. Quality control and dockyard test procedures were adapted from the submarine refitting systems. The final trials and acceptance programme followed a pattern to be used for later projects, and the Department of Defence project management methods developed and matured.

Cockatoo was also responsible for the largest integrated logistic support task yet undertaken for the RAN in Australia. It included the preparation of comprehensive manuals, parts lists, maintenance procedures, training films and an extensive computer database for 'through-life' support of the ship.

HMAS *Success* was the last ship built at Cockatoo. She was soon to prove useful, not only during routine operations but especially in support of RAN ships during Operation Morris Dance in May 1987, when RAN units were sent to provide contingency evacuation support for Australians in Fiji. When the destroyer tender HMAS *Stalwart* was paid off in December 1989, *Success* became flagship of the Royal Australian Navy.

During the Gulf War in 1990–91, HMAS *Success* supported RAN ships and other allied warships in the Persian Gulf for several months, the longest deployment of any allied warship.

A second ship, AOR 02, had been planned to follow *Success*, and Cockatoo had been asked to submit a tender for this ship in 1980. This was deferred in view of the contractual difficulties with *Success* at that time, and in due course AOR 02 was dropped from the Defence programme. The need for a second replenishment ship remained, and studies continued into less expensive alternatives. In September 1989 the RAN leased the 40,000-ton Royal Fleet Auxiliary *Appleleaf* for a period of five years, which was commissioned as HMAS *Westralia*.

The completed *Success* at sea shortly before hand over to the RAN. *Success* is the largest naval vessel ever built in Australia, and the first ever built to a French design.

Chapter Seven

SHIP REPAIR AND CONVERSION

In 1912, the dockyard's last year of operation by the New South Wales Government, 47 ships were docked in the Fitzroy and Sutherland docks. In addition to New South Wales Government vessels and other merchant ships, 14 were naval ships. The most notable was HMS *Drake*, an armoured cruiser and flagship of the Australia Station between 1911 and 1913.[109] HMS *Drake* was the flagship of Admiral Sir George King-Hall, the last flag officer commanding the Australia Station. In January 1913, his flag was transferred to HMS *Cambrian*, a second class protected cruiser, which was docked for the last time at Cockatoo Island in May 1913 before leaving for Britain in October 1913.

In 1913, in its first year as the Commonwealth Naval Dockyard, 21 ships docked at the island, the lowest number for many years to come. The arrival in Australian waters of the ships of the new Australian Navy, and the outbreak of war in 1914 saw the workload of the dockyard increase considerably. The flagship of the new navy, the battle cruiser HMAS *Australia*, docked for the first time at Cockatoo on 11 May 1914.[110]

During World War I, Cockatoo Dockyard was busy with the docking and repair of RAN ships and merchant ships. In particular, the dockyard fitted out 21 ships as transports between August 1914 and October 1915. Nine ships had been converted by the end of 1914, and all were completed quickly.

The work done on the P&O Steam Navigation Company's SS *Berrima*, was typical. This passenger and cargo ship was fitted out as an expeditionary ship to carry 1500 officers and men in six days, between

12 and 18 August 1914, at a cost of £4513. Improved signalling arrangements were fitted on the bridge, and four 4.7-inch guns were mounted, two on the fore-castle and two on the poop deck, together with the necessary structural stiffening. A hospital was built in existing accommodation on the upper deck, and further cabins were dismantled to make way for baggage rooms, guardrooms and cells. Troop accommodation was arranged in the holds with latrines and wash places fitted below the poop deck. Magazines for the 4.7-inch guns and small arms ammunition were built on the lower deck forward and aft. The ship was commissioned on 19 August 1914 as the auxiliary cruiser HMAS *Berrima*, and sailed carrying the Australian naval and military expeditionary force for New Guinea.

More work was done on *Berrima* at Cockatoo between 30 October and 7 November 1914, prior to her departure with the second contingent of the Australian Imperial Force to the Middle East. The hospital was enlarged with 33 extra berths, a steriliser room and additional latrines. Additional troop accommodation was built in wood on the bridge and upper decks and the troop accommodation on the main deck rearranged. Galley facilities were extended and extra latrines and wash places were built on the upper deck forward and aft.

Six more ships were converted between October 1917 and February 1919, and a further 214 refits of 112 transports were completed during the war, with some ships being taken in hand nine times.

In addition to the fitting out of accommodation for troops and horses, the work on transports included the overhaul of machinery, the fitting of additional pumps and services, and the overhaul of electrical systems. In all, the transports were fitted to carry 4459 officers, 5900 non-commissioned officers, 112,500 other ranks, 1800 munition workers and navvies, and 17,100 horses.

Work on transports continued after the war, with 67 ships being partly reconditioned for normal service with fittings dismantled and stowed on board or taken ashore. Eight transports and two tugs (*Heroic* and *Heroine*) were fully refitted for merchant service.

Many other ships were refitted, docked or

repaired during the war years. Ships from other navies to visit Cockatoo Island included the auxiliary cruisers HMS *Orama* and HMS *Otranto*, the battle cruiser HMS *New Zealand* (a sister ship of HMAS *Australia*), and the Japanese second class cruisers *Hirado*, *Chikuma* and *Yahagi*.[111]

Many small ships and boats were also slipped, repaired, refitted or converted at Cockatoo during the war years. Over 400 such jobs were completed by the end of 1918.

BETWEEN THE WARS

During the early years of the 1920s, the docks at Cockatoo continued to be busy, with most of the work being ships of the RAN or the Commonwealth Government Line of Steamers. The number of ship dockings grew from 59 in 1919, to 175 in 1926. The sale of the Commonwealth ships and finally the whole line in April 1928, resulted in a fall in the use of the docks, but a respectable 64 dockings were still completed in 1932, the year before the dockyard was leased.

When built in 1924, the quadruple screw motor vessel *Aorangi* was the largest and fastest motor liner in the world. She measured 17,491 tons gross, and had an overall length of 600 feet. This handsome ship first docked in the Sutherland Dock in March 1928. During her long career, *Aorangi* was to visit Cockatoo 43 times, the last in August 1951.

Although the bottom of the Sutherland Dock had been widened to accommodate the ship, there was not much room to spare when the battle cruiser HMAS *Australia* was in the dock.

SS *Berrima* about to undock on 18 August 1914 after conversion to an expeditionary ship.

Other famous Union Steamship Company ships were regular visitors to Cockatoo: *Niagara* and *Monowai* were overhauled many times, however the outstanding 13,482 ton *Awatea* (which was lost off Algeria in November 1942) came to Cockatoo on only nine occasions between July 1937 and August 1941. In July 1937 she had suffered severe damage to her main propulsion reduction gearing and repairs were completed by Cockatoo to the satisfaction of her builders, Vickers Armstrongs of Barrow in Furness.[112]

Australian coastal passenger ships regularly docked at Cockatoo, and *Manoora*, *Manunda*, *Duntroon*, *Wanganella*, *Westralia* and *Kanimbla* came to the island in peace and war. In most cases, the work involved routine hull cleaning and painting, plus hull, machinery and electrical repairs to satisfy survey requirements.

The extensive engineering capability of Cockatoo enabled the yard to tackle any unusual job without difficulty. In early 1934 the P&O liner RMS *Cathay*[113] broke a tail shaft and lost the port propeller in the Indian Ocean. When the ship arrived at Cockatoo, it was found that the forward portion of the port main engine crankshaft was also damaged. The floating crane *Titan* removed the crankshaft from the ship through the after funnel (which provided ventilation to the engine room). Cockatoo forged a new journal and coupling from a 35-inch diameter, 13-ton bloom. The machined forging was then shrunk and dowelled into the crank web. After final machining the crankshaft was returned to the ship with *Titan*, and the engine rebuilt. Two new tail shafts and propellers were shipped out from Britain, and after preparatory work, the old shafts were removed, the stern tubes re-bored, and the new shafts and propellers fitted.

Another unusual repair was that of the Norwegian motor tanker *Vardaas*.[114] She ran aground at Danger Point, south of Brisbane on 3 March 1936, severely damaging her hull, effectively breaking the ship's back. Repairs began at Cockatoo on 25 April 1936, and were completed in a little over two months at a cost of some £40,000. Two hundred men were engaged on the repair, which involved separating the hull into two sections for realignment. Machinery repairs were also carried out before the ship sailed from Sydney on 7 July 1936.

In the immediate pre-war years, naval refit work at Cockatoo was mainly routine docking work in support of refits at the Garden Island Naval Dockyard. However in 1938, the cruisers *Adelaide* and *Australia* were taken in hand at Cockatoo for modernisation.

The refit of HMAS *Adelaide* began in January 1938. The major part of the work involved conversion to oil burning. The two foremost boilers and the forward funnel were removed, and the remaining six coal fired boilers were modified to burn oil only. The ship's armament was also modernised. One forward 6-inch gun was removed, with the other moved to the centreline, and three 4-inch HA Mark IV gun mountings (removed from HMAS *Australia*) were fitted aft. An HA director, also removed from *Australia*, was fitted on the foremast. Garden Island completed final installation of the weapons equipment and *Adelaide* was recommissioned on 13 March 1939.

During 1933–34 the British Admiralty developed plans for the modernisation of the Kent class heavy cruisers, to the extent possible within the available weight margin allowed by the Washington Treaty. The Royal Navy ships were modernised between 1936 and 1938. HMAS *Australia* was paid off for a similar modernisation on 24 April 1938. During the refit a 4.5-inch armour belt was fitted for protection of engine and boiler rooms, the aircraft and boat

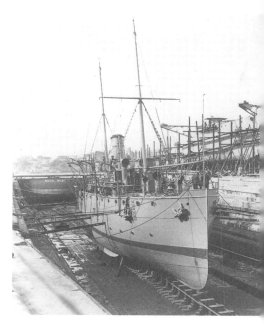
HMAS *Gayundah* before undocking on 31 July 1914. The ship had been extensively modified as a training ship with the bows built up to provide additional space and improve sea keeping. (J C Jeremy Collection)

A paravane for protection against mines. Many of these were fitted to ships at Cockatoo during World War I.

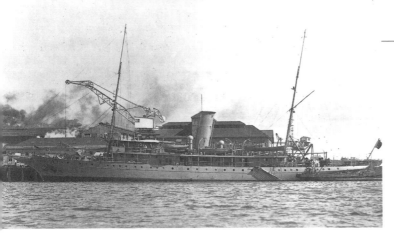

handling arrangements were improved, the single 4-inch HA guns replaced with four twin 4-inch HA mountings and new HA directors were installed.

The refit had been planned to be completed by March 1939, but the widespread differences between all ships of the class delayed the work, as the Admiralty guidance drawings had to be modified for *Australia*. HMAS *Australia* was recommissioned on 28 August 1939, however work was not quite complete by the outbreak of war on 3 September. After further trials, the ship finally left Cockatoo on 28 September.[115] A less extensive modernisation had been planned for the cruiser HMAS *Canberra*, to be undertaken by Garden Island with the assistance of Cockatoo, but the war intervened and the job was cancelled. A modernisation of the cruiser HMAS *Sydney*, intended for Cockatoo Dockyard, was also cancelled.

The sloop HMAS *Una* at the Destroyer Wharf in January 1917. *Una* was built in 1911 as the steam yacht *Komet* for service with the German authorities in New Guinea. She was commissioned into the German Navy when the war began in 1914. Captured on 11 October 1914 she was converted by Garden Island and Cockatoo for RAN service and commissioned as HMAS *Una* on 19 November 1914. She returned to Cockatoo Island on several occasions for further modifications.

Cethana during a docking in March 1919. The first of four C class wooden motor ships built in the United States for the Commonwealth Line, and the first merchant ship built overseas to the order of the Commonwealth Government, the *Cethana* leaked badly on her delivery voyage in late 1918 and was docked at Cockatoo in September of that year for caulking.
(J C Jeremy Collection)

WORLD WAR II

The pace of work at Cockatoo increased rapidly in the months preceding World War II. On 31 August 1939, the Aberdeen and Commonwealth liner *Moreton Bay* arrived at Cockatoo for conversion to an armed merchant cruiser. Built to carry refrigerated cargo and passengers, the ship required extensive modification to cargo holds for the construction of magazines, ammunition trunks and hoists. Gun mountings, stiffening of structure and gunnery control systems were also completed during the seven-week refit, which was completed on 19 October.

On 1 September 1939, the SS *Changte* began conversion to a victualling issue ship. Holds were converted for the storage of general provisions, and the passenger accommodation was rearranged to provide office space and store rooms for the stores staff. Gun crew accommodation was also fitted out, and a 4-inch gun installed. During docking, paravane gear was also fitted for protection against mines. *Changte* left the dockyard on 17 September.

Moreton Bay and *Changte* were the first of many such conversions to be completed by Cockatoo during the war. Between 1939 and 1945 some 250 ships were converted, overhauled or repaired. (The major refits and repairs are listed in Appendix 8.) This work included 15 troop transports, two stores ships, and two hospital ships.

The fleet oiler *Kurumba* in the Fitzroy Dock in the early 1920s. Built in Britain in 1916, the *Kurumba* served the RAN until 1948. The ship was sold into merchant service, and was finally scrapped in 1966.

The transport *Boorara* in the Sutherland Dock in September 1919. *Boorara* (A42) was originally the German *Pfalz. Pfalz* had been stopped by gunfire from the Nepean Battery at the entrance of Port Phillip Bay on 5 August 1914. The ship was found to be manned by German Navy reservists and carrying war stores, including 4-inch guns. (J C Jeremy Collection)

An unusual way to bring a ship upright for docking: the Commonwealth Line's *Australcrag* in December 1923. Six tons were suspended from the derricks, 12 tons were placed on deck, and the port lifeboats were filled with water. The *Australcrag* was one of 15 ships bought for the Commonwealth Line in 1916. She was built in 1907 and was sold in 1924.

Cleaning the hull of RMS *Niagara* in the 1930s. This was a labour-intensive process, working from punts using brooms and scrapers.
(J C Jeremy Collection)

The dockyard handled many famous ships. Amongst the troopships, the most notable were the Cunard liners *Queen Mary*, *Queen Elizabeth*, *Aquitania* and *Mauretania*. Others included the *Orford*, *Orion*, *Orcades*, *Strathaird*, *Strathnaver*, *Nieuw Holland*, *Nieuw Zeeland*, *Indrapoera*, *Empress of Japan*, *Empress of Canada* and *Zealandia*.

In April 1940 the liners *Queen Mary* (80,774 tons gross, 1019 feet LOA), *Mauretania* and *Aquitania* arrived in Sydney. Too big to secure alongside, the *Queen Mary* was anchored in Athol Bight in Sydney Harbour, where Cockatoo began work on 17 April. Work on the conversion had started in New York in March with the removal of much of the furniture, carpets and other valuable equipment. In Sydney most of the remaining furnishings (and the cabin doors) were removed for storage. Additional bunks were fitted in cabins and other spaces throughout the ship, and shops were converted to military offices. Dining tables and benches to seat 2000 men were made and fitted.[116] Engineering and boiler repairs were also carried out. On 3 May 1940 the work of conversion to carry 5000 troops was completed.

The work in *Aquitania* (12 to 16 April) and *Mauretania* (27 April to 3 May) was similar, but much easier as both ships were berthed alongside wharves.

The liner *Queen Elizabeth* (84,000 tons gross, 1031 feet LOA) arrived in Sydney on 21 February 1941. On 25 February, Cockatoo workmen began to complete the job of conversion that had been started in Singapore in the final months of 1940. Bunks for 5000 men were fitted, and dining rooms became mess halls. Hospital accommodation was also increased.[117] The work was completed on 31 March 1941. Further work was done on most of these liner conversions during later visits to Sydney.

The conversion of liners to troopships was helped by the existence on board of the essential services necessary to carry large numbers of people. Later in the war, the US liberty ship *William Ellery Channing* was fitted out as an invasion ship to carry 1500 troops. Steel structures were fitted to carry troop and tank landing barges abreast of the hatches, and the ships handling gear modified. Troop accommodation was built in the holds, with ventilation, lighting and semi-permanent stairways at each hatch. Three field kitchens were built, and washing and latrine facilities provided on deck. The work was completed between 12 February and 12 April 1943.

Early in the war, Cockatoo also converted two liners to hospital ships, a much more complex job than the transports. The first was the Adelaide Steamship Company's *Manunda*, which was converted between 27 May and 31 July 1940. Cabins were extensively dismantled to create wards fitted with hospital beds, with considerable rearrangement of ventilation and electrical services. Galleys were enlarged and patient lifts, a laundry and storerooms built.

The conversion of the Dutch liner *Oranje* between 4 April 1941 and 30 June 1941 was a more elaborate task. Cabins were stripped on several decks to allow for the fitting of single and double tier berths to accommodate 670 patients in 26 wards. An operating theatre block

The cruiser HMAS *Adelaide* at the Sutherland Wharf about to start modernisation in 1938. (Phil Bushell)

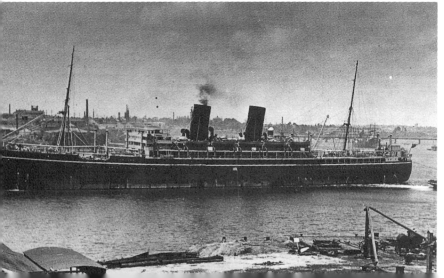

RMS *Cathay* arriving at Cockatoo Island for repairs in 1934.

HMAS *Adelaide* on completion of modernisation in 1939. (RAN photograph)

consisting of preparation, X-ray, plaster and sterilising rooms, laboratory and operating theatre — was fitted out. Decontamination facilities and storerooms were provided, as well as a cot lift and stretcher landing platforms. Splinter protection was also provided for the wheelhouse and wireless rooms.

Some of the most notable work done at Cockatoo Dockyard during the war was the repair of ships damaged in the Pacific, particularly between August 1942 and March 1943. Cockatoo was then the main ship repair facility in the south-west Pacific and heavy demands were placed on the resources of the dockyard.

A torpedo from a Japanese destroyer hit the cruiser USS *Chicago*[118] during the Battle of Savo Island on 9 August 1942. The bow of the cruiser was extensively damaged, and on arrival at Cockatoo on 29 August it

RMS *Queen Mary* dwarfing *Titan* in Athol Bight during her conversion to a troopship. Cockatoo Dockyard worked on the *Queen Mary* and *Queen Elizabeth* many times during their visits to Sydney. (J C Jeremy Collection)

was decided to complete temporary repairs only. Damaged structure for a length of 50 feet and a depth of 35 feet was cut away and a modified bulbous bow built using some 30 tons of steel plate and sections. Work was completed in three weeks, with the ship leaving on 19 September.

On 20 October 1942, the cruiser USS *Chester*[119] was torpedoed in the forward engine room whilst supporting operations in the Solomon Islands. After emergency repairs at Espiritu Santo, *Chester* steamed to Sydney, arriving at Cockatoo on 11 November 1942. Another temporary repair was undertaken, with damaged structure and machinery being removed before a new shell section (some 70 feet long) was built. Many deep indentations in the keel were fitted with doubler plates. In

addition to the structural repairs, main feed, steam and exhaust pipes were run from the forward boiler room to the after engine room, and the outer propellers were removed. *Chester* left Cockatoo after five weeks on 23 December 1942. USS *Chester* was later sent to the Norfolk Navy Yard for permanent repairs, and on 4 August 1943 the Commandant of that yard sent Cockatoo a letter of commendation for the excellence of the repairs carried out in Sydney.

The pressure of work increased dramatically in December 1942 with the arrival of the US cruisers *Portland*[120] and *New Orleans*[121]. On 2 December 1942 the *Portland* was slowly approaching Sydney when she was met at sea by the new Cockatoo built destroyer *Warramunga*, then conducting a full power trial. *Warramunga* circled *Portland* to give dockyard officers their first view of the job ahead.

Portland had been hit towards the stern by a torpedo in the battle of Guadalcanal. It destroyed the two inboard shafts, jammed the rudder, and blew part of the upper deck against the guns of the after 8-inch turret. Despite extensive flooding, the ship continued operating at reduced speed.[122] Temporary repairs, including strapping the damaged stern to the rest of the ship with a steel girder, had been completed before the passage to Sydney.

When docked on 24 December 1942, it was found that the stern of the ship was badly twisted and had dropped. The structure was realigned, by lifting it up to 5.5 inches and moving laterally up to 2 inches. New structure was built using some 85 tons of steel and about 40,000 rivets. The original electro-hydraulic steering gear had at first been considered beyond repair, with the hydraulic rams, about 18 inches in diameter and 14 feet long, bent up to 5 inches. The rams were straightened, the damaged hydraulic cylinder reconstructed with

HMAS *Australia* at the Cruiser Wharf at Cockatoo Island during her 1938–39 modernisation.
(J C Jeremy Collection)

HMAS *Canberra* at the entrance of the Sutherland Dock in the 1930s, attended by the tugs *Heroic* and *Hero*.
(RAN photograph)

The hospital ship *Oranje* after conversion by Cockatoo in 1941. (Phil Bushell)

1.5-inch steel plate, and the final repair was tested to 1500 pounds per square inch. The flooded and damaged electrical equipment was rebuilt. Repairs were completed on 14 February 1943.

USS *New Orleans* was also torpedoed, in the battle of Lunga Point on 30 November 1942. A heavy explosion, which removed 150 feet of the bow forward of the second 8-inch gun turret, followed the hit. Temporary repairs to allow the ship to return home for reconstruction started at Cockatoo on 28 December 1942. Initial work involved cutting away torn plating and the removal of damaged pipes and fittings to enable a false bow to be fitted forward of the second turret. This

Right: USS *Portland* in the Sutherland Dock in December 1942. The temporary structure that held the stern of the ship on can be clearly seen.

Below: Ward A4 on board the hospital ship *Oranje* after conversion.

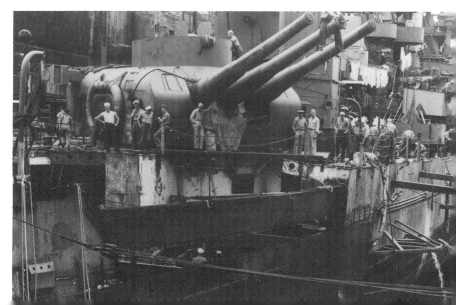

false bow measured about 30 feet in length at the upper deck, and 8 feet at the keel. When completed the 70-ton unit was transferred from the shipyard to the Sutherland Dock by *Titan* for fitting to the ship. Some 130 tons of steel were worked into the repair. *New Orleans* was completed on 6 March 1943.

These major repair jobs placed a considerable load on the resources of the dockyard, which was then busy with a substantial shipbuilding programme. The government recognised that the demand for labour for shipbuilding and ship repair at the peak period of the war was likely to present difficulties for the yards involved. Accordingly, the Australian Shipbuilding Board had established a committee comprising representatives of the Directorate of Manpower, Department of the Navy, the British Ministry of War Transport, various trade unions, and the contractors to help build up the necessary manpower.

The dockyard could not meet the need for labour at Cockatoo at the end of 1942 alone. The ASB committee, with the help of the Metal Trades Employers Association and the trade unions was able to locate 120 boilermakers and ironworkers in land shops which were loaned to the dockyard to enable the peak demand of December 1942 to March 1943 to be met.[123]

Despite these special measures, the times were not without their tensions. In early February 1943, the US Navy expressed concern at the progress of repairs on the US ships:

> The progress of work at Sydney has been very disappointing since the Christmas holidays ... Higher efficiency will be obtained if a definite policy were established and adhered to regarding the priorities of combatant ship repairs relative to new construction both naval and merchant ships.[124]

Notwithstanding these understandable strains, the achievements of the dockyard at that time were remarkable.

As well as a wide range of work on allied warships and merchant ships, 1943 saw interesting repairs to three US tank landing ships. In June, *LST 464* was fitted out with a mobile first aid unit. The tank deck was fitted to accommodate 66 patients in three tier bunks, and an operating theatre complete with laboratory, sterilising and isolating treatment, dark and X-ray rooms, was provided.

LST 469 and *LST 471* required almost identical repairs after torpedo damage in the stern. In both cases some 130 tons of steel was used

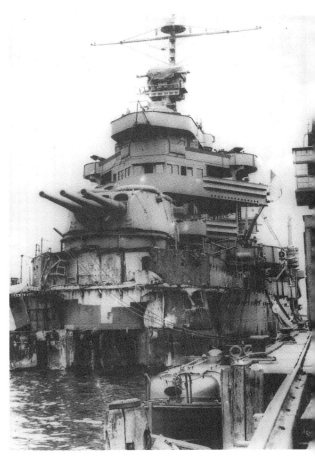

USS *New Orleans* on arrival at Cockatoo Island for temporary repairs in December 1942. The bow structure is completely missing forward of B turret.

to rebuild the stern, and new crew accommodation, galleys, magazines, cold stores and provision rooms were built and fitted out. To simplify the repairs, standard equipment as fitted in the class was shipped from the United States for installation. The wrecked propeller shafts were replaced and new propellers fitted. Improved armament was fitted in *LST 471*, with new gun and gun direction platforms. The work on *LST 469* was undertaken between 12 July 1943 and 16 February 1944, and that on *LST 471* between 2 December 1943 and 17 August 1944.

Many repairs to Royal Australian Navy ships were also carried out during the war years, as well as routine refits. The cruiser HMAS *Australia* was docked in April 1942 for repairs to a badly damaged port outer shaft. Extreme wear to a shaft bracket bush necessitated the fitting of a spare shaft and renewal of the bush. Other routine work was done and additional Oerlikon guns fitted during the seven-day docking.

The temporary bow for the *New Orleans* being lowered into the Sutherland Dock by the floating crane *Titan*.

Shortly afterwards *Australia* took part in the battle of the Coral Sea.

Australia returned to Cockatoo on several occasions, the most notable after severe damage from five Kamikaze attacks at Lingayen Gulf in January 1945. The ship arrived at Cockatoo on 30 January 1945, where preliminary work on the construction of new funnels had begun whilst the ship was returning to Sydney. Two were replaced and the third repaired. In addition to other structural repairs, the aircraft catapult structure was removed, a new deckhouse containing a radar mess, bosun's store and ready-use magazine was constructed and fitted out. One 8-inch turret (Y turret) was removed and the barbette space converted to a spare gear store. Two new 50-kilowatt generators were fitted and an oil fuel system was fitted to the bulge tanks. *Australia* left Cockatoo on 24 May 1945.

The largest repair carried out to a RAN ship during World War II, was to the cruiser HMAS *Hobart*, which was torpedoed near Espiritu Santo on 20 July 1943. The torpedo hit the ship's port quarter, causing severe structural damage. Both port propellers were blown off, and the starboard inner propeller damaged. Steering was lost, and only the starboard shell was holding on the stern of

USS *New Orleans* on the way home for permanent repairs. (J Goldsworthy Collection)

the ship. Temporary repairs were made enabling the ship to steam to Sydney, where she arrived on 26 August 1943.

Repairs at Cockatoo began on 6 September. On docking, the extent of the damage became apparent. The damaged 6-inch turret (Y turret) was removed, the barbette stripped out and the damaged shell and deck plating cut back to suitable butts. The aft end of the ship was twisted and had dropped. A large wooden cradle, on sliding ways, was fitted athwartships before the stern section was cut away from the rest of the ship.

The stern was repositioned by hydraulic jacks in four operations, each taking an average of 2.5 hours. The forward section of the stern casting, which was twisted and cracked, was removed and straightened in a hydraulic press, heat-treated and replaced. Approximately 100 feet of shell plating was replaced on the port side, and 70 feet on the starboard side was replaced or repaired. Three new shaft brackets were fitted. The barbette plating was re-rolled, replaced and the gun ring machined. All skylights, hatches, fittings and wood decking in the way of the damage were renewed. New steel furniture was fitted in rebuilt cabins and offices.

The engineering repairs were extensive. Both HP and LP turbines in the forward engine room were opened up for survey. The port turbines from the aft engine room were removed from the ship for complete overhaul. The LP astern rotor wheel, which had become slack from racing after the torpedo hit, was replaced, and the blading on this rotor renewed. All gear cases were opened up for inspection, the manoeuvring valves were reconditioned, and steam pipes rejointed. Several lengths of propeller shaft were straightened, and one intermediate and one tail shaft were renewed.

During the repairs *Hobart* was extensively modernised. The 4-inch guns were repositioned and Oerlikon and small arms mountings were removed and replaced by director-controlled twin and single 40-millimetre Bofors mountings. Existing magazines were modified and new magazines constructed. Both masts were replaced to take new radar equipment fitted during the modernisation.

HMAS *Hobart* completed her modernisation and repair on 6 February 1945, having been recommissioned on 7 December 1944.

After September 1944, Cockatoo Dockyard began to see more of the ships of the British Pacific Fleet as the

USS *Chester* in the Sutherland Dock in November 1942. *Chester* had been torpedoed in the forward engine room. Temporary repairs were completed by Christmas 1942.

USS *LST 471* in the Fitzroy Dock at an early stage in the repairs. Note the badly damaged port propeller shaft.

concentration of the war effort moved to the Far East. Repairs and dockings were carried out to aircraft carriers, cruisers and destroyers, as well as support ships. In June 1945 the dockyard repaired the Royal Navy carrier HMS *Formidable*,[125] which had been damaged by a Kamikaze hit on the flight deck. The 3-inch armoured deck was ruptured, and the island superstructure and arresting gear was also damaged. Two armoured plates from the flight deck, each weighing 14 tons, were removed and straightened under a hydraulic press. A third plate was beyond repair, and it was replaced by a double strake of 1.5-inch special quality steel plates. The island structure was repaired and an admiral's staff cabin and a radar workshop fitted out.

In addition to tasks done directly by Cockatoo Dockyard, assistance was also given to the Garden Island Naval Dockyard, particularly for specialised work in the newly completed Captain Cook Dock. One such job involved another British aircraft carrier, HMS *Indomitable*.[126] On 22 July 1945, the Commanding Officer of *Indomitable* reported to the Flag Officer in Charge, Sydney:

1. I have the pleasure to inform you that during the recent refit of His Majesty's Ship under my command the spirit of cooperation among all concerned was excellent, the amount of work done more than expected and the standard of workmanship high.

2. This ship was the first big job undertaken in Captain Cook Dock. The following remarks are submitted either to encourage by appreciation or to remedy by criticism.

3. The biggest item in the defect list was the repairs to the centre shaft, which involved the removal of the rudder and propeller and the withdrawal of the shaft. In spite of the lack of appliances and with unexperienced help the work was done quickly and well by Cockatoo Dock Company. Six weeks was estimated as the time required, but it is now apparent that this can be cut to four weeks.

4. The general impression gained in the ship was that, within limitations imposed by rigid observance of Trade Union rules, everyone was dead keen to send the ship to sea in as good a condition as possible. The standard of workmanship throughout was excellent particularly in welding and electrical work. The latter was better than any that has been put into the ship, either during building or when making good damage in the United Kingdom or the United States of America.[127]

Not all that he had to report was good news. He concluded:

10. Some cases of drunkenness and improperly leaving the ship occurred through members of the ship's company being given or buying a most virulent 'wine' from workmen in the Dock heads or sheds. A warning about this and the prevalence of thieves should be given to His Majesty's Ships before docking.

11. My Ship's Company and I are grateful for a most satisfactory refit.

I have the honour to be,

Sir,

Your obedient servant,

(Signed.) Jas. Eccles

Captain, Royal Navy[128]

HMAS *Hobart* under repair in the Sutherland Dock. The stern of the ship has been completely severed for realignment. The break in the hull can be seen just aft of the remains of the barbette for Y turret. Further forward on the port side, the derrick that was used to remove the port turbines from the aft engine room can be seen.

The passenger liner *Manoora* on trials after reconversion for merchant service.

In his response, the engineer manager at Garden Island considered that the problems outlined in paragraph 10 of the letter probably arose from dock construction workers, not dockyard employees!

By the end of World War II, Cockatoo Dockyard had completed 20 major conversions, major repairs to 31 warships, and three merchant ships, fitted defence equipment to 42 ships, and carried out extensive alterations or repairs to large passenger liners on 45 occasions.

In the docks, there had been 355 naval dockings and 395 merchant ship dockings; totaling 3,855,446 gross tons of shipping.

POST-WAR ACTIVITY

The workload of the dockyard did not slacken with the end of the war. The return of ships to commercial service ensured a steady demand for the docks, and 1947 was a particularly busy year, with 204 slippings or dockings, the greatest number in any one year in the yard's history.

The refit and restoration for merchant service of HMA Ships *Manoora* and *Kanimbla* employed much of the yard's capacity between 1946 and 1950.

The first class saloon lounge in *Manoora*.

The infantry landing ship (LSI) HMAS *Manoora* was paid off on 6 December 1947, and was returned to the Adelaide Steamship Company on 31 August 1949. During her refit at Cockatoo, her machinery was fully overhauled, all military features were removed, and her crew and passenger accommodation was extensively modernised.

The last passenger ship to be taken in hand at Cockatoo was the McIlwraith McEachern's *Kanimbla*. She also ended her war service as an LSI and was paid off in Sydney on 25 March 1949. Her wartime conversion had been one of the most extensive carried out to an Australian passenger ship, and had included the stripping out of most of the accommodation, the removal of lifeboats and other equipment, and the fitting of landing craft with special davits. The main mast was also repositioned and heavy lifting gear for other landing craft fitted.

The refit at Cockatoo began in April 1949 and was completed on 13 December 1950. All the wartime equipment including additional splinter protection, boat handling gear and troop fittings were removed and the ship and her machinery completely surveyed to determine the work needed to restore her Lloyd's classification, and for compliance with Commonwealth Navigation Act requirements.

The hull was completely chipped internally, and sandblasted externally. Many hull plates were removed for renewal or fairing. The main and auxiliary machinery was completely refitted, the main mast replaced and the whole of the cargo handling equipment renewed. New boat davits were fitted to take the original boats and several new ones. The whole of the teak deck sheathing was lifted for preservation of the steel decks, and much of it renewed.

More teak was used for new handrails and two new accommodation ladders. All tanks were cleaned and tested and all sparring and ceilings renewed in the holds. The insulation in the coldrooms was also replaced, and the galley equipment completely overhauled or replaced with new gear made in Australia.

All passenger accommodation was rebuilt with new bulkheads and new furniture when original furniture was missing or beyond repair. The public rooms were completely rebuilt. New accommodation was also provided for the crew to the highest standards of the day.

All electrical wiring was renewed throughout the ship, and all

Kanimbla leaving Cockatoo Island in December 1950. One of the Q class destroyers can be seen at the Plate Wharf before conversion to a Type 15 frigate.
(The Fairfax Photo Library)

HMAS *Queenborough* in the floating dock *AFD 17* towards the end of conversion to a Type 15 frigate.

Not an attempt to tow the island to sea but heeling trials for *Queenborough*. During these trials machinery and equipment is run at various angles of heel to prove that it will continue to work if the ship is damaged.

electrical machinery overhauled. New radar and radio equipment was fitted.

The re-conversion of *Kanimbla* was the largest of its type ever undertaken at Cockatoo and one of the largest in Australia.

Fewer warships came to Cockatoo after the opening in March 1945 of the Captain Cook Dock at Garden Island, although visitors in late 1945 and 1946 included the Royal Navy light fleet carriers *Vengeance* and *Glory*, and the cruisers *Euryalus*, *Black Prince* and *Newfoundland*.

The RAN destroyer HMAS *Arunta* returned to her builders in July 1945 for a major refit to incorporate modifications to bring her to the same standard as HMAS *Bataan*, completed earlier that year. The work included fitting a lattice fore mast, new radar, additional ventilation and improved accommodation. The top steam drum of No. 1 boiler was also removed from the ship for major repair in the boiler shop.

Bataan also came back to the island, during the Korean War. She returned to Sydney for refit in June 1951 after 11 months in Korean waters. Her next deployment was delayed by major propulsion plant defects which developed during the post-refit work up, and the repairs, which included retubing No. 1 boiler and the superheater of No. 3 boiler were not completed until January 1952.

Arunta began a modernisation at Cockatoo in September 1950. The after 4.7-inch mounting was removed and the after deckhouse extended to accommodate the handling room for a Squid anti-submarine mortar which was fitted on the quarterdeck. New radar, improved communications, and other changes were completed to improve her anti-submarine capability. The secondary gun armament was also modernised. *Arunta* was recommissioned on 12 November 1952. A similar modernisation to HMAS *Warramunga* was completed at Garden Island between 1952 and 1954. (*Bataan* was never modernised.)

On 15 May 1950, Cockatoo began a much more extensive modernisation of the Q class destroyer *Queenborough*. HMAS *Quiberon* was also taken in hand in November 1950. Both these ships had been built in Britain during the war as part of the 3rd Emergency Flotilla. Of the eight ships of the class, *Quadrant*, *Quality*, *Queenborough*, *Quiberon* and *Quickmatch* were commissioned in the RAN on loan. (They were presented permanently on 1 June 1950.)

All the Australian Qs, except for *Quality*, were converted to Type 15 frigates, similar to others converted in Britain for the Royal Navy. The Type 15 frigate conversion was intended to make use of the many available war-built destroyer hulls to provide a counter to the greatly improved underwater speed of the modern submarine, and as a stop gap until the new Type 12 frigates became available.

The conversion was very extensive, with the ships being stripped of all armament, structure and fittings above the upper deck. The main machinery was thoroughly overhauled, including in *Queenborough* the removal of the gear wheel from the starboard gearbox for machining of the trunnions. A new superstructure of riveted aluminium was built, which extended almost to the stern. The new armament comprised two Mark 10 anti-submarine mortars, a twin 4-inch gun mounting aft and a twin 40-millimetre Mark V mounting forward of the enclosed bridge. New radar, sonar and communications were fitted and accommodation standards were greatly improved, with extensive air conditioning and enlarged galley and laundry facilities.

The first ship to be completed in Australia was HMAS *Quadrant*, at the Williamstown Naval Dockyard in Victoria in July 1953. Progress on the Cockatoo ships was delayed by the shortage of skilled people which was also affecting the construction of the Daring class destroyers. Whilst the conversions were based on the Royal Navy Type 15 frigates, the Q class were distinctively Australian, and delays in the preparation of working drawings frequently resulted in work at the ships being stopped while the drawing offices at Williamstown, Navy Office and Cockatoo caught up. *Queenborough* was handed back to the RAN at sea on 1 December 1954 and was commissioned on 7 December, but in *Quiberon* the shortage of outfitting trades prevented much other than the structural and machinery overhaul work to be done at Cockatoo. At the end of 1954 *Quiberon* was transferred to Garden Island for completion and she was finally commissioned on 18 December 1957.

Some preliminary work for the conversion of *Quality* was also done at Cockatoo, but the refit was never started and the ship was sold for scrap in 1958.

The Type 15 frigate conversion proved successful and *Queenborough* finally retired from RAN service in 1972, after a career of nearly 30 years.

Despite the heavy workload of reconversions, modernisation and new construction, commercial ship repair continued to provide significant business for the dockyard during the late 1940s and 1950s.

Since before the war, Cockatoo

HMAS *Arunta* returning to Cockatoo Island in 1952 during trials after modernisation. (Marine Photography)

HMAS *Queenborough* as a Type 15 Anti-Submarine frigate. The ship returned to Cockatoo Island for refit in 1968, 1969 and 1970. (The Fairfax Photo Library)

had been the agents in Australia for the Kort Propulsion Company of London for the manufacture of the Kort nozzle, a propeller shroud for tugs which greatly increased their propulsive efficiency at towing speeds. Kort nozzles were made at Cockatoo until the 1960s. One of the most unusual applications was to the Fenwick tug *Hero* in 1947. Built of iron in England in 1892, the tug sank in Sydney Harbour in September 1940, was raised in March 1944 (by *Titan*), refitted and returned to service. After the Kort nozzle was fitted her performance was so improved that she remained in service as a relief tug until 1960.

Apart from a number of unusual hull and machinery repairs, most commercial ships came to Cockatoo for routine docking and survey work. Most were coastal passenger and cargo ships, and ferries, but overseas visitors included the largest ship to dock between 1945 and 1991, the P&O liner *Mooltan* (20,952 tons gross) in 1950.[129] In the 1950s and 1960s the cargo passenger ships of the Royal Interocean Line, for example *Straat Banka*, *Straat Clarence*, *Straat Cumberland*, and *Tjinegarra* were regular visitors.

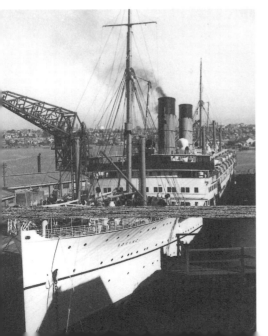

RMS *Aorangi* in the Sutherland Dock in July 1948. This docking was at the end of a nearly two-and-a-half year refit after war service, managed by the Union Steam Ship Company and undertaken by a number of Sydney firms at Darling Harbour. *Aorangi* resumed commercial service in August 1948. (J C Jeremy Collection)

Commercial dockings steadily declined in number during the 1960s and became a rare event in the final years of the dockyard. A number of factors contributed to this trend: shipowners' reluctance to repair ships in Australian yards because of a perceived unreliable industrial climate, increased time between dockings, and fewer ships in the Australian trade were all factors in the general decline in the Australian ship repair industry in the 1970s and 1980s. Not only were the docks at Cockatoo too small for modern ships, they were unsuitable for the modern machinery widely adopted overseas for ship cleaning and painting, and they became uncompetitive, even with other docks in Australia.

The diverse range of skills at Cockatoo and the adaptability of the workforce were tested on a number of occasions. In March 1951 the P&O refrigerated cargo ship *Palana*[130] came to Cockatoo for major repairs after severe grounding damage. The work included reinsulation of cargo spaces, realignment of the main machinery, and extensive refit of equipment damaged by flooding. Repairs were completed in late October 1952. Occasional collisions also provided work for the dockyard, as with the Australian National Line's *Boonaroo* and *Bulwarra* during the 1960s.

On 10 February 1964, the flagship of the RAN, the aircraft carrier HMAS *Melbourne* collided with, and sank, the Cockatoo-built destroyer *Voyager* during night flying exercises of the south coast of New South Wales. The bows of *Melbourne* were severely damaged, and the ship came to Cockatoo on 14 February for repairs. Damaged structure was cut away, and internal repairs progressed whilst a new prefabricated bow section was built in the shipyard. The ship was removed from the dock to enable the new 38-ton bow unit to be positioned by the floating crane *Falcon*, then redocked for the completion of repairs.[131] The work was particularly difficult as the ship was a very tight fit in the dock, leaving very little room for access. The repairs were completed on 27 April 1964, and the Company subsequently received a letter of commendation from the Minister for the Navy, F C Chaney.

A similar accident occurred on 3 June 1969 when the *Melbourne* collided with the destroyer USS *Frank E. Evans* during exercises in the South China Sea. Temporary repairs were made in Singapore, and the ship arrived at Cockatoo on 16 July. The repairs were almost identical to those of 1964, and were completed in early September. However a protracted industrial dispute over a demand for increased wages resulted in the ship being held 'hostage' in the dock. Finally the government,with the agreement of the Company, decided to undock the ship using Navy resources. With the assistance of the dockyard management, *Melbourne* was finally undocked on 11 October.

Despite the delay the Flag Officer Commanding the Australian Fleet sent the following message to the Company:

> It has been most pleasing to me as the Fleet Commander to observe the workmanlike manner in which you have tackled the repairs to my flagship.
>
> It is to your great credit that you completed repairs ahead of originally estimated date. None of us could have foreseen that strong winds would delay movement of ship out of dock.
>
> Please pass my personal thanks to those concerned for a job well and speedily done.[132]

The P&O liner *Iberia* was damaged in collision in early 1956 and was repaired by Cockatoo Dockyard in Pyrmont with the help of *Titan* from mid-April to early May. The Cockatoo-built dredger *Hercules* (completed in 1915) lies off the liner's port side.

HMAS *Melbourne* entering the Sutherland Dock on 14 February 1964 for repairs after colliding with and sinking the destroyer *Voyager* on 10 February 1964.

The new bow section for *Melbourne* being placed in the dock during the 1969 repair at the Sutherland Wharf. The new bow section was placed in the bottom of the dock and the ship redocked over it. The new section was then moved into position and the repairs completed.

At the time of the second repair to the *Melbourne*, the dockyard was once again busy with Navy surface ship refit work. The increased workload on the naval dockyards at Garden Island and Williamstown in Victoria during the Vietnam War, and the major modernisation of HMAS *Melbourne* at Garden Island during 1968, resulted considerable work being directed to Cockatoo.

The troop transport HMAS *Sydney*, which had been converted for that role from an aircraft carrier at Garden Island in the early 1960s, was given a major refit at Cockatoo in 1967. Very active in a logistic support role during the Vietnam War, the ship had not been refitted for over two years, and after being surveyed, extensive repairs to hull structure and services were found to be needed. The ship's boilers were retubed, and modifications included the removal of sponsons and the fitting of davits for LCM 6 landing craft. A further refit of *Sydney* was completed in 1969, when the ship's habitability was improved. (Between 1965 and 1972 HMAS *Sydney* transported 15,600 soldiers.)

The fleet tanker HMAS *Supply* became a regular visitor to Cockatoo, being refitted in 1967, 1969, 1970, 1971 and 1977. A number of intermediate dockings were also carried out. Built for the RAN in 1955 as *Tide Austral*, *Supply* first came to Cockatoo for five weeks in 1962, shortly after her first arrival in Australia, having spent seven years with the Royal Fleet Auxiliary. The 1971 refit was particularly extensive, and included fitting the ship with an enclosed bridge and the capability to carry aviation gasoline (AVGAS).

The destroyer *Vampire* completed a refit at Cockatoo in April 1968, and in 1969 her sister ship *Vendetta* was refitted before deploying to Vietnam for service with the US Seventh Fleet. Extensive structural repairs were completed in *Vendetta* including the replacement of a portion of the shell plating in way of B boiler room with a prefabricated section. The ship was also fitted with probe refueling to assist operations with US replenishment ships.

Other RAN ships to refit at Cockatoo between 1968 and 1980 included the destroyer tender *Stalwart*, the destroyer *Duchess* (twice), the frigate *Queenborough* (three times), the minesweepers *Ibis* and *Hawk*, the research ship *Kimbla*, the survey ship *Paluma*, and the training ship *Jervis Bay*.

In June 1969, the patrol boat HMAS *Attack* began a refit at the dockyard, the first of 43 refits and 48 other slippings of RAN Attack class patrol

HMAS *Torrens* in the Fitzroy Dock during the 1988 intermediate docking.

A busy Cockatoo Island from the east in 1969. Early construction work is underway on the new submarine refit facilities and the reconstruction of the Sutherland Wharf. HMAS *Melbourne* is in the Sutherland Dock for repairs after collision with USS *Frank E Evans*, two Attack class patrol boats are in refit in Timber Bay, HMAS *Vendetta* is completing a refit at the Destroyer Wharf before being deployed to Vietnam, *Torrens* is fitting out at the Bolt Shop Wharf, and the troop carrier HMAS *Sydney* is refitting at the Cruiser Wharf. (RAN photograph)

boats between 1969 and 1978. The refits were nominally of nine weeks duration, and the work included an exchange of the main diesel engines with refitted spares. Delays in the supply of spare engines extended the time of many a refit. The first patrol boat to come to Cockatoo was the appropriately named HMAS *Ardent*, which had been badly damaged by a galley fire, and was repaired between May and September 1969.

In the mid-1970s the RAN began a programme of modernisation of the first four of the Type 12 destroyer escorts. *Parramatta*, *Stuart* and *Derwent* were given an extensive reconstruction at the Williamstown Naval Dockyard. HMAS *Yarra*, completed by Williamstown in July 1961, was allocated to Cockatoo to fill a gap in the Oberon class submarine refit programme. *Yarra* was not modernised, but given a half-life refit to extend the ship's life by about ten years.

The refit of *Yarra*, which began in October 1976, included removal of the Mark 10 anti-submarine mortar, structural repairs, and a complete overhaul of weapons, machinery and accommodation. As the ship was the trials ship for the Australian Mulloka sonar system, the refit was given a high priority and was the only one of the four to complete on time and within budget. *Yarra* was recommissioned at Cockatoo Island on 16 December 1977.

High pressure water blasting was introduced for cleaning ships' hulls at Cockatoo in the 1970s. There are no side shores supporting the *Silver Harrier* and the ship is supported by bilge blocks to leave the sides clear for access. Whilst this process was much more efficient and greatly reduced the number of men needed for the job, the use of stages suspended from the cranes was inefficient as it prevented them from being used for other purposes. There was little choice in the Sutherland Dock, because its old design and uneven floor made the use of 'cherry pickers' difficult for most ships.

The tanker *Express* (built by the State Dockyard in Newcastle) in the Sutherland Dock with the Australian National Line's bulk carrier *Musgrave Range* at the Sutherland Wharf in 1974. The *Express* was a relatively small coastal tanker. The rapid growth in the size of commercial ships after 1945 relegated the Sutherland Dock to the small dock category.
(Douglass Baglin)

After 1980, RAN surface ships came to Cockatoo less frequently. Even rarer was the opportunity to repair a United States naval ship. In 1982 the USNS *Yukon*, a 24,000 DWT tanker came to Cockatoo for repairs after colliding with an iceberg and the icebreaker *Polar Sea* in Antarctic waters. This was the first visit of a US flag ship since the Trans Pacific liner *Mariposa* in 1966.

Most of the docking and repair work carried out at Cockatoo in the last 15 years of operation was for the RAN, in line with the general decline in commercial ship repair in the Port of Sydney.

Cockatoo Island on 23 February 1944: *Titan* is at the Fitzroy Wharf with (moving clockwise) *LST 471* at the Sutherland Wharf, HMAS *Australia* in the Sutherland Dock, the *River Hunter* under construction on No. 1 slipway, TSS *Nairana* at the Plate Wharf, HMAS *Hobart* at the Cruiser Wharf, *Bataan* at the Bolt Shop Wharf, HMAS *Arunta* at the Destroyer Wharf, USS *Gilmer* in the Fitzroy Dock and *Barcoo* under construction on No. 3 slipway.

Naval work included inclining experiments for the guided missile destroyers *Perth*, *Hobart* and *Brisbane* and dockings for underwater painting or propeller repair of the guided missile frigates *Adelaide* and *Canberra*. The latter ships were docked in the Sutherland Dock stern first to allow their large single propeller to take advantage of the pit in the bottom of the dock, which had been dug for the destroyers' sonar domes in the 1960s.

The last RAN surface ship refits at Cockatoo were those of HMAS *Supply* (in 1985–her last refit), the amphibious heavy lift ship HMAS *Tobruk* (in 1986), and the destroyer escort HMAS *Stuart*. *Stuart* began her 30-week refit in February 1987, her first refit since Williamstown Dockyard completed the half-life modernisation in 1981, and also her last. Several RAN ships came to Cockatoo in this period for intermediate dockings, including the fleet flagship HMAS *Stalwart*, HMAS *Tobruk*, the destroyer escort *Parramatta*, and the British bicentennial gift to Australia, the sail training ship *Young Endeavour*.

The intermediate docking of the destroyer escort HMAS *Torrens* in March 1988 was the first RAN docking for many years to be carried out anywhere on a fixed price basis, a successful exercise for both the Company and the Navy.

Most of this work was routine, however the intermediate docking of HMAS *Jervis Bay*, which began on 24 April 1987, happened to

Cockatoo Island in February 1982: the BHP bulk carrier *Iron Curtis* is at the Sutherland Wharf, USNS *Yukon* in the Sutherland Dock, *Success* under construction on No. 1 slipway, *Titan* at the Cruiser Wharf, HMAS *Orion* on the slave dock at the Bolt Shop Wharf and HMAS *Ovens* at the Destroyer Wharf.

The guided missile frigate (FFG) HMAS *Canberra* in the Sutherland Dock in December 1982.

coincide with the political crisis in Fiji, and the possible need to evacuate Australian citizens by sea. Four days before the ship was to undock, the Navy asked the dockyard to modify the ship to enable it to land the Sea King helicopter, the largest in RAN service. An existing deckhouse was removed, and following the necessary design work, additional deck stiffening and changes to the guardrails at the deck edge to allow them to be lowered for flying, operations were completed. The ship sailed for her new task on schedule.

HMAS *Jervis Bay* returned to Cockatoo in March 1989 under subcontract to Garden Island, who was responsible for her regular refit. Cockatoo fitted a flight control station and modified the flight deck arrangements, in addition to the normal docking work on shafts, propellers, underwater valves and painting. *Jervis Bay* had the misfortune to be trapped in the Sutherland Dock during the long strike in protest at the government's plans to sell the Island, and was not undocked until August: a sad conclusion to the dockyard's long record of achievement in support of the Royal Australian Navy's surface ships.

HMAS *Stalwart* in dock in the 1980s.

SUBMARINES

Cockatoo Dockyard's involvement with submarines started at the very beginning of the RAN submarine service and the maintenance and refit of RAN submarines became the main task of the dockyard for its last 25 years of operation.

The first serious proposals for the establishment of an Australian Navy that were tabled by the Admiralty at the Imperial Conference of 1909 included three submarines of the C class, together with the necessary support ships and facilities.[133]

In 1912 two submarines of the British E class were ordered from Vickers of Barrow in Furness, for the RAN.

The E class design was developed just before World War I. The RAN boats, *AE1* and *AE2* were commissioned on 28 February 1914. They had a surface displacement of 660 tons, and were 181 feet long with a beam of 28 feet 6 inches. The E class was notable in that they were the first British submarines to be subdivided by transverse watertight bulkheads and to be fitted with transverse torpedo tubes, one 18-inch tube discharging on each beam. A third tube was fitted in the stern.

AE1 and *AE2* arrived in Sydney for the first time in May 1914 and docked together in the Fitzroy Dock at Cockatoo between 6 June and 25 June 1914. This first association of the dockyard with submarines was not to last long. *AE1* disappeared without trace off New Britain on 14 September 1914. *AE2* docked again briefly at the end of November 1914, and was sunk in the Sea of Marmora on 30 April 1915.

Australia's next submarines were six J class submarines of the Royal Navy, which were presented to the RAN by the British government in 1919.

HMA Submarines *AE1* and *AE2* in the Fitzroy Dock in June 1914.

The first six of the J class had been ordered under the emergency war programme of 1915. Intended for speed in fleet operations, the J class submarines were quite large with a submerged displacement of 1820 tons, an overall length of 275 feet 6 inches, and a beam of 23 feet. They were designed for a surface speed of 19.5 to 20 knots, and 10 knots submerged. Partial double-hull boats of the Fiat-Laurenti type, they were armed with four 18-inch torpedo tubes in the bow and two 18-inch tubes on the beam. The J class boats were the first and only British submarines with three shafts. [134]

The first six boats, *J1* to *J6* were completed between April and August 1916. *J6* was accidentally sunk in the North Sea in 1918. A seventh submarine was ordered in May 1916, specifically for the Royal Australian Navy. *J7*, completed in November 1917, was similar to the earlier boats, but slightly shorter at 274 feet 9 inches overall. The main difference was the location of the control room, which was moved from just forward of the beam torpedo tubes to just forward of the motor room, 60 feet further aft.

The six survivors arrived in Sydney in June 1919. They were not in good condition, and were immediately taken in hand for refit at Garden Island and Cockatoo Island. During these refits all the submarines were docked at Cockatoo, but the most extensive work done at the island was the complete refit of *J7*. The work began on 11 December 1919. The refit was suspended between 23 March and 14 July 1921, and it was not completed until 15 May 1922.

The refit of *J7* included a number of alterations and additions to services and systems. By the time the work had been completed, the decision had already been taken to pay off all the submarines. The economic conditions of the time and the high cost of maintenance had brought the brief service of the J boats to a premature end. All six were sold for scrap between 1924 and 1929.

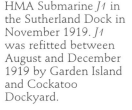

HMA Submarine *J1* in the Sutherland Dock in November 1919. *J1* was refitted between August and December 1919 by Garden Island and Cockatoo Dockyard.

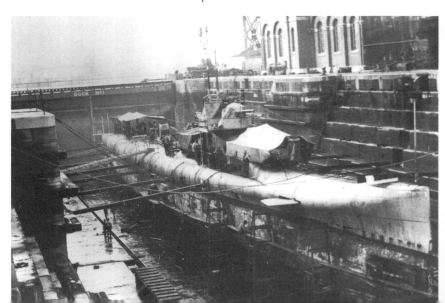

The 1924 naval construction programme, which included the cruisers *Australia* and *Canberra* and the seaplane carrier *Albatross*, also provided for the purchase of two submarines of the British O class.

The O class submarines were the first post-World War I British design, and were known as the overseas patrol type. Seven were built for the Royal Navy. *Oxley* and *Otway* were ordered from Vickers at Barrow in Furness in 1925. They were completed in 1927. They differed from their Royal Navy contemporaries, with a pressure hull 4 feet 6 inches longer and increased fuel and fresh water capacity. They had an overall length of 275 feet and a beam of 27 feet 7 5/8 inches and were armed with eight 21-inch torpedo tubes (six forward and two aft), had a submerged displacement of 1872 tons and a speed of 15 knots (on the surface) and 9 knots (submerged).

Vickers had redesigned the diesel engines for *Oxley* and *Otway*, increasing the power from 2700 to 3000 brake horsepower (BHP). Problems developed with these engines on the delivery voyage to Australia, and the submarines did not arrive in Sydney until 14 February 1929. The cuts in defence expenditure as a result of the depression resulted in both submarines being paid off at the end of that year. In view of the limitation of British submarine tonnage following the London Naval Treaty of 1930, the Australian

HM Submarime *Telemachus* in the Fitzroy Dock in 1950. *Telemachus* was a Royal Navy submarine based in Sydney as part of the Fourth Submarine Squadron.
(J C Jeremy Collection)

Government decided to hand over the submarines as a gift to the Royal Navy, and they were transferred on 10 April 1931.[135]

HMA Submarines *Oxley* and *Otway* had docked at Cockatoo Island on five occasions each between April 1929 and March 1931.

No further submarines were to come to Cockatoo until the Dutch submarine *K XIII* was overhauled between 26 May 1942 and 9 August 1942. Another Dutch submarine *K IX* was accepted into the RAN as a training submarine and commissioned on 26 June 1943. A small submarine of 712 tons submerged displacement, HMAS *K IX* was refitted for RAN service at Cockatoo between 17 May and 8 June 1943. She was paid off in March 1944, and was docked at Cockatoo again in September of that year.

After World War II, the Royal Navy submarines *Truncheon*, *Tireless* and *Totem* were docked at Cockatoo in June and July 1946; andbetween 1949 and 1969, the Royal Navy maintained the 4th Submarine Squadron in Australia, based in Sydney. The submarines regularly docked at Cockatoo, although their refits were undertaken elsewhere. From 1950 to the end of 1960, there were 27 dockings of T class submarines at Cockatoo (HM Submarines *Telemachus*, *Tactician*, and *Thorough*) and 10 of A class submarines (HM Submarines *Aurochs*, *Andrew* and *Anchorite*).

In 1960, consideration was again being given to the purchase of submarines for the RAN. To provide experience in the refit of submarines for future support of a RAN squadron, the Royal Navy agreed that the submarines of the 4th Submarine Squadron should be refitted in Sydney at Cockatoo Dockyard. The refits were managed by the RAN and paid for by the Department of the Navy.

At that time modernised submarines of the same class also replaced the unmodernised T class submarines. The first to arrive, HMS *Tabard* began a refit at Cockatoo in November 1960 which was completed in March 1962. Subsequently, HM Submarines *Trump* and *Taciturn* were also refitted. *Trump* and *Tabard*, which were both refitted twice, had a submerged displacement of about 1,740 tons, an overall length of 293 feet 6 inches and a beam of

HMS *Tabard* was recommissioned at Cockatoo Island in December 1965 after her last refit.

26 feet 6 inches. *Taciturn* was smaller at 1700 tons and 287 feet 6 inches overall. All were armed with six 21-inch torpedo tubes, four forward and two aft.

The work required for these refits was done by Cockatoo, except for that on radar, radio, sonar, torpedo control systems, gyro compasses, masts and periscopes and main batteries which was undertaken by Garden Island, although Cockatoo mostly removed and replaced these items.

The five refits were largely routine, although that of *Taciturn* between January 1963 and March 1964 involved the replacement of a pressure hull plate 27 feet by 5 feet, and extensive repairs to systems which were showing their age.

Despite the relatively small experience in the dockyard in major submarine work, the customer was well pleased. In a letter of 4 April 1962 to the dockyard managing director following the completion of the first refit of HMS *Tabard* the Commander of the 4th Submarine Squadron, Commander P R Wood DSC RN said:

> While the proof of the pudding will be in the eating, I would like to offer you my sincerest congratulations on the standards of workmanship which Cockatoo Island Dockyard have achieved in this your first submarine refit.
>
> The results of the inspections and trials reported to me have on the whole been most satisfactory, and the state of the Submarine and the finish achieved on Completion Date was very good indeed by any standards. That all this was achieved at a first refit, and not after experience gained from a succession of refits, is extremely creditable to all concerned.
>
> ... There is no doubt that so long as future refits are tackled in the same manner as this one, whilst use is made of experience gained, we can all look forward to refits of outstanding quality and reliability.[136]

The last T class refit, the second for HMS *Trump*, was completed on 10 October 1966, and the submarine was recommissioned that day at the Bolt Shop Wharf at Cockatoo Island.

HMS *Trump* leaving Cockatoo Island after recommissioning on 10 October 1966. HMAS *Stalwart*, launched on 7 October, lies at the Cruiser Wharf.

OBERONS

Whilst much was learnt during the refits of the T class, the specialised facilities for submarines at Cockatoo were minimal. The decision of 1963 to acquire a squadron of Oberon class submarines for the RAN, and that they should be refitted at Cockatoo, was to result in many changes in the dockyard, as already described.

As the first Oberon refit was not due to start for some years, the Company pressed the Navy to fill the gap with further British submarine refits, preferably of the Porpoise class, to maintain continuity of experience. It was a faint hope, and in any case it was soon realised that the refit of more modern submarines than the T class could not be done without the new facilities and specialised test equipment.

The Scotts Shipbuilding and Engineering Company, at Greenock, Scotland built the RAN Oberon class submarines. The first four, *Oxley*, *Otway*, *Ovens* and *Onslow* entered service between March 1967 and December 1969.

A further two submarines were approved in 1970. Cockatoo expressed interest in building at least one of these, however *Orion* and *Otama* were also ordered from Scotts and completed in June 1977 and April 1978. Until 1988 all six submarines were based at HMAS *Platypus* in Sydney.

The Oberon class submarine is a long-range diesel electric patrol submarine and is a development of the Porpoise class, the first submarines to be built for the Royal Navy after World War II. Seven Porpoise class and 13 Oberon class submarines were built for the RN, with a further three Oberons for Canada, two for Chile and three for Brazil.

The submarines have a submerged displacement of 2417 tons, an overall length of 295 feet 3 inches, and a beam of 26 feet. As built they had eight torpedo tubes, six 21-inch forward and two aft (later removed in the RAN boats).

The Oberon class submarines were built with a double hull, comprising a circular pressure hull with an external hull containing ballast tanks and fuel tanks. The pressure hull, which is constructed of high strength steel, is divided into five watertight compartments. The pressure hull contains the admiralty standard range diesel engines of 3600 BHP driving generators to supply the two 6000 SHP electric propulsion motors. The remaining space is filled with air-conditioned accommodation for a crew of about 68, the battery and its supporting systems and weapons, weapon control systems, and other electronics.

Although the new facilities being built at Cockatoo for the Oberon refits were not complete, the first refit of HMAS *Oxley* began in March 1971. Despite the experience gained during the

Making the best use of available facilities: two submarines and a slave dock together in the Sutherland Dock.

T class refits the Dockyard underestimated the work required for an Oberon refit, a much more exacting task. Although planned to take 64 weeks, the first refit was not completed until 23 March 1973, after nearly 104 weeks in hand. An ill-defined work package, incomplete facilities and a lack of technical information also contributed to the delays.

Despite the problems with the first refit, later work adopted a routine pattern, and with the refit cycle firmly established, the programme at Cockatoo became predictable and reliable.

The refit cycle for the Oberon class submarine was at first based around an operational period of three years between refits. The RAN was the first Navy operating these submarines to extend this period to five years. A refit cycle of five years in service, broken for

HMAS *Oxley* leaving Cockatoo Island on completion of her modernisation refit. HMAS *Otway* is on the slave dock at the Bolt Shop Wharf (background).

three intermediate dockings and one mid-cycle survey docking, followed by a two year refit became standard and until 1990, all the refits and most of the dockings were done at Cockatoo.

For some years, the refit programme at Cockatoo was 'single stream', that is, only one submarine in hand at any time. From 1978 to 1990, the programme was 'two stream', with, in general, one submarine nearing completion and one starting its refit each year. This arrangement was most suitable to the dockyard, as it provided the best balance of labour, an important consideration in view of the specialised knowledge and skills needed for submarine refitting. It also led to the occasional accusation that the entire submarine programme was built around the needs of the refitting dockyard, however the timing also balanced the number of operational submarines and the naval personnel needed to man them.

The refit philosophy adopted in Australia for the support of the Oberons borrowed much from that used for nuclear submarines. The aim of each refit was to restore the submarine to 'as new' performance and reliability. The Navy required Cockatoo Dockyard to establish modern planning and costing systems, and to develop a quality control system (the first ever in an Australian dockyard or shipyard) to assure them that the work met the required standards. The quality system took some years to develop, partly because of the extent of education and attitude change required in a dockyard accustomed to many years of naval overseeing. In addition the Oberons had not been built under any quality system, and a full set of standards had to be developed by Cockatoo and the Navy for the refits.[137]

After five years, full responsibility for the technical definition, authorisation and documentation of the refit work, together with the responsibility of setting to work and trials (in harbour) was delegated to the dockyard, with the naval overseers assuming an audit role. Navy Office remained the technical authority for the submarines, providing guidance drawings for alterations and additions and class modifications, but Cockatoo prepared the bulk of the working drawings. Full-scale mock-ups of the comcentre and the control room tailored to the actual dimensions of each submarine were frequently used to prove arrangements. Later in the programme a computer aided design system was used as well.

An Oberon class submarine refit was a complex task requiring some 1,300,000 man-hours over a period of between two and two and a half years. The design of the submarine, with many hard systems (piping systems exposed to full diving depth pressure), and very limited access made it a very labour intensive task, and very sensitive to delays caused through lapses in the supply of information, materials and equipment.

The dockyard developed the planning systems that were used for the refits. They combined proprietary packages with software written by the company's EDP staff, as no completely suitable systems were available commercially at the time. In the 1970s the submarine refit programme was one of the largest applications of network analysis techniques in Australia.

In October 1977 HMAS *Oxley* began her second refit. It was the first in a series of modernisation refits that became known as the Submarine Weapons Update Programme (SWUP). This RAN developed programme involved the fitting of an advanced digital fire control system, new sonars and the capability to fire both the US Mark 48 wire-guided homing torpedo, and the Harpoon submarine launched air flight guided missile. SWUP was the first such modernisation of the Oberon class submarines undertaken anywhere in the world.

Although there were many problems with the first SWUP refit, following refits benefited from the experience gained from that of *Oxley*, and the modernisation of all six submarines was completed, as planned, in 1985. Operationally the programme proved very successful, and the RAN gained some of the most capable conventional submarines in the world. The Canadian Navy and the Royal Navy later adopted similar modernisation programmes.

Following the completion of the SWUP, the regular refits became more routine, however the opportunity was taken at each refit to update the submarine's equipment and systems. Later, mid cycle dockings were successfully extended to include selected alterations and additions to hasten the modification process.

The stripped control room of HMAS *Otway* during refit.

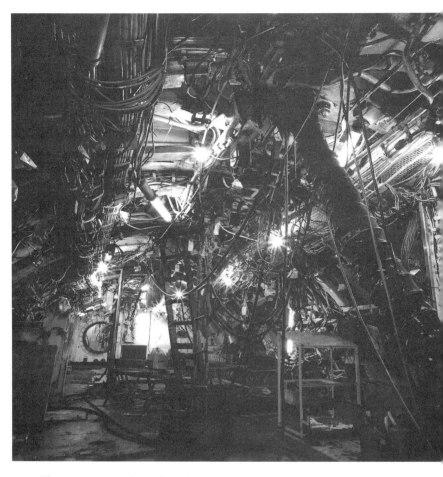

Changes introduced included the fitting of facilities for docking with the US Navy's deep submergence rescue vehicle (DSRV), and regular updating of communications and other electronics.

As the Australian submarines grew older, more work was needed to replace worn out valves and fittings. Whilst the early refits depended heavily on the supply of spares from the United Kingdom, local industry gradually became qualified for the supply of some parts, reducing this dependence. The supply of spares (some 30,000 individual items were usually required each refit) was always a major problem, and frequently the many skills of the Cockatoo people were called upon to meet an urgent requirement, either for a submarine in service or in refit.

Several refits of the older submarines required the fitting of substantial pressure hull plates over the engine rooms to replace corroded structures.

Cockatoo also regularly provided assistance at short notice to operational submarines and their base at HMAS *Platypus*.

THE SUBMARINE REFIT PROCESS

A submarine is perhaps the most complex marine craft devised by man. It operates in a very hostile environment, and its crew depends entirely for their safety on the quality and integrity of the submarine and its systems. The refit of a submarine is, therefore, a most rigorous process, with an attention to detail comparable to the maintenance of aircraft.

A submarine would arrive at the dockyard in a de-stored and de-fuelled condition. The first phase of the refit was equipment removal, all of which went through the existing five hatches: no access holes were cut in the pressure hull. To gain access to the battery, the accommodation area was stripped, with all bunks, lockers and minor bulkheads being removed for repair in the joiners' shop. The battery, comprising 480 cells each weighing half a ton, was removed through the accommodation space and conning tower hatches. Weapons, radio and radar electronics were removed, together with all electrical and mechanical machinery, except for the main motors and the main generator bedplates and main frames.

All minor bulkheads, ship's side linings, deck coverings, ladders, gratings, floor plates, furniture and stowages, together with about 70 per cent of ventilation trunking and 60 per cent of pipe work was removed.

Early in the refit, the submarine was placed on the slave dock, where it would remain for about sixty weeks, either at the Sutherland Wharf or the Bolt Wharf. The submarine was then grit blasted externally and in the tanks. Following initial preservation, the hull was extensively surveyed. This included the measurement of the thickness of the hull plates and the integrity of the welds using ultrasound. To help this process, the permanent ballast about 7500 ingots weighing 150 tons) was removed for re-preservation.

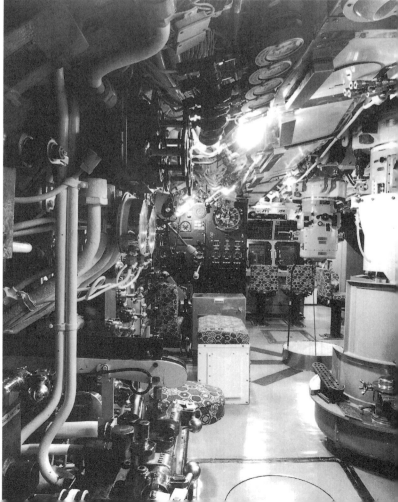

The completed control room of HMAS *Oxley* after her modernisation refit.

All equipment and systems remaining on board were surveyed for repair as necessary. Any pipes or electrical cables that were in poor condition were replaced. The machinery remaining on board (mainly the main motors) was surveyed and repaired *in situ*. During the docking, the torpedo tubes, hydroplanes and steering gear were refitted. Any structural repairs or structural changes were completed while the submarine was on the slave dock, with parts being fabricated as required in the shipyard or the boiler shop.

The atmosphere in a submarine in service is generally damp, salty and contaminated by oil fumes. Equipment that can not be readily reached in service is usually greasy and dirty when removed for refit.

All items removed from the submarine, whether directed to electrical, electronic, mechanical or hull shops, were subjected to essentially the same routine. The first task was to strip, identify and clean the equipment.

Mechanical equipment was directed to the dirty transit store where it was held until work could start. In the cleaning area of this store, the equipment would be dismantled into its component parts, and each part would be tagged with a metal tag, which identified the part and its origin. Grease and dirt was removed by steam cleaning. Paint corrosion products and marine growth were removed in chemical cleaning baths, and the parts were chemically brightened and washed before being dried.

When the submarines were built, almost all parts were painted, usually with epoxy paint. This was removed during the cleaning process, and to reduce the amount of painting needed, and future cleaning work, many parts were left in a 'bright metal' condition and not repainted.

Electric motors and switchgear were treated in a similar way in the electrical production shop.

Pipes removed from the submarine were cleaned by chemical treatment. Electronic components were usually ultrasonically cleaned, although cabinets were chemically cleaned to remove dirt and paint.

After cleaning, all equipment was surveyed by measurement and examination to determine the repairs required, and then repaired to the 'as new' performance and reliability standard. Pipes were pressure tested for defects.

After being repaired, equipment would be reassembled and then painted where required. This was necessary as access for painting in a submarine is extremely limited and if the equipment was not properly preserved during a refit it could be up to seven years before it could be done again.

On completion of repair, as much equipment as possible was subjected to a shop test. All pipes and valves were pressure tested, and electric motors and their associated control equipment were tested under load before they rejoined their mechanical components. This involved connecting the motors to a load (a fan brake) in the electrical assembly shop. Completed mechanical equipment was tested in the functional test rooms, which were provided with all power and fluid services required. The equipment was then run as it would in the submarine. Noise and vibration trials were also done in these rooms. Special test rigs were used for torpedo firing equipment, where compressed air was used to test and to set to work the valves and fittings comprising the systems.

A similar repair routine was used for electronic equipment. After cleaning, any faulty components were replaced, and the equipment tested. The equipment was set to work in test rigs which accurately simulated the systems in the submarine, and held in these rigs prior to re-installation on board.

Accommodation minor bulkheads and furniture were cleaned and refitted in the joiners' shop. Damaged linings (usually a melamine paper laminate like Formica) were replaced, locks and door handles repaired and repolished or replaced, and timber surfaces repolished. Similarly, sheet metal lockers and boxes (and ventilation trunking) were cleaned and repaired in the sheet metal shop.

After all the on board repair work was complete, and shortly before undocking, the new battery was shipped. The accommodation spaces could then be rebuilt. The submarine was painted before undocking with the final paint scheme, although the final coats would be applied later.

The submarine was undocked when the trials programme required water around the hull. As systems were rebuilt on

To mark the completion of each major refit it was usual to hand each submarine back to the Navy with some ceremony. Here Captain D J Dalton RAN (general overseer and superintendent of inspection) signs the completion certificate for HMAS *Orion* on 12 August 1983. He is being watched by John Jeremy (managing director) and LCDR G V Dikkenberg RAN (Commanding Officer, HMAS *Orion*).

board, they were tested, and then subjected to a comprehensive trial. Main engines and main motors were run extensively, to charge and discharge the batteries. The propellers were used to provide the load for the batteries and for this reason temporary 'hack' propellers were fitted to the shafts to avoid the risk of damage to the operational propellers from any debris in the water around the island. The submarine was berthed at the Destroyer Wharf during these trials.

Towards the end of the trials period, the submarine would undertake a basin dive. This was usually done at the entrance of the Captain Cook Dock at Garden Island, where there was sufficient depth of water (about 40 feet) in an enclosed basin. By this stage the submarine was substantially complete.

After the basin dive, the submarine would enter dock (usually the Fitzroy Dock) for final docking. During this docking the final paint coats were applied, the hack propellers replaced with the operational items, and any other outstanding underwater work completed.

After undocking and a final cleaning and painting period, the submarine was returned to the navy, and this occasion marked the end of the refit. Sea trials were carried out after the refit, with the submarine operating out of HMAS *Platypus* at Neutral Bay. The dockyard would send a number of people to sea on trials to help with rectification of any minor defects as they arose. Any major defects arising from trials were usually fixed at the base; it was very rare for a submarine to return to Cockatoo after refit for any reason.

SUBMARINE BUILDING PLANS

In December 1979, Cockatoo again raised the possibility of building submarines at Cockatoo Island. Noting that the Oberons would start reaching the end of their lives in about ten years, the Company proposed to the Department of Defence that it undertake a study into the feasibility of building modern submarines in Australia.

The Department of Defence adopted the proposal, and in March 1980 a contract was signed for the study. It was to be partly funded by the Commonwealth, and partly by the Company. The study was primarily based on the British Type 2400 submarine design, although other European designs, selected in consultation

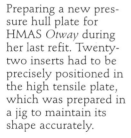

Preparing a new pressure hull plate for HMAS *Otway* during her last refit. Twenty-two inserts had to be precisely positioned in the high tensile plate, which was prepared in a jig to maintain its shape accurately.

with the RAN, were examined in order to test the sensitivity of the findings of the study to the selection of a different submarine.

The report was completed in March 1981.[138] It confirmed the practicability of building modern submarines in Australia, and identified many opportunities for Australian industry to participate in the supply of materials and equipment. Outline plans and cost estimates for the modernisation of Cockatoo Dockyard, and programmes for the construction of the submarines were prepared. The study also concluded that all of the designs examined were suitable for Australian construction, and emphasised the benefits to the future support and refit of submarine, which would be gained from local construction.

In 1981, the new construction submarine project began with government approval to proceed with the project definition phase. The Commonwealth invited tenders for the design and construction of a new class of submarine for the RAN, which was intended to be based on an existing proven design. The preference was for a consortium of companies, including the designer and suitable Australian companies, to assume total responsibility for the project, including design and construction of six and possibly eight submarines. At least some of the submarines were to be built in Australia, possibly at a new site.

During the tender phase, Cockatoo and the holding company, Vickers Australia, held extensive discussions with the submarine designers in an effort to secure a preference for Cockatoo as the Australian construction location. With assistance from the UK shipbuilding consultants A & P Appledore, detailed plans and cost estimates were prepared for the construction of suitable facilities, both at Cockatoo or at a new site. A management plan was also developed for an appropriate company structure and management systems to make use of the considerable expertise built up during the Oberon refitting programme.

During 1982 and 1983, the project attracted considerable public interest, and state governments began to compete for the project with offers of construction sites and other assistance. It became clear that the outcome of the project definition study would be influenced by many factors unusual in a naval shipbuilding project.

Whilst the European contenders recognised that Cockatoo possessed the only concentration of submarine expertise in Australia, they did not greatly favour the use of Cockatoo Island as a building site for a number of reasons. The location of the yard on an island, with poorly laid out old facilities and an entrenched industrial culture were seen as major disadvantages. There was also little political support for Sydney as the construction location.

Moreover there were negative attitudes within the Department

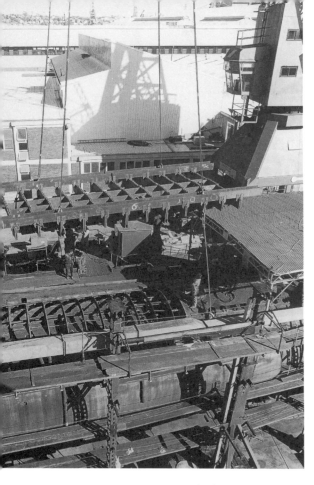

of Defence, where some people felt that the existing relationship between the Company and the Commonwealth, and the obligation under the lease for the Commonwealth to fund major modernisation, would not work to the advantage of the project. The Company felt that revised trading arrangements could overcome any perceived difficulties, and was prepared to participate at a new site if that was the preferred solution.

In the event, the project definition study, which began in May 1985, did not seriously explore the Cockatoo option. Two contracts were let, one to a consortium including the HDW/IKL team from West Germany, offering the IKL 2000 design, and the other to a consortium with Kockums, of Sweden, offering the Kockums Type 471 design.

In May 1987 the Kockums design was selected, and on 3 June 1987 a contract was signed with the Australian Submarine Corporation for the construction of six Type 471 submarines at a new facility to be built at Adelaide.

Shipping the replacement plate to HMAS *Otway*, still firmly held in its jig.

THE END OF THE REFITS

Meanwhile, the regular cycle of submarine refits at Cockatoo was severely disrupted by the government's decisions of April and May 1987 about the future of the dockyard.

Those of HMAS *Ovens* and HMAS *Orion* (the thirteenth and fourteenth at Cockatoo) began as planned in September 1987 and November 1988. Two further refits were then planned before the RAN's new Collins class submarines entered service, those of HMAS *Onslow* (January 1990 to December 1991) and HMAS *Otama* (December 1990 to December 1992).

In January 1989 the Navy sought interest and subsequently tenders from alternative contractors for the last two refits to be done either at Garden Island in Sydney or in the Fremantle region of Western Australia.

The uncertainty of the future refit plans and doubt about real government intentions for Cockatoo Island prompted the crippling 14-week strike at Cockatoo between May and August 1989, which caused long delays to the refits in hand. The aim of the strikers was to persuade the government to leave the last two refits at Cockatoo. Whilst this was not inconsistent with the Company's view, government policy decisions cannot readily be changed by industrial action, however logical the cause.

In June 1990 the government decided to place the last two Oberon refits with Australian Defence Industries at Garden Island, notwithstanding the cost penalties and delays involved. Concerns over a possible repetition of the industrial problems of 1989 were a contributing factor in the decision. In November, the refit of HMAS *Onslow* finally began at Garden Island, nearly a year late.

The forward torpedo compartment of HMAS *Oxley* at the end of her modernisation refit in December 1979.

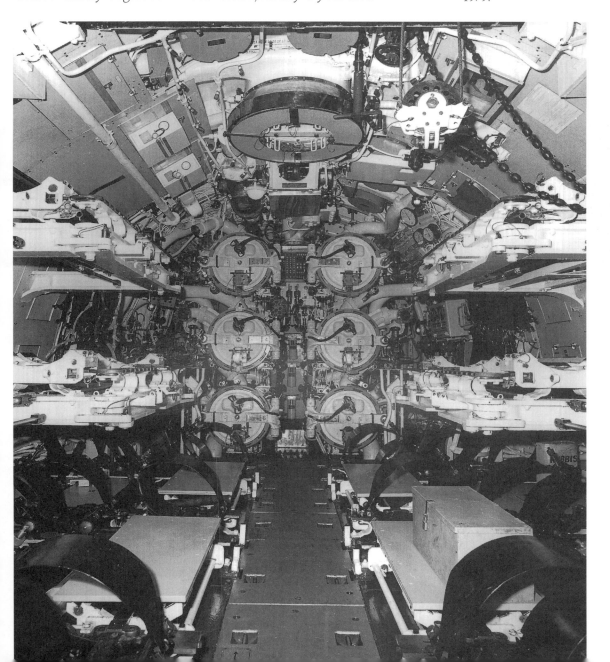

Taken shortly after the Fitzroy Dock had been opened in 1957, this photograph shows the half-finished dockyard workshop building, which was built of stone quarried on the island.

The following month Cockatoo Dockyard entered into an agreement with Australian Defence Industries (ADI) to provide access to the know-how developed over the many years of submarine refitting at Cockatoo, providing some assistance for the newcomer to this complex and demanding task.

On 4 June 1991, the last refit of an Oberon class submarine to be undertaken at Cockatoo Island was completed, and HMAS *Orion* was returned for service with the RAN Submarine Squadron, bringing to an end the dockyard's 134 years of service to the navies of Australia.

ENGINEERING

When the Fitzroy Dock opened in 1857, the large stone work-shop building on the eastern shore was incomplete. Within a few years the workshop had been equipped with a range of machine tools driven by a 6 horsepower engine. In 1860 additional pumping machinery for the dock was built in the workshop, which enabled the dock to be emptied in 4 hours.[139] After the Harbours and Rivers Branch took control, the range of work grew, and in the last decades of the nineteenth century, much of the machinery and equipment for the tugs, dredgers and other small craft built at Cockatoo was made on the island. The yard also built much of its own machinery.

The dockyard also carried out a wide range of work for other departments, for example (in 1893) repairs to the Glebe Island Bridge and to cranes on Spectacle and Garden Islands, and the manufacture of a 15-ton crane and machinery for the torpedo workshop at Garden Island. Some attempts by the dockyard to widen the scope of the engineering work were frustrated. The Managing Committee reported in 1904:

> During the year advantage was taken of the Railway Commissioners inviting tenders for the local manufacture of sixty locomotives, to place before them a proposition that these engines should be built at the dockyard. The tender from the dockyard was the lowest received, and serious consideration was given to the advisableness or otherwise of placing the contract with the dock-yard, but finally it was decided that a Royal Commission should inquire into the whole matter of manufacturing locomotives locally as against direct importation. The finding of the Commission was, that the dockyard was not considered a suitable place for the purpose, the water carriage being, in the estimation of the Commission, a distinct drawback.[140]

A steam locomotive for the Barren Jack Dam narrow gauge railway. (D J Mitchell)

The first marine water-tube boiler designed and built in Australia was made at Cockatoo for the torpedo boat *Countess of Hopetoun* in 1910. (PWD)

Looking east over the foundry buildings in about 1908. The ship in the background is the school ship *Sobraon*.

Some railway rolling stock work was done on the island however. About 1909 the workshops built a locomotive and trucks for a narrow gauge railway built for the construction of the Barren Jack (Burrenjuck) Dam in southern New South Wales.[141] A large amount of other work was also completed for the Railway and Tramway Construction Branch of the Public Works Department, including points and crossings, turnouts and loops of various descriptions.

By 1898 a brass foundry had been built behind the stone workshop building, but it was not until 1902 that an iron foundry was established, when other local foundries were unable to meet the needs of the dockyard. The new foundry could handle castings up to 12 tons. It was expanded by 1908 into new buildings and in 1910 it produced 260 tons of cast-iron outlet pipes 4 feet 6 inches in diameter for the Barren Jack Dam. That year a complete set of Channoine shutters was also completed for the Berembed Weir. Each shutter was 14 feet high and 3 feet wide. The combined width was 165 feet and they were the largest built in Australia so far.[142]

A water tube boiler, the first of the type to be designed and built in Australia was completed at Cockatoo in 1910. The boiler was designed at Cockatoo in 1909 by H Goldsmith for the Federal torpedo boat *Countess of Hopetoun*.

By the time the Commonwealth took over the yard, Cockatoo had well established, but quite small, machine and fitting shops, supported by a forge, the foundries, a boiler shop, copper, sheet metal and plumbing shops, and a new joiners' shop.

When Cockatoo built *Warrego* in 1911–12, the main machinery for the destroyer, which consisted of Parsons direct drive steam turbines driving three screws, with three Yarrow water tube boilers, was

imported from Britain. The turbines for the *Huon*, *Torrens*, and *Swan* were completely assembled at Cockatoo.

Cockatoo also built the boilers for the cruiser *Brisbane*. Her turbines developed a total of 25,000 shaft horsepower on four propellers. The cruiser *Adelaide* had more powerful machinery, with the same power delivered to only two propellers. These Parsons turbines were built at Cockatoo, and were very substantial, weighing some 120 tons. *Adelaide's* 12 Yarrow water tube boilers, which could burn either coal or oil fuel, were built in the dockyard's boiler shop.

The considerable workshop capacity provided on the island during World War I enabled Cockatoo to build most of the main and auxiliary machinery for Australian built warships for many years.

A view of the dockyard workshops in 1907, looking north. (PWD)

During the World War I the yard also manufactured propellers (21 for the destroyers) and shafts, and many other parts and fittings needed for the new ships. During the war the yard built three sets of high-speed vertical engines of 370 IHP, complete with condensers and boilers for the Flinders Naval Base power plant. A 6 cylinder 110 BHP kerosene engine was built for a motor launch for Williamstown, and a 4 cylinder 75 BHP kerosene engine for the 50 foot picket boat of HMAS *Australia*, which the dockyard converted from steam propulsion in 1919.

A 300-ton hydraulic press built for the dockyard in its own workshops in 1907. (PWD)

New rotors and blading were made during extensive turbine repairs in the troopship *Loongana* between May and December 1917. The *Loongana* had been built in Scotland in 1904 for the Union Steam Ship Company of New Zealand for the Bass Strait passenger service and it was the first ocean-going steam turbine powered merchant ship.[143]

As part of the wartime shipbuilding programme a large number of parts were made for the ships at the dockyard. These included doors, hatches, bollards, fairleads, valves, and flanges, guardrail stanchions and rudder stocks. A large number of electrical fittings were also made in the yard, including switches, junction boxes, plugs, lamps and so on.

A very wide range of general engineering work was also completed in the war years. It included a steel radio mast, rolls for the manufacture of steel plate for BHP, 75- and 100-ton crane hooks for BHP, cranes and many minor machinery parts. The records also show that the yard made 200 4.7-inch projectile boxes, 126 midshipmen's sea chests, 700 hospital cot frames, 363 canvas cots, 3350 seamen's kit bags, 550 lifebelts and 1560 hammocks. A further 14,450 hammocks and 17,400 life rafts were repaired on the island.

The joiners' shop made the furniture for the Cockatoo-built ships,

Part of the dockyard machine shop in February 1914.

and also produced high quality office furniture for the dockyard itself, and other Commonwealth Government departments, including the GPO and the Taxation Department.

After the war, Cockatoo built the machinery for the collier *Biloela* and the boilers and main engines for the *Fordsdale* and *Ferndale*, which were each fitted with quadruple expansion steam engines of 5500 IHP, and six scotch boilers, the largest of the type built in Australia.[144]

The reduced level of activity in shipbuilding during the 1920s encouraged the dockyard to seek other ways to use its many skills, which resulted in the tender for the Bunnerong Power Station machinery, described earlier. The loss of this job left the workshops short of work, and greatly limited the amount of non-government work the dockyard could obtain.

The lease of the yard to the Company in 1933 removed all these restrictions. During the 1930s, Cockatoo began to increase its general engineering work. It ranged from the repair and overhaul of steam turbine machinery to the manufacture of milk processing plant for the dairy industry. 'Codock' brand stainless steel cream holding and neutralising vats and 'Lesco' pasteurisers were made on the island. Heavier engineering included a 125-ton hot metal ladle for BHP, and presses and guillotines for leather and metal fabrication industries.

When the Bunnerong Power Station was expanded in 1937 Cockatoo won a contract to build the condensers, work that continued into 1939.

The contract for the sloops *Yarra* and *Swan* included the manufacture of their Parsons steam turbines and Yarrow boilers, and the main machinery of the later two ships of the class and the Tribal class destroyers was also built on the island. The Tribal class turbines developed 22,000 shaft horsepower on each shaft and were the most powerful yet built at Cockatoo. Three Admiralty three-drum watertube boilers with superheaters provided steam.

In addition to the machinery for the warships built at Cockatoo, the yard also made the main engines for the *River Clarence* and *River Hunter*, and six ship sets of Bauer Wach exhaust steam turbines for the A class standard steam ships. Three Lentz type double acting compound steam engines of 1850 IHP were built for the D class standard freighters, together with thrust blocks, poppet valves, valve cam gear, piston rings, main regulating valves, engine mountings and propellers for another seven ships. A considerable quantity of auxiliary machinery and parts for the World War II merchant ship building programme was also made at Cockatoo.

The manufacture of ships' boilers was one of the outstanding engineering achievements of Cockatoo during World War II. Cockatoo made all but 12 boilers for all warships built in Australia during the war, and they were supplied to shipbuilders throughout the country. At one time boilers were being delivered at the rate of two per week. The number of boilers built is shown in the table below, and a list of all boilers and the ships for which they were delivered is given in Appendix 9.

BOILERS BUILT AT COCKATOO DOCKYARD DURING WORLD WAR II

TYPE OF SHIP	COCKATOO SHIPS	OTHER YARDS	TOTAL ORDERED	TOTAL COMPLETED
Sloops	4		4	4
Minesweepers	16	92	108	108
Boom defence vessels	6		6	6
A class standard steamships	4		4	4
Tribal class destroyers	9		9	9
River class frigates	4	22	26	26
D class standard steamships		14	14	14
A and B class tugs	6	6	12	
TOTAL	49	134	183	171

Preparing for a large casting in the iron foundry during World War I.

One of the 12,500 SHP turbines built for HMAS *Adelaide* in 1920. It weighed 120 tons.

The manufacture of boilers and turbines for naval vessels continued after the war. Two ship sets of Parsons turbines, each developing 50,000 SHP, with Admiralty three drum water tube boilers were built for the Battle class destroyers *Tobruk* and *Anzac*. They were followed by three sets of English Electric turbines with Foster Wheeler boilers for the Daring class destroyers. These turbines, which developed 27,000 SHP per shaft, and were the most powerful ever built at Cockatoo.

Y100 steam turbines of 15,000 SHP per shaft were also built under licence from the English Electric Company for the Type 12 frigates that were built at Cockatoo and Williamstown. Main and cruising turbines were built for the first four ships, although the cruising turbines were removed before completion. Y136 turbines were built for the last two ships, *Torrens* and *Swan*. Completed in 1968, they were the last turbines to be built at Cockatoo. The Foster Wheeler boilers for the first four ships were also built at Cockatoo, but the boilers for the last two were imported.

In 1945, the heavy engineering capability of Cockatoo was probably unequalled in Australia, and over the next three decades the yard completed a very wide range of general engineering work. The following jobs were typical:

◆ fabrication of dam gates for the Snowy Mountains Scheme and New South Wales water supply dams

◆ fabrication of container handling cranes

◆ machining of propeller shafts and rudder stocks for ships under construction in other Australian shipyards

◆ casting and machining of ship's propellers up to 15 tons weight

◆ manufacture and machining of parts for the iron and steel industry, including mill spindles, slab mill manipulator shafts, jack shafts and couplings, rope drums and heavy duty hoist barrels. Extensive equipment overhaul was also carried out, for example the repair of three 90-ton mill drive armatures.

◆ manufacture of mine winder drums, up to 5.5 metres diameter, and complete mine winders, including drums, pedestals, and base frames

◆ manufacture of mill shells for the cement industry, the largest of which weighed 70 tonnes

◆ manufacture of mill shells for power stations, including seventy 47-tonne coal pulverising mill shells for the New South Wales power stations at Eraring, Bayswater and Mount Piper. This work included the white-metalling and proof machining of 112 ball mill main bearings. The coal pulverising mills had a diameter of 4 metres and a length of 8.3 metres.

◆ manufacture of fixed wheel gates and radial gates for flood mitigation

◆ manufacture of many thousands of spare parts for naval ships and equipment for the RAN

◆ the repair of mechanical, electrical and electronic equipment for power generation authorities, the Navy and Army, oil refineries, mines and many other industries

◆ the rehabilitation of various types of sugar mill crusher/shredder-drive turbine rotors for the sugar industry.

The joiners' shop continued to build furniture for ships until the dockyard closed. This photograph was taken in the 1960s.

Below: A 'Lesco' pasteuriser made at the dockyard in the 1930s.

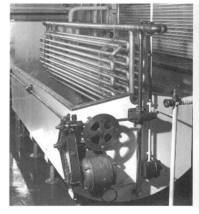

Left: The quadruple expansion steam engines built for the cargo ship *Fordsdale* in 1923.

A condenser for the Bunnerong Power Station under test in the boiler shop.

A set of turbines for HMAS *Voyager* under test with their gearbox. (RAN photograph)

A 30-ton mill spindle after machining from a 50-ton forging.

Less typical was the support given by Cockatoo to the Australian challengers for the America's Cup, notably the first by Sir Frank Packer's *Gretel* in 1962. Cockatoo lent a ship draughtsman to the designer of the yacht, Alan Payne, to help with the working drawings, and many of the special parts needed for the boat were made on the island.

The lead keel, which weighed 19 tons, was cast in the foundry to a pattern supplied by the yacht's builders, Halvorsens. The casting was then marked off and machined on the top surface, and holes drilled accurately for the securing bolts. It was perhaps the largest lead casting then made in Australia, and its handling and machining presented many problems.

Forty floor plates, six web frames and the mast step were fabricated from mild steel with careful control of dimensions and weight. Over 100 other items, including deck and mast fittings, steering sheaves and rudder fittings, shroud plates, mainsheet sheaves and blocks were cast or fabricated in Superston bronze, aluminium alloy, monel metal or gunmetal. All were finished to a high standard of finish for yacht use.

In time the facilities at Cockatoo became more widely duplicated throughout industry, and the dockyard became less competitive for some classes of work. This change resulted in the decision to cease making castings on the island and the foundries closed in 1968. The island location, with no road or rail access, increased transport costs. Priority often had to be given to ship repair work in the docks, which had adverse effects on deliveries. Consequently the work that came to Cockatoo tended to be the more unusual or difficult jobs, which benefited from the wide experience of the workforce and their skills at adapting to difficult circumstances.

The long experience at Cockatoo in the manufacture and repair of marine steam turbines ensured that there was a constant stream of steam turbine work through the shops. During the 1970s the number of ships with steam turbine propulsion visiting Australian waters gradually declined, and diesels or gas turbines propelled newer navy ships. However, this was compensated by a substantial increase in work from commercial industry and power generation authorities.

Steam turbine repair work came to Cockatoo from all states in Australia, plus New Zealand and Fiji. The biggest jobs came from power generation authorities, but the greatest number came from commercial industry such as oil refineries, chemical plants, sugar and paper mills, and other industry wherever turbines were used for power.

In the 1970s and the 1980s Cockatoo completed a large volume of major turbine repairs for power authorities. Much of this work arose from the catastrophic failure of an 87 megawatt turbo alternator at the Hinkley Point nuclear power station in Britain in September 1969. The turbine disintegrated whilst undergoing a routine overspeed test. The LP rotors involved had been made by shrinking the disks onto the rotor shaft, and failure was believed to have been caused by stress corrosion cracking at the disk keyway. A worldwide programme of examination of similar rotors revealed widespread similar defects. In 1973, the New South Wales Electricity Commission asked Cockatoo to dismantle for inspection and possible repair a 22-ton 100 megawatt LP rotor from the Tallawarra Power Station. The rotor was found to be defective, and was repaired at Cockatoo. Many more similar rotors from Australia and New Zealand followed it.[145]

The bearing journals of a 47-tonne mill shell being machined in the Craven lathe. This is just one of the 70 built for the New South Wales power stations at Eraring, Bayswater and Mount Piper.

Cockatoo was also called upon frequently to straighten bent turbine rotor shafts. In the five years 1974 to 1979, over 26 rotors from nine different manufacturers were straightened, a complex operation often involving heating, pressing and machining.

Cockatoo had formal agreements for turbine and compressor repairs with overseas manufacturers like Elliot and Turbodyne of the United States, and Stal Laval of Sweden. Nevertheless, some 30 other overseas manufacturers often called upon Cockatoo to provide service for their equipment.

A typical view of the turbine shop in the 1980s.

An oil refinery turbine rotor being repaired in 1984.

Preparing to disassemble a power station turbine rotor in the turbine shop in 1978.

The range of heavy machine tools on Cockatoo Island, some dating from World War I, assisted the turbine repair work. In the 1970s a large balancing machine, owned by the New South Wales Electricity Commission was installed in the turbine shop. In 1976 the dockyard acquired the largest lathe in Australia, a Craven lathe with a 14 feet 6 inch diameter face plate. It had been made during World War II and installed in the workshops at Garden Island. Rarely used there, it was removed in the 1960s and later installed at Cockatoo. With these facilities Cockatoo was able to handle the largest turbines installed anywhere in Australia.

The largest single customer for turbine and other rotating machinery repairs was the Electricity Commission of New South Wales. In the 1980s, Cockatoo completed about fifty major turbine repairs for them, as well as repairs to 11 small turbines, 126 bearings, seals and thrust pads, 17 oil coolers and heat exchangers, 14 generator armatures and exciters, 17 river pumps, 79 boiler circulating pumps, 18 other pumps and over eighty other off-site and miscellaneous repairs. Often, repair techniques were used at Cockatoo for the first time in Australia.

With the closure of the dockyard in 1991, some of the experienced people from Cockatoo moved with some of the equipment to a new turbine repair facility established by GEC Alsthom in the Hunter valley.

The steering gear for the guided missile frigate HMAS *Newcastle*, built under licence from Jered Brown in the United States, under test in the turbine shop.

The floating crane *Titan* lifting a mill shell for delivery to the mainland. A submarine in refit on the slave dock lies at the Bolt Wharf.

Chapter
Ten

OTHER ACTIVITIES

SHIP DESIGN

When the Commonwealth took over in 1913 the technical capacity of
Cockatoo Dockyard was small. The new management steadily built up
the drawing offices with people from the United Kingdom, and particularly from Vickers, at Barrow in Furness. A number of experienced
draughtsmen were brought to Cockatoo under contract. Most
remained after their contracts expired. Their work involved the
detailed design and preparation of working drawings for the torpedo
boat destroyers, the cruiser *Brisbane* and the many conversions of merchant ships to transports, all done by a drawing office staff of only
about sixty in a dockyard with 2500 employees.

In July 1916, 10 people were sent to Britain to study submarine and
warship building. By the time they returned in January 1918, plans for
submarine construction had been dropped, however their experience
was to be very valuable to Cockatoo, particularly when the J class submarines arrived for refit and repair in 1919.

The order for the cruiser *Adelaide* to a substantially modified design
from that of her near sister ship *Brisbane*, resulted in an expansion of
the drawing offices. Throughout the 1920s most of the work was in
detailed design and working drawings, with little basic ship design
work apart from the Commonwealth steamers. Some design proposals
were prepared, particularly for commercial tenders.

When the Company took over the dockyard in 1933 a nucleus of
design skills was acquired with those staff taken over from the
Commonwealth. Their design workload expanded considerably as the
Company sought new business, and they designed tugs, oil lighters and

The patrol vessel
Vigilant on trials on
Sydney Harbour in
August 1938.
(J C Jeremy Collection)

other small ships, some of which were built at the yard. One interesting design of the period was that of the patrol vessel *Vigilant*, which was designed and built by Cockatoo for the Department of Trade and Customs in 1938.

The naval ships built during the 1930s were based on British Admiralty designs, and the RAN acquired working drawings from the Admiralty for use in Australia. All the necessary design modifications were prepared in detail by Cockatoo. This procedure was changed for the Tribal class destroyers, when the Navy asked Cockatoo to arrange for the supply of working drawings direct from a British shipbuilder. They were obtained from the Vickers Armstrong's yard in Newcastle upon Tyne, where four Tribal class destroyers had been built. Cockatoo had enjoyed a long working relationship with Vickers, and this programme further encouraged the association. During this period the Company also developed a useful working relationship with the British firm of naval architects and marine engineers, Graham and

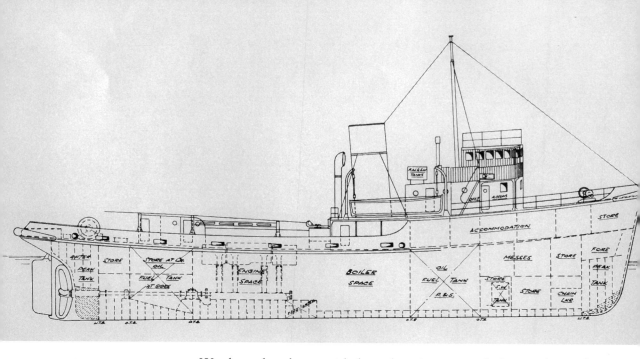

Within the diagram: AFTER PEAK TANK, STORE, STORE AT CR. OIL, FUEL TANK AT SIDES, ENGINE SPACE, BOILER SPACE, OIL FUEL TANK, STORE, C.W. TANK, STORE, CHAIN LKR, FORE PEAK TANK, ACCOMMODATION, MESSES, STORE, STORE, ANSER TANK, CABINS, ROOMS

Cockatoo designed the A class ocean-going tugs that became Cockatoo Ships number 180, 181 and 182. They were cancelled in September 1945.

Woolnough, who provided much assistance with the purchase of materials and equipment from Britain and Europe.

The technical staff was being over-worked by 1937, and to help meet the demand the Company increased the numbers of young men taken on as apprentices for training, particularly as naval architects. This helped to provide the skills that were to be much in demand during the war years. Many of the people trained at Cockatoo during those years went on to fill important positions in Navy Office, the Australian Shipbuilding Board and other shipyards throughout Australia. A number of experienced draughtsmen were also brought out from Britain.

Most of the technical workload of Cockatoo during World War II, involved detailed design and the preparation of working drawings for naval ships built at Cockatoo and by other Australian yards, as well as the many drawings needed for the ships which came to Cockatoo for repair or conversion.

During the merchant shipbuilding programme begun in 1941, Cockatoo prepared working drawings for the A class standard steam ships. Loft templates were also prepared for use, not only at Cockatoo, but also by the other yards involved.

The A class standard ship programme was curtailed in 1943, and the War Cabinet approved the construction in Australia of a number of smaller ships for the Australian coastal trade. Ten vessels each of 6000 DWT and 4000 DWT capacity and two of 2000 DWT capacity were planned. Cockatoo did most of the design work for these ships for the Australian Shipbuilding Board, although the dockyard built none.

The designs became known as the B, D and E classes. The B class ships were single screw, shelter deck, general purpose cargo ships of about 6500 DWT capacity, 405 feet 2 inches long overall, and 53 feet in beam. The main engine was a triple expansion steam engine with exhaust turbine supplied with superheated steam by two Babcock boilers fitted with Erith-Roe mechanical stokers. The maximum speed was about 13 knots. The design was later modified for oil firing and a diesel-powered version was also built. Ten ships were completed, two by Mort's Dock, three by BHP at Whyalla, and five by Evans Deakin.

The D class were single screw, single deck, general-purpose cargo vessels of about 2950 DWT. They were 290 feet 9 inches long overall, 46 feet in beam, and powered by a double-compound four cylinder reciprocating steam engine of 1850 IHP, with two water tube boilers. Nine ships were built three at Whyalla, four at the State Dockyard Newcastle, and two at Evans Deakin.

The five E class were built by Walkers Limited and were propelled by a Mirrlees HFR 6 diesel engine of 540 BHP. They were single shelter deck type ships with a raised quarterdeck. Capacity was about 620 DWT, and they were 181 feet 9 inches long overall with a beam of 29 feet 6 inches.

By the end of the war, Cockatoo had an experienced and capable design team. They were to be very busy for some years with the reconversion for commercial service of the liners *Manoora* and *Kanimbla*,

The drawing office at the end of World War II.

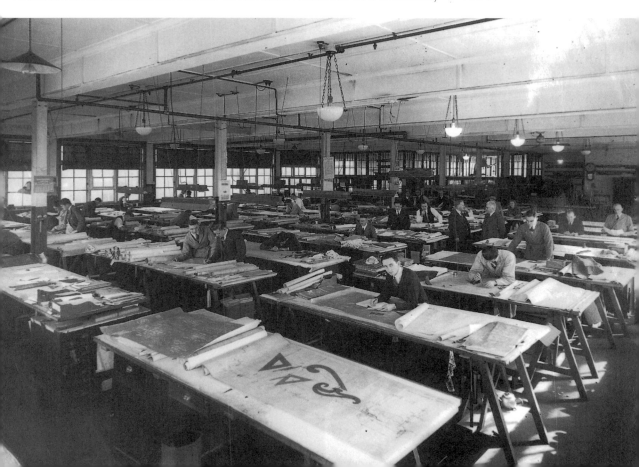

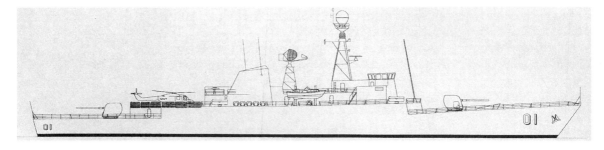

The RAN concept of the light destroyer in 1968. It was intended as a relatively simple ship that could be built with different armament configurations to suit a variety of roles. (J C Jeremy)

and the detailed design and working drawing work for the post-war naval shipbuilding programme. Their experience enabled them, working with Navy Office and the Williamstown Naval Dockyard, to incorporate many uniquely Australian features into the Battle and Daring class destroyers, the Type 12 and 15 frigates, and the modernised Tribal class destroyers.

New RAN ships were being designed in Australia by 1960, although this was limited to non-combatant types. The designs included the survey ship *Moresby*, the Attack class patrol boats, and the escort maintenance ship HMAS *Stalwart*, which was built at Cockatoo. For the *Stalwart*, the basic design was done by Navy Office, with Cockatoo completing the detailed design and working drawings. At this time, the naval capability of Navy Office, Cockatoo and Williamstown was complemented by a considerable merchant ship design capacity in the Australian Shipbuilding Board's ship design group, and the drawing offices of the shipbuilders like the State Dockyard, Newcastle, the Whyalla Shipbuilding and Engineering Works, and Evans Deakin, Brisbane. By the end of the next decade this hard won capability had been lost.

The successful Australian designed naval ships of the 1960s engendered sufficient confidence for the new construction programme (approved by the government in 1969) to proceed on the basis of ships designed in Australia, specifically for Australian conditions. The design of the fast combat support ship (AOE) was undertaken by Navy Office, with assistance from Cockatoo (for the structural design) and Y-ARD of Glasgow for the machinery installation design. The small hydrographic survey ship approved then was built by Williamstown (as HMAS *Flinders*) based on a design by the Australian Shipbuilding Board for a survey ship which had been built by Walkers for the Philippines.

The most ambitious of the projects approved in that programme was for the construction of a class of light destroyers. A sketch design had been prepared by Navy Office for a ship of 2100 tons displacement, 335 feet long, a beam of 40 feet and a maximum speed of about 32 knots. The ship was to be adaptable for different roles, and the patrol version was to be armed with two 5-inch guns and a light helicopter. It was intended to place the contract for the preliminary design of the light destroyers with an Australian contractor in order to build up the local capability for warship design.

Naturally, Cockatoo was very keen to get this work, however the Company recognised that whilst it had significant detailed design capability, the drawing offices had no basic warship design experience and a credible tender would only be possible in partnership with experienced overseas firms.

Some time previously, Vickers had proposed to the RAN that they be funded to establish a naval design office in Australia, and so Vickers Barrow were an obvious part of the Cockatoo team. As the RAN was gradually moving towards United States standards, and the selection of weapons for the sketch design confirmed, the US firm of naval architects and marine engineers, Gibbs & Cox of New York joined the team.

The contract for the preliminary design of the light destroyers (DDL) was awarded to Y-ARD (Australia) for $800,000 in July 1970. During the design process the staff requirements for the ship were changed considerably, and by the time the design was completed in September 1971, the DDL had become a general purpose destroyer of over 4000 tons, armed with one 5-inch gun, the Tartar surface to air guided missile, and two helicopters. The cost of the ship had also risen, and the likely number fell to three, all to be built at Williamstown.

Despite uncertainty over government approval for construction of the DDL, in September 1972 the government did approve the invitation of tenders for the detailed design phase of the project. Y-ARD, Cockatoo and Litton Industries (of the US, through an Australian subsidiary) were invited to submit a detailed tender. Littons later dropped out of the competition.

The detailed design phase included the preparation of working drawings and the integrated logistic support activity, work that would extend through the shipbuilding phase, if approved. As Vickers Barrow was then heavily committed with other work, the Cockatoo team was altered to include Cockatoo's Canadian associated company Canadian Vickers. Cockatoo as prime contractor would be responsible for the management of the project, Gibbs & Cox would undertake the detailed design, and Canadian Vickers would do most of the working drawings. Much of the work would have been done in Australia.

The Gibbs & Cox version of the light destroyer that emerged from the design review in 1973. By this time the ship had grown into a large and capable but expensive ship. Modifications were needed to the preliminary design to improve damaged stability. One modification in this proposal was the introduction of a break in the upper deck which was unusual in warship designs after World War II.
(J C Jeremy)

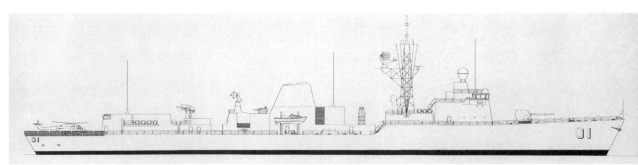

Tenders closed on 1 February 1973, and Cockatoo's final price estimate for the project was $31,923,066. Indecision continued, and to keep the process moving whilst the new Labor Government, which had won the December 1972 election, considered the project's future, contracts were given to both Y-ARD and Cockatoo for a design review and appraisal task. This work, known as Task B, was an early part of the detailed design process intended to examine the integrity of the preliminary design of the ship (which had been further modified since 1971), and to validate plans for the construction of the ships at Williamstown.

Cockatoo undertook to validate the construction programme, and Gibbs & Cox studied the design. The work which began in April 1973 was not finished when the DDL and AOE projects were cancelled in August. Both contractors had to continue for several weeks to complete work on projects already cancelled. It was a very discouraging process for the people involved.

The design review revealed some problems with the ship design, principally with damaged stability, which could be overcome by some rearrangement. Nevertheless, cancellation was probably the correct course of action, as subsequent experience with the construction of HMAS *Cook* at Williamstown and later *Success* at Cockatoo revealed some of the problems which would probably have made the construction of the DDL in Australia very protracted and expensive.

Cockatoo learned a great deal through its participation in the DDL project, and gained some new skills and capability in modern naval ship design and support. However the demise of the DDL did much harm to the ability of Australia to design and build its own naval ships. The scrambling for experienced people by the tenderers in a very restricted market dissipated much of the experience that had been gained since the war. Much worse was the loss of confidence by government in the undertaking of such work in Australia. Opportunities for Australian industry to take a leading role in naval design were lost as the selection of ship designs was based on minimum technical risk criteria which resulted in the choice of existing, proven designs from overseas.

After the cancellation of the DDL, the government instructed the RAN to examine a range of existing designs to identify those that might be suitable as the RAN's new destroyer. The range of options was wide, and based on the involvement with Vickers Barrow in the 1974 Vickers Vedette proposal for Indonesia, Cockatoo, with guidance from Barrow, developed 'Australianised' versions of the Vedette which became known as Types 633 and 642.

The work mainly involved altering the Vedette design to incorporate US weapons and other RAN specific requirements. The Vickers Vedette was a private venture design for a small, simple and inexpensive patrol corvette, with excellent sea keeping ability and low 'through life' cost. The designed displacement was around 1200 tons on a waterline length of 72 metres and a beam of 10 metres. Propulsion machinery comprised two diesel engines for cruising and one gas turbine for high speed, driving two shafts. Maximum speed was to be about 34 knots.

The Vedette Type 633 was armed with one 5-inch gun, two 35-millimetre Oerlikon guns in a twin mounting, two triple Mark 32 torpedo tubes, and eight Harpoon surface-to-surface missiles. In the Type 642, the secondary armament was reduced and a helicopter and hangar fitted.

The Vedette was considered too small to satisfy the RAN's needs, and suffered because it was not a 'proven' design, however good its design origins. The work on the design did, however, provide interest for the Cockatoo technical people at a time when there was little alternative work on the horizon. The RAN finally selected the US Navy guided missile frigate (FFG 7) design, which had a similar armament to the DDL. Two ships, which became HMAS *Adelaide* and HMAS *Canberra*, were ordered from the United States in August 1974.

In the early 1970s the number of technical people at Cockatoo fell as the workload shrank to that needed to support the submarine refits, the design of the slave dock *SD 3201* and the other minor shipbuilding projects of the time.

Despite this reduction in capacity, it was thought to be sufficient to support the construction of HMAS *Success* when that contract was won in 1979, as a complete set of working drawings was to be supplied by the Navy from France. The extent of the work needed to modify the drawings to include Australian materials and equipment and to incorporate RAN design changes proved to be much greater than expected. The problems were magnified by the different design philosophy of the French Navy, and the often poor quality of the original drawings.

Additional staff was recruited from other major Australian shipyards, which were progressively closing in the late 1970s, and more were obtained from the United Kingdom. Technical resources remained in short supply throughout the project, despite the technical departments, including planning and quality control, growing to about 210 people, the largest in the dockyard's history.

The Vickers Vedette Type 633. This version of the Vickers private venture design was prepared at Cockatoo to incorporate US weapons.

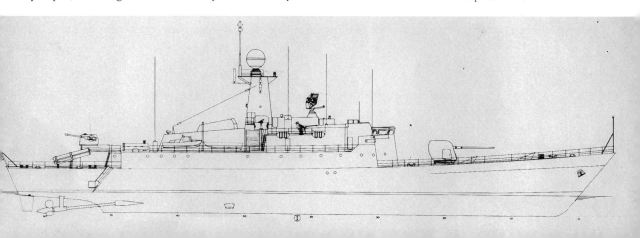

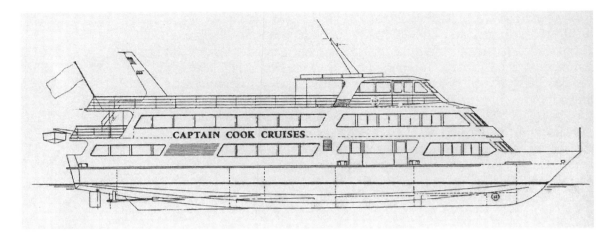

The Ship Technology Unit designed this 350-passenger 38.6-metre harbour cruise vessel for Captain Cook Cruises. It was built by Carrington Slipways at Tomago for service on Sydney Harbour.

In 1978 the dockyard developed a concept for a small air-operated floating dock. This is the *Vickdock 30* being launched in Sydney in August 1980. Others were built in New Zealand and Indonesia.

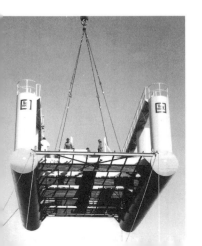

The need to have well-qualified technical support for modern ship-building and ship repair encouraged the Company to expand the design capacity of the dockyard when an unusual opportunity arose in 1980.

Until then, the Australian Shipbuilding Board had administered the subsidy scheme for merchant shipbuilding in Australia. Within the Board, a ship design group (SDG) provided technical support, and ship design and technical services for ships ordered by the Board on behalf of Australian ship owners.

With the passage of the *Bounty (Ships) Act 1980*, the role of the Board changed, and the need for the ship design group to continue within the public service was questionable. The SDG was however one of the few remaining centres in Australia capable of major ship design tasks, and also provided unique technical support services to commercial shipbuilders.

Following extensive negotiations with the Commonwealth Department of Industry and Commerce, which then operated the SDG, Cockatoo took over the group in a reduced form in September 1981. The group was established in offices in North Sydney and operated as the Ship Technology Unit (STU).

For the next six years STU continued to provide shipbuilders, ship owners, Commonwealth and State government departments and Statutory Authorities with a wide range of services, including ship design, ship and machinery performance recording and analysis, technical investigations and noise and vibration analysis.

Projects undertaken by the unit included feasibility studies for coal projects in the Philippines and ship repair facilities in Malaysia, the recording of sea trials performance data for most commercial shipbuilders in Australia, and the design of ships ranging from a Sydney Harbour cruise vessel to an update of the design of HMAS *Flinders* for the RAN.

Despite a continued demand for the Unit's specialised services, the reduced size of the Australian shipbuilding industry limited the work available. It was not profitable, and the STU was sold in 1987.

With the loss of the Unit and the completion of HMAS *Success* the technical workload of Cockatoo shrank to that required to support commercial work and naval refits, in addition to the maintenance of the Oberon class submarine drawings and the support of the refits. This Oberon work was particularly important, as Cockatoo was the only place in Australia that maintained a complete database on the RAN submarines, including all quality records from the fourteen refits of Oberon class submarines completed at the dockyard.

AIRCRAFT

In the early decades of the 20th century, it was not unusual for shipbuilders to become involved in some way with aircraft. In England, Vickers Sons & Maxim, at Barrow in Furness were approached by the Admiralty in 1908 and asked to submit a price to build a rigid airship for the Naval Air Service. Vickers' high reputation as a submarine builder, and innovative approach to new developments attracted the responsible officers to the yard. In 1909 they began construction of No. 1 Rigid Naval Airship.[146] In Germany, Blohm+Voss began to build aircraft

A Walrus seaplane about to be lifted by the Destroyer Wharf crane.

during the Depression as a means of diversification.[147] In Australia, Cockatoo Dockyard became involved in the aircraft industry almost by accident.

In 1924, the Royal Australian Air Force established the RAAF Experimental Station at Randwick, in Sydney.[148] The brain child of Wing Commander L J Wackett, the Station's first big task was the design and construction of a single engine flying boat with a wooden

Building a new wing for the *Southern Cross*.

Preparing the *Codock*
for its first flight in
March 1934.
(J C Jeremy Collection)

hull. The *Widgeon I* was the first flying boat to be designed and built in
Australia. It was built in about eighteen months, and was succeeded by
the larger and more powerful *Widgeon II*.

The Station also repaired aircraft and engines, manufactured propellers and spares, and grew to have a staff of about eighty. In 1929,
under some pressure from the British aircraft industry, the government
decided to close the Experimental Station as an economy measure. The
closure would save about £25,000 per year, and although resisted by
the Air Force, the decision was implemented.

Wackett decided to leave the RAAF, but was unwilling to see his
efforts in establishing an aircraft industry wasted. He had developed a
friendship with the manager of Cockatoo, Jack Payne, who agreed to
help. With the support of the Chief of the Air Staff, the best of the skilled
men from the Experimental Station and the essential plant were transferred to Cockatoo Island. The government approved the move, and
agreed that the Air Force should divert some repair work to the dockyard.

The Aircraft Department was set up on the top of the island, in the
drawing office building, and the drawing offices moved to the old
prison buildings. Repairs were carried out on civil and military aircraft,
including the Walrus amphibians carried on the seaplane carrier HMAS
Albatross.

At Randwick, Wackett had repaired the propellers of the famous Fokker monoplane *Southern Cross* for Sir Charles Kingsford Smith after his first crossing of the Tasman Sea in 1928. After the *Southern Cross* crashed at Mascot in 1932 on the night of the celebrations for the opening of the Sydney Harbour Bridge, Kingsford Smith gave the repair job to the aircraft department at Cockatoo.

The *Southern Cross*, which had a wingspan of 70 feet, was extensively rebuilt with over fifty per cent of the entire structure being replaced, including the wing.

Soon after, Kingsford Smith became interested in starting a small airline in New Zealand, and asked Wackett to design and build a six passenger aircraft for the service. The twin engine monoplane design was completed in mid-1933, and named the *Codock*, after its birthplace.[149] The contract price for the *Codock* was £3700, and it first flew at Mascot on 6 March 1934. The plane had a wingspan of 52 feet, a length of 34 feet 4 inches, and a height of 10 feet 5 inches. It had originally been designed for de Havilland Gipsy engines, but Kingsford Smith arranged with Napier for two more powerful Javelin engines at a low price. They developed 185 horsepower each, giving a maximum speed of 140 miles per hour at sea level. The plane cruised at 185 miles per hour at an altitude of 3000 feet.

The plans for the New Zealand service failed, and in August 1934 the *Codock* was sold to Northern Airways for use on the Sydney–Newcastle run. The engines gave a lot of trouble, mainly because fuel of sufficiently high octane content was not available in Australia at the time. The plane crash-landed on at least one occasion, and in due course changed hands again. (It ended its days in a paddock at Minchinbrook, west of Sydney, as an advertisement for Penfolds Wines.)

Wackett prepared a design for a four-engine version of the *Codock* called the *Corella*, and he used the basic design of the *Codock* for the very successful *Gannet*, 12 of which were built. Wackett was also interested in high speed racing boats, and whilst at Cockatoo he built two stepped hydroplanes, the *Century Tire II* and *Cettein*, for men wanting to win the Australasian championship. They were powered by aircraft engines of 400 horsepower, for a maximum speed of around 70 miles per hour. One held the championship for 15 years.

Wackett also designed a 45-foot double step planing hull fast ferry, which the aircraft department built in mahogany and Queensland maple. It was powered by a 350 horsepower 12 cylinder Rolls Royce aero engine, and achieved 35 knots on trials. Named *Clifton*, the 35 passenger boat was completed in December 1933, and offered to Sydney Ferries for a proposed high-speed service from Circular Quay to Clifton Gardens. After trials, the offer was not taken up, and the *Clifton*, which had cost £2500, was finally sold in February 1936 for £100 to a man who planned to convert it into a private motor yacht.

The economies imposed by the new Company which ran the dock-yard after February 1933 ('a firm of gelatine makers' according to Wackett in his autobiography[150]), and a claim by the shipwrights for coverage of the aircraft work, resulted in the closure of the aircraft department in 1934. Plans for development at Cockatoo, including the building of a substantial hanger between the docks, remained only drawings.

Wackett soon formed a small company, the Tugan Aircraft Company, which within a few years was to form the nucleus of the Commonwealth Aircraft Corporation. Under the leadership of Wackett, later Sir Lawrence, it went on to become a major enterprise, which by 1949 had built 1380 aircraft (mostly fighters and trainers) for the Royal Australian Air Force, and 1610 aircraft engines.

The remains of the cruiser *Sydney* towards the end of demolition at Cockatoo Island. (J C Jeremy Collection)

SHIPBREAKING

Following the sale of the Common-wealth Government Line of steamers in 1928, when the future of Cockatoo Dockyard was still under considera-tion, the government decided to allo-cate the cruiser HMAS *Sydney* to Cockatoo for breaking up as a means of preserving jobs.

The plan to scrap *Sydney* at Cockatoo was announced on 7 January 1929, shortly after the deci-sion to call tenders for the lease of the dockyard. It was expected that the job would occupy the yard until the new operators took over.

The demolition of such a famous ship attracted considerable public attention, particularly when the dockyard offered for sale souvenirs and parts of the ship to help recover the cost of the scrapping. Today, relics of *Sydney* can be found throughout Australia. A section of the bows is mounted in the sea wall under the Sydney Harbour Bridge, and in 1934 the tripod foremast was erected on Bradley's Head by the float-ing crane *Titan*.

Time was to take its toll on the mast, and *Titan* returned to Bradley's Head in May 1964 to bring the mast back to Cockatoo for repair. The fighting top was severely corroded, and was replaced by a 'look alike' welded structure (not a replica). The standards of conserva-tion at that time were not demanding. After it had been sandblasted and repainted the mast was returned to Bradley's Head in August 1964.

In October 1929, the destroyers *Parramatta*, *Yarra*, *Warrego*, and *Swan* were also sent to Cockatoo to be broken up, along with the depot ship *Penguin*, previously the cruiser *Encounter*. The destroyers *Huon* and *Torrens* followed them later.

These ships were stripped of valuable non-ferrous metals and other useable materials. The hulks of *Parramatta* and *Swan* were sold to the New South Wales Department of Prisons for use as accommodation ships on the Hawkesbury for road building. Never used for this purpose, they both found final resting places in the river where their remains still lie today. *Huon* and *Torrens* were sunk at sea as targets, and *Yarra* scuttled. The stripped hull of *Encounter* foundered off Bondi Beach in September 1932 whilst being towed to sea for scuttling.

It had been intended that *Warrego* should also be sunk at sea, however Sydney weather was to intervene. By July 1931, the hull had been stripped, loaded with scrap steel and ashes from *Titan*, and prepared for tow. Whilst waiting, a period of heavy rain filled the old ship with water. This would not have been a major problem, but the dockyard had earlier removed the two 'peace oil' tanks, located below the upper decks at the ship's sides amidships, greatly reducing the vessel's freeboard. *Warrego* sank alongside the Sutherland wharf.

An attempt was made to raise the wreck, using 'camels' at each end, and the *Titan* amidships. The hull was raised to the surface, however when some camels broke free, a massive load was placed on the slings of *Titan*. Fortunately, the weakened hull broke in two releasing *Titan* and the ship sank for the final time.

During World War II, the wreck became a problem for ships using the Sutherland Wharf. It was substantially demolished by explosives in April 1943, and *Titan* was used to lift parts of the ship for recovery as scrap. One section of the bows was retained as a relic at the main

Cockatoo Island in about 1930. The cruiser *Encounter* (centre front) can be seen lying alongside the remains of the *Sydney* with other parts of the ships being broken up in the shipyard.
(Government Printing Office Collection, State Library of New South Wales)

After shelling by
HMAS *Canberra*, the
hull of *Torrens* is sunk
by a demolition charge
on 24 November 1930.
(RAN photograph)

entrance to the dockyard at the Parramatta Wharf. It is now in the
Navy's historical collection on Spectacle Island. The two oil tanks that
had been removed in 1931 were used as oil tanks at the Power House
for many years until the late 1960s.

The wreck of *Warrego* came to light again in the late 1960s when
the Sutherland Wharf was being rebuilt to a new alignment. The contractors had great difficulty driving some of the new steel piles, and
divers discovered the obstruction to be the remains of *Warrego*. Parts
raised to make way for the piles were in remarkably good condition.
Today, the first modern warship built in Australia remains buried under
the wharf at the yard that built her.

Between June 1932 and September 1932 the sloops *Mallow*,
Geranium and *Marguerite* were also sent to Cockatoo for dismantling.
Proposals were developed to adapt *Mallow* and *Geranium* for commercial service, and to convert *Marguerite* to a salvage ship for the newly
formed Pacific Salvage Company. Nothing came of these plans and,
after stripping, the three ships were sunk by gunfire as targets at sea off
Sydney between April and August 1935.

No more ships were broken up at Cockatoo, although in April
1984, when a declining workload was again threatening jobs, the
Company did consider offering to buy the aircraft carrier *Melbourne* for
scrapping. The large quantity of asbestos in the ship made the proposal most unattractive, and she was ultimately broken up in China.

TITAN

The floating crane *Titan* was to be a familiar sight around Sydney Harbour for over seventy years after it was completed in December 1919. It made a major contribution to the industry of the port and the development of public infrastructure in the city.

Titan was designed to lift a maximum of 150 tons at 90 feet radius, and up to 100 tons at 125 feet radius. The total displacement of the crane pontoon, with a maximum lift was 2125 tons. The pontoon had an overall length of 176 feet 10 inches, and a beam of 79 feet 8 inches, and the maximum height of the top of the jib above the deck was 190 feet, ensuring that the crane was a prominent feature of the harbour.

Even floating cranes deserve a proper ceremony: the launching of *Titan* on 5 December 1917.

The crane was not self-propelled, but relied on two or three tugs for movement around the harbour. Power for working the crane was provided by two steam driven generators, each of 220 kilowatt at 220 volts, and an auxiliary generator of 44 kilowatt. A coal fired cylindrical boiler 11 feet diameter and just over 10 feet long supplied steam.

Three motors of 80 horsepower drove the main hoist and auxiliary hoist. The jigger hoist, jigger racking gear and slewing mechanism motors were each 40 horsepower. Derricking was controlled by two motors of 60 horsepower. Most of the crane's work required the use of the main or auxiliary hoist, with a rate of lift varying from 50 feet per minute with a 15 ton load, to 8 feet per minute when handling the maximum load of 150 tons. The jigger hoist could be used for loads up to 10 tons, and could travel outwards or inwards along the jib by means of the traversing mechanism. This avoided the need for the much slower derricking of the jib, which was the only means of moving a load in those directions when using the main or auxiliary hoists.

The slewing mechanism was inside the pontoon. It could rotate the crane bodily upon its axis, taking about 8 minutes to complete a full revolution with a maximum load. Derricking took about 20 minutes from the lowest to the highest position.

Counterbalancing of the jib and load was by a combination of fixed cast iron ballast (attached to the derricking screw cross beam and in the ballast box under the lifting machinery cabin) and by out-of-balance machinery weight. The pontoon could also be trimmed by water ballast, but this was rarely done.

The control room was located high up in the main structure, where the operator could have a clear view of the load and surroundings.

The crane used large quantities of steel wire rope in the hoists. The main hoist was of two 5.5-inch circumference cables, each 1880 feet long, passing through two 75-ton pulley blocks, which could be operated together or separately. The auxiliary hoist was 1330 feet of 4.5-inch wire with a 30-ton block. The jigger hoist had 760 feet of 3.75-inch wire, and the racking wire was 330 feet of 4-inch rope.

Titan provided an essential service for the dockyard, handling machinery and boilers for ships under construction, and other heavy machinery on and off the island. With no road or rail access, there was no other way heavy equipment could be handled without great difficulty and cost. The height of the crane was also useful, enabling equipment like crankshafts, to be removed from ships for repair.

Titan's largest lift before World War II was the unloading of the 145-ton French cargo ship *Le Phoque* off the deck of the German freighter *Stassfurt* in October 1938. During the 1930s, *Titan* launched several small ships built at Cockatoo, and also launched the new caisson for the Fitzroy Dock, which had been built on the island in 1931–32, a lift of 120 tons.

During World War II, *Titan* usually worked seven days a week, and often 24 hours a day, providing valuable services in the port of Sydney, which was for a time the main supply and repair base in the south-west Pacific. Large numbers of small craft, ranging from assault barges to small tugs, up to 80 tons displacement, were shipped to Sydney as deck cargo and unloaded by *Titan*. The crane lifted over 100,000 tons of material during the war.

Titan was very useful at Cockatoo Island for work that was beyond the capacity of the wharf cranes. Here *Titan* is handling weights for the testing of the boat davits of *Stalwart* in 1967.

In post-war years, the crane continued to be busy, not only serving the needs of the dockyard, but also helping with public works around Sydney, including the construction of the Iron Cove, Spit and Gladesville bridges. Similar work in earlier years had included the construction of the inverted siphon across Middle Harbour for the Northern Suburbs sewerage system, which consisted of 90 foot sections of reinforced concrete pipe, lowered by the crane into a trench dug in the bottom of the harbour.[151]

Other major lifts included boiler drums and steam turbines for New South Wales power stations, and on many occasions turbine rotors up to 60 tons in weight, and armatures, from power station plants.

By the 1960s the crane was starting to show its age, and after an extensive survey a modernisation was planned which was to include the replacement of the steam plant with diesel generators. Much work had been done on the crane structure and the pontoon when the Navy decided that there was little requirement to justify the retention of the crane for naval purposes, and the modernisation was cancelled in 1975.

Despite the high cost of operation, there was still use for the unique unit in Sydney, and the crane was essential for the handling of large equipment to and from Cockatoo Island. The Company decided to keep the crane in service as long as possible, and installed a portable diesel generator to power the crane machinery, and air compressors were carried on deck to power the winches, allowing the old steam plant to be taken out of service.

Throughout its 70 years *Titan* lifted many ships of all shapes and sizes, including tugs built at Cockatoo, and a tall ship arriving in Sydney for the Bicentennial celebrations of 1988, the Irish sail training ship *Asgard*. During the World War II the crane helped to salvage the remains of the Japanese midget submarines from the bottom of Sydney Harbour after the raid in May 1942. In 1985 *Titan* returned the pieces of two of them to Cockatoo for restoration by the dockyard apprentices for the Australian War Memorial in Canberra.

Titan raising the Sydney ferry *Karrabee* from the bottom of Circular Quay on 22 January 1984.

Other vessels rescued from the bottom of Sydney Harbour by *Titan* included the wooden coaster *Gosford* and the tug *Emu*.

The salvage of the ferry *Karrabee* in 1984 was the last salvage job for the crane and one of the most public.

The Urban Transit Authority's ferry sank at its jetty at Circular Quay on 22 January 1984, after taking part in the annual ferry race on the Harbour as part of the Australia Day celebrations. On 24 January *Titan* was berthed at the end of the wharf, and four bale slings, each made from 7-inch wire, and forming part of the normal heavy duty lifting gear of the crane were used for the salvage.

Two 60-foot slings were passed under the ferry in trenches prepared by divers. A 45-foot sling was then attached to both ends of each of the 60-foot slings by shackles. The main hoists of *Titan* were then positioned directly above *Karrabee* and the free ends of the 45-foot slings attached to them. *Karrabee* was then raised slowly until clear of the bottom. The operation was stopped periodically, once the ferry had broken surface, to allow water to drain off.

When the main deck could be seen the remainder of the lift continued very slowly, as it was not intended to lift the vessel above water level. Finally, pumps were placed on board, and hoisting was stopped when the main deck was about 18 inches clear of the water. *Karrabee* was lowered slowly as the water was pumped out, until the ferry was floating free, and the salvage, watched by a large crowd, was complete.

In 1989 the surveyors who regularly surveyed *Titan* for the renewal of its port craft licence declined to issue a certificate of operation for more than three months. Whilst the hull was basically sound, they were concerned about the condition of the thousands of rivets, most of which had been driven when the pontoon had been built. With limited demand for the crane's services, a full refit of the pontoon could not be justified, and *Titan* was taken out of commercial service in 1990. Short-term operating permits were issued for the crane to off-load and re-load the steam locomotive *Flying Scotsman* in 1991. The crane was also used that year at the island to dismantle the 50-ton Butters crane in the shipyard for scrapping; a final duty for the dockyard the old crane had served so well.

With the closure of the dockyard the Commonwealth decided to finally dispose of *Titan*. Despite the considerable interest in the community for the retention of the crane because of its historical value, it was not a practicable proposition. Nevertheless, some parts were in near original condition and worthy of preservation if possible. In particular, the engine room was essentially unchanged from its 1919 appearance, with most of the original electrical and mechanical equipment intact and in excellent condition.

At the request of the Commonwealth, the Company recommended that the steam driven generators complete with auxiliaries valves and condensers, and the switchboard be removed from the crane before disposal. These items could then be reconstructed in working condition on the island at some future date. The Commonwealth included this extent of equipment removal as a condition of sale.

Titan was sold in April 1992 to a New Zealand company. The new owners hoped to return the crane to service, and sought (and received) permission to retain all the electrical equipment on board, and to leave the condensers in place to avoid cutting large access openings in the pontoon for their removal. Consequently, only the steam engines and the steam driven auxiliaries were saved. By late 1992 the new owner was convinced that there was no viable prospect for the operation of the crane in Sydney, and sold *Titan* in early December to a Singapore company.

The provisions of the *Protection of Movable Cultural Heritage Act 1986* covered *Titan* (as it had been built in Australia before 1930 and was in use before 1920). Accordingly there were restrictions on the export of the crane but a permit was granted on the condition that it was returned to Australia before July 1995.

After preparation *Titan* left Sydney on the afternoon of 23 December 1992 under tow by the former New Zealand research ship *Rapuhia*, bound for Singapore.

Titan was towed stern first as was usual because it was more manageable that way. Slow but steady progress was made up the New South Wales coast until Christmas Day 1992 when the two vessels had reached Smoky Cape. At about 10:50 that evening, the crew of *Raphuia* felt a pronounced jerk, and found that the towline had parted. No sign of *Titan* could be seen but after a search of the area the pontoon was found floating bottom up.

Titan had capsized. The crane assembly, including the jib and crane tower had fallen off the central mast, which was bent towards *Titan's* bow. The capsize had occurred at a place where the east coast current was strong, and the capsized pontoon was towed south by *Rapuhia* to a position off Camden Head out of the current. After several days it was decided that the pontoon could not be salvaged, and it was prepared for sinking. It sank in 33 metres of water at around 9:00 pm on 29 December, about two miles south-east of Camden Head.

The Department of Transport and Communications subsequently investigated the loss of *Titan*.[152] The inquiry found that it was probable that the working of the crane in the seaway had caused rivets to fail in the after starboard section of the pontoon, allowing a large volume of water (probably between 500 and 700 tonnes) to enter the hull. This would have reduced the intact stability of the pontoon, and the shipping of seas on deck and the probable immersion of the deck edge would have had the effect of reducing the pontoon's reserves of stability. The report also noted that a number of factors were present and if they coincided they may have contributed to the capsizing moment. The factors included the plunging of the pontoon due to the loss of buoyancy at its towed end, the periodic rolling, wind heel effect in wind gusts and small movements of the jib, which would have contributed to the roll.

The long history of *Titan* was finally over.

Not all the tall ships that came to Australia to help celebrate the Bicentenary sailed to Sydney. The Irish brigantine *Asgard II* came by ship and was unloaded at Darling Harbour by the *Titan*.

THE PEOPLE
OF COCKATOO
DOCKYARD

The real strength of Cockatoo Dockyard was always its people. Nothing was ever too difficult for Cockatoo, and its ability to respond to any requirement reflected the wide range of skills available within the yard. In the early years the convicts provided a basic labour force for ship docking and cleaning, but in due course a permanent workforce was established as the facilities on the island developed.

The work of the yard was often demanding, with working conditions that no worker would accept today. Inevitably these conditions caused friction, and the island was fertile territory for the developing trade unions. The Ship Painters and Dockers Union was very active at Cockatoo during the latter part of the nineteenth century, and by the turn of the century the growing number of unions represented on the island inevitably meant that disputes arose, particularly over demarcation issues.

The 1903 Royal Commission commented that the action of over-zealous delegates seemed to be interfering with 'good discipline and economy of working'.[153] The considerable political influence over dockyard affairs made it difficult for the management to exercise their authority, as the unions readily bypassed them. This problem was to reappear on occasions throughout the dockyard's history, often because of the close relationship with the government, both as owner and as the principal customer. The dockyard was always a major employer of labour, and a ready target to establish a precedence for industry generally in major national campaigns, such as those for the 44, 40 and later 38 hour weeks.

The situation did not improve greatly after the yard became the Commonwealth Naval Dockyard. The number of people employed on the island grew considerably and they came from many other places in Australia and overseas. This ensured that the General Manager, John King Salter, and his team had much of their time taken up by industrial issues. In 1915 he complained to the Parliamentary Joint Committee of Public Accounts:

> Here I am, working under 51 awards, and new ones keep cropping up every day. How on earth can a man run an establishment of this sort and meet the contending forces of 51 different awards ... Several Unions cover one industry. There are two painters' unions; there are three carpenters' unions. The labourers have many unions, and many awards and conflicting awards. It is absolutely impossible to try to run this dockyard on economic lines, when you have so many conflicting rates of pay and overtime, and all that sort of thing, and different rates for night shift. One of the great difficulties here is the multiplicity of labourers' unions necessitating the employment of a much larger number of men than is necessary. One union allows its members to handle steel and iron, another union only allows its men to handle wood.[154]

There were many disputes over demarcation, and King Salter was constantly involved in trying to resolve the differences. One of his major problems was his lack of standing in the State Industrial Courts, as the Commonwealth Government was not recognised as an employer under the terms of the state Arbitration Act. King Salter proposed that the dockyard should be put under a Federal industrial award, but the unions resisted this.

John King Salter (second from the left in the middle row) with members of his management and the officers of the destroyer HMAS *Swan* in 1916.

In the event, the dockyard management and unions came to terms for practical purposes, particularly during the war period. Nevertheless, the problems that plagued King Salter continued for many years, constantly absorbing management time and unnecessarily increasing cost. After 1933 the Company was able to benefit from its membership of the Metal Trades Employers' Association (now the Metal Trades Industry Association or MTIA) and always worked strictly to the meaning of the appropriate awards with reference to the industrial courts if necessary to settle disputes.

During World War I many people came to Sydney from Britain, bringing with them the special skills needed for the warship building programme. Many of these men remained at the dockyard for years, and helped train young Australians in shipbuilding. Among them was John Wilson, who had served his apprenticeship with Vickers at Barrow between 1901 and 1906. There he rose to be assistant to the chief of the Technical Department, working on all classes of ships including battleships, battlecruisers and passenger liners.

Wilson came to Cockatoo in 1913, as assistant chief ship draughtsman. He became chief ship draughtsman in 1914 and assistant manager of the dockyard in 1922. He was acting general manager after the death of Jack Payne in 1932 until the Company took over in 1933. He continued to work for Norman Frazer as manager until he retired.

Of the executives the new Company took on in 1933, several were to play a major role in the development of industry in Australia. They included the aircraft superintendent, Lawrence Wackett, the engineering superintendent James Morton, the naval architect David Mitchell, the assistant hull superintendent David Carment, and the accountant Henry Morgan. Wackett left in 1934, but the others spent the rest of their working lives at Cockatoo and left a permanent mark on the shipbuilding industry.

Described as a dour Scot with high principles, James Cowan Morton was born in Glasgow, and served his apprenticeship as a fitter and turner at the Fairfield Shipbuilding and Engineering Company, builders of the prefabricated destroyer *Warrego*. He left Fairfields in 1912 to migrate to Australia.

After a few weeks at Mort's Dock, Morton was appointed chief engine draughtsman at Cockatoo, where he became deeply involved with the construction of the cruiser *Brisbane* and the three destroyers. He remained a 'temporary' public servant until the Company took him on in 1933. He continued in his position as chief draughtsman until he retired at the age of 74 in 1950. He trained many men in his 37 years at Cockatoo. In 1950, the superintendent of technical colleges, and the chief designing engineer (and his assistant) at the Metropolitan Water Sewerage and Drainage Board were all men who had served their time with him. Morton's grandson, another James Morton, served his apprenticeship at Cockatoo, later becoming the yard's last production manager.

D J Mitchell was born in Pyrmont in 1885, and started his apprenticeship at Cockatoo in 1904. He remained in the drawing office after he finished his time, and became assistant chief ship draughtsman in 1914. In 1916 he went to Britain as part of a team of 10 to study warship and submarine construction, returning in 1918. After 1933 he became the Company's naval architect for ship construction work, until he retired in 1955, with over 51 years service. His son Alan also served his time in the drawing office at Cockatoo, and remained at Cockatoo, apart from a spell with Vickers in Barrow as a ship manager during the construction of the aircraft carrier HMAS *Melbourne*. Together, David and Alan Mitchell worked at Cockatoo for just over 99 years.

The dockyard management team during World War II, (back row, left to right) George Roe (engineering superintendent), James Morton (chief designing engineer), Bert Ross (assistant manager), Noel Self (electrical engineer) and Harold Overton (shipyard superintendent), (front row) David Carment (chief estimator), John Wilson (manager), Norman Frazer (managing director), Harry Morgan (secretary) and David Mitchell (naval architect).

David Carment was also an Australian, born in Sydney in 1885. He had a great interest in ships, and wanted to become a naval architect, an unusual ambition for a young Australian of his generation. In 1906 he travelled to the United States, and later to Britain where, at Glasgow University he graduated with a Bachelor of Science degree in Naval Architecture with a Certificate of Efficiency in Engineering. He worked on Clydebank until he returned to Sydney in 1916 to take a position at Cockatoo. He remained with the dockyard until he retired in 1954. During the war he was the naval architect in charge of the design and drawing work for the many conversions and repairs carried out on ships like the *Queen Mary* and the US cruisers in 1942–43.

Carment also gave much of his time to helping others obtain knowledge of naval architecture and shipbuilding. He became a part-time teacher in the shipbuilding trades course with the New South Wales Department of Technical Education in 1919. Much later he became head teacher for the Naval Architecture Diploma course at the Sydney Technical College, and played a part in the establishment of the degree course in naval architecture at the University of New South Wales.

Carment had a great interest in yachting, and raced his yacht *Athene* with the Royal Sydney Yacht Squadron for many years. He was the Squadron's honorary measurer, and issued the Measurement Certificate for the Australian America's Cup Challenger *Gretel* in 1962. This 12-metre yacht had been designed by one of his former students, Alan Payne. Like many Australian naval architects, Alan Payne served his apprenticeship in the drawing office at Cockatoo. Carment was also involved in the formation of the Australian Branch of the Royal Institution of Naval Architects, and was president of the branch for a time.

H E Morgan became secretary of the Company, and a director in 1953. He died in office in 1959, having worked at Cockatoo for over 42 years. He was a meticulous man, who gave a lot to the company and

The shipwrights photographed against the starboard fore poppet of *Voyager* before launching. In the foreground (seated or squatting) are Mel Phillips (assistant foreman shipwright), George McGoogan (assistant foreman shipwright), Jim Cochrane (foreman shipwright and dockmaster), Bert Ross (manager), Ron Joselin (shipyard superintendent) and Harry McGoogan (chargehand shipwright).

contributed much to its success. He was also a great writer and record keeper, and many of his long memoranda to his managing director survive today. Although he had spent many years in the public service before the Company took over the yard, he found bureaucratic attitudes hard to take. There is no better illustration than his memo to Captain Hutcheson in 1957 complaining of the attitude of a senior Navy official to his estimate of 60 per cent for the dockyard overhead. The official believed that 57 per cent was a more appropriate figure. Morgan said:

> I explained ... that the whole subject was most complex, and that when [all the] 'intangibles', 'imponderables', 'unknowns' and so on, were taken into account, sound business judgement dictated that 60% was the only practical percentage for Naval Estimates ....

> We must, in short, have the strength of Hercules, the eyes of Argus, the judgement of Solomon, the speed of Mercury, and the patience of Job, and in addition possess the gift of prophecy. And *with* all these we reach 60%.

> The plain truth is, that we at Cockatoo have to answer with our economic lives for our judgement, and if we ran our business on the lines followed by the abstract figurers, we should quickly go bankrupt.

> But what a futile journey we have been forced to take, merely to come back to where we started.[155]

Many managers at Cockatoo have shared his frustration over the years. Morgan also held firm views on the value of man-hours as tool for job costing and estimating — a method introduced in 1956. In another long memo to Captain Hutcheson he said:

The man hour system though useless and misleading as a basis for comparison, is praised as a method of *control*. It helps management! This is a blunder of the first order. 'Man hours' at best is a *record* and records are history. By the time the record arrives the money is spent. The damage is done. It is too late. There is only one way to *manage*, and that is by effective *supervision*. Get the best return, by the best methods, under the prevailing economic conditions; by efficient supervision. The *result* of such supervision will be reflected in the *money* cost

Cockatoo Island after trying all types of management and control has placed its emphasis on efficient supervision, followed by practical and economic accounting. All useless elaboration has been discarded. This accounting is based upon, and revolves about, *money*. Every operation in the accounting from Time Sheet and Material Issue note, to Final costing and Balance Sheet is intimately related and is expressed in money terms. It is an integral system — a living *body*. It cannot be touched at any point without injury to the corporate system.[156]

(It must be remembered that he was writing at a time before high inflation and computers.)

A contemporary of Morgan's in senior management was H G (Bert) Ross. He started at Cockatoo in March 1912 as an apprentice fitter and turner. He moved to the drawing office and became a ship draughtsman, later transferring to the estimating office. About two years after the Company took over he was appointed assistant to the general manager, John Wilson.

He became shipbuilding superintendent, and later works manager. When Wilson's successor, Charles Inglis, resigned in 1955, Ross was promoted general manager. He retired in November 1960, after more than 48 years service to the Dockyard.

Ron Joselin, who had started at Cockatoo in 1938 as a trainee boilermaker, followed Ross as general manager. Joselin was appointed to the board in 1963 (as director of production), and retired in 1975. The management structure was then changed and the position of general manager ceased to exist.

The resident principal naval overseers made a major contribution to the running of Cockatoo as a successful dockyard. Until 1939 the engineer manager of Garden Island acted as the Navy's overseer for all their work at Cockatoo, but the approach of the war and the increased activity in the dockyard resulted in the appointment of Engineer Commander G I D Hutcheson RAN as the principal overseer at Cockatoo. Since 1939, 26 naval officers have held the position, the longest serving being the last, Commander Mike Davidson RAN, from 1982 to 1991.

Even in the early years of their training, apprentices were often involved in the production work of the yard. Here first and second year fitting and turning apprentices are repairing valves from the submarine HMS *Tabard* in January 1965. The foreman of the training school, Jim Irwin, is supervising Roger Sawyer. Intent on their work at the same bench are (left to right) Ronald Wilkins, John Jeffrey and Stanley Livingstone.

Several principal overseers went on to Flag rank, and some became general manager of the Garden Island or Williamstown Naval Dockyards. Amongst the latter were Hutcheson and Commander R G Parker RAN. Both later came to Cockatoo as managing director.

Hutcheson was an outstanding engineer. 'Hutch', as he was known, was a fast thinker and a fast talker who earned the respect of the allied navies whose ships came to Cockatoo during the war. It is said that the Americans invented the expression 'hutching', meaning to do things at top speed. He was also well respected by the people of Cockatoo, and as managing director was a familiar figure as he strode around the island, his hands clasped behind his back. He was also listened to in Canberra, so much so that some referred to him as the 'Fifth Naval Member'. (The Naval Board had four members.)

Hutch was also widely involved with industry matters outside Cockatoo. He became chairman of the Standards Association of Australia, President of the Institution of Engineers Australia, vice president for Australia of the Institute of Marine Engineers, and president of the Chamber of Manufactures.

Like his predecessor Norman Frazer, Hutch became president of the New South Wales Branch of the MTIA. The later managing directors of Cockatoo, Parker, Humbley and Jeremy all served on the MTIA Council, and Jeremy was New South Wales president between 1989 and 1991, when Cockatoo became the only Company to fill the position on three occasions. He went on to become national president of the Association. Jeremy was also a member of council of the Australian Branch of the Royal Institution of Naval Architects from 1971, and was president from 1978 to 1985. During his term as president the Branch became the first Division of the RINA.

Other executives of Cockatoo were active on industry bodies and associations, including the Australian Shipbuilders Association (of which Cockatoo was a foundation member), the Australian Ship Repairers Group, and the Australian Welding Research Association. The Company always supported professional associations like the Institute of Marine Engineers and the Royal Institution of Naval Architects, and Cockatoo people held many positions on their councils.

The wide range of experience and long service evident in the management of Cockatoo was reflected in the workforce. Many people came to Cockatoo from Britain, but others came from Australian industry. A major source of skilled people was the dockyard's own apprentice training scheme. Thousands of young men, and a very few young women, learned their trade at Cockatoo. Some remained at the island for all their working lives, others left as soon as they completed their time, some to go to sea, and others to other industries. Generally, Cockatoo would expect to keep only about 20 per cent of the apprentices as they completed their training.

Opposite: All the dockyard apprentices assembled at the Fitzroy Dock for a group photograph in 1947.
(J C Jeremy Collection)

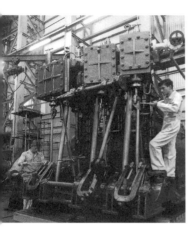

Joseph Pitar (left) and Jeffrey Scobie make adjustments to the triple expansion reciprocating marine engine restored in 1983 by fitter and turner apprentices for the Powerhouse Museum. Built in about 1879 the engine was installed in the steamers *Pheasant* and *Karrabee* and was in continuous use until about 1935.

In 1986 the dockyard's apprentices restored the parts of two of the Japanese midget submarines that attacked Sydney in May 1942. The work was done for the Australian War Memorial in Canberra.

At times, the yard employed over 400 apprentices, and the range of training opportunities was so broad that the total occasionally approached half the number of tradesmen employed. Apprentices were indentured in most trades, including fitters and turners, electricians, plumbers, sheet metal workers, coppersmiths, joiners, painters, shipwrights and draughtsmen. Whilst this method of training the future workforce was tried and true, it became clear in the 1980s that changes were needed to meet the demands of modern industry.

The Australian shipbuilding industry has suffered in the past from an unfortunate reputation for poor industrial relations, seeming to the general public as racked with demarcation and other disputes. Cockatoo shared this reputation and long industrial campaigns like that in 1981 for a shorter working week reinforced the impression. Towards the end of that campaign, which lasted a year, the yard was on strike for six weeks. For four of those weeks transport to the island was withdrawn. The dispute was finally broken when the government directed the Navy to provide transport for the management and the approximately 800 staff and apprentices who were still at work, but unable to get to the island in the usual way.

In reality of course, the yard was working normally most of the time, as the management and unions worked out their problems on a day-to-day basis. Disputation was, however, common. Even during World War II Cockatoo lost over 750,000 man hours, often as a result of a demarcation dispute. Disputes over demarcation, wages and conditions continued throughout the 1950s and 1960s, encouraged by the many unions and different award conditions applying in the yard.

In 1968 the employers on the Sydney waterfront negotiated an industrial agreement with the combined unions in an attempt to reduce the level of disputation in the industry. The Port of Sydney Shipbuilding and Ship Repairing Industry Industrial Agreement was one of the first of its kind in Australia. It provided for common wages and conditions throughout the signatories, and removed many of the inequities of the past that had caused dispute. It also contained a dispute settlement procedure intended to resolve disputes without lost time, but old habits died hard and it took time for the management and workforce to get used to new ways. The Agreement gained the status of a Federal Award in 1976.

The Waterfront Agreement, as it was known, worked reasonably well whilst the workforce was stable. It was less effective in times of growth. Between 1979 and 1982, when many people were being recruited to help build HMAS *Success*, disputes again grew as people unfamiliar with the ways of the industry joined the Company. Moreover, people from industries like the construction industry, with worse work practices and bad habits, tried to introduce them to the shipyard.

It became clear that radical change was needed if the shipbuilding

As part of the Bicentennial celebrations, in 1987 the apprentices built a replica of an eighteenth-century jolly boat for the Lane Cove Council to commemorate Lieutenant Ralph Clark's exploration of the Lane Cove River in 1790. The boat was built to plans from the National Maritime Museum at Greenwich and was launched by the member for Lane Cove, John Dowd MP on 21 October 1987.

industry was to have a viable future in Australia and those changes would have to be initiated from within the industry itself. Many inefficient work practices had become entrenched by the trade structure and even by decisions by the Courts within the conciliation and arbitration system, where the resolution of disputes had a higher priority than the efficient use of labour. The training structure was also sustaining the work practices. Even though shipwrights, boilermakers, sheet metal workers and fitters and turners all belonged to the same union, their training defined the boundaries of their skills.

In early 1984 the Company negotiated an agreement with the combined unions which provided for two important changes. Firstly, it agreed to the introduction of training to improve the skills of the painters and dockers, but more significantly it provided for more flexible working arrangements and common training and qualification for metal workers, with the aim, in time, of removing the distinction between the traditional trades.

The agreement did not take effect, not least because it depended for its success on the co-operation of the technical colleges and other employers to achieve some common approach and uniformity. This co-operation was not forthcoming, as a complete restructuring of training courses for a single employer was not regarded as practical. The 1984 agreement was ahead of its time. Within three years the metal industry employers and unions, with strong support of the government and the technical training authorities, had agreed on a restructuring of the metal industry award, and the introduction of a new trade training structure. Whilst this change has taken longer than first planned, it has achieved all that was intended by the Cockatoo Agreement, and more. Unfortunately by 1987 the future of Cockatoo Dockyard had been decided.

The presentation of awards for long service was not introduced at Cockatoo Dockyard until 1982. In view of the large number of potential recipients, the first awards were made to those with 35 or more continuous years of service at the dockyard. The 37 recipients had an average of 41 years of service.

A 60-year old racing snub nose 18-footer, *Yendys* was restored by the apprentices and taken for its first sail on 4 December 1982.

Other industrial agreements have been set in place at new facilities like the Australian Submarine Corporation in Adelaide and at the Tenix Defence Systems Williamstown shipyard. The old Williamstown Naval Dockyard had employed members of 23 unions working under 30 awards. There were 390 trade or work classifications. Demarcation disputes were endemic. After the change to private operation, and a period of difficult change, the yard now employs members of only three unions working under one award with two classifications. Productivity is said to have increased some 600 to 700 per cent.[157]

Whether such changes could have been achieved in a well-established dockyard like Cockatoo, with all its traditions and history, will now remain a matter of speculation.

IN RETROSPECT

Shipbuilding and ship repair is a labour intensive business, with a large component being the mere handling of material. Whilst access to the sea is an obvious requirement for any shipyard, access by road and rail are equally important. Access to Cockatoo Island is only possible by water. Every worker and every visitor had to travel to the island by boat or ferry, a movement at times of thousands of people a day. Every ton of material and every item of equipment needed on the island also had to be carried by water, sometimes more than once if sub-contractors on the mainland were involved.

The location of the dockyard on an island in the middle of the harbour was recognised as a major problem for many years, yet none of the schemes to connect the island to the mainland ever got off the drawing board. The development of the Commonwealth Naval Dockyard during World War I provided the dockyard with a wide range of excellent facilities which enabled it to be largely self-sufficient, minimising the handicap imposed by the island location. Even after the substantial development of Australian industry during World War II, Cockatoo remained somewhat unique.

By the 1960s, the facilities and services on the island were showing their age, yet the dockyard still had an important role to fulfil in support of the Royal Australian Navy. The modernisation begun then, had it been completed, would have overcome many of the problems of the aging dockyard, but the problem of access would have remained.

With a substantial workload the overheads imposed by the location and aging facilities were manageable. During the 1970s and 1980s the steady programme of submarine refitting provided an ideal base of high quality and high value work for the yard. With the combined

Success, the last ship built at Cockatoo Island, leaving Sydney on trials on 17 December 1985. Building a large ship like this on an island was a major exercise in logistics. Every piece of material, every part and component of this 17,800-tonne ship was delivered to the waterfront in Sydney by road, rail or ship, transshipped to a barge or boat and carried across the water to Cockatoo Island. On arrival nearly everything had to be handled again to a truck or trailer for movement to store or to the ship.

occurrence of this work ending in the 1990s, modern naval ships needing less intensive maintenance, a move of a substantial part of the RAN to Western Australia, and the naval shipbuilding work going elsewhere, closure of the dockyard on Cockatoo Island was probably inevitable by the end of the century.

Cockatoo Island was owned by the Commonwealth, and the Commonwealth was responsible for most of the dockyard's infrastructure. The Royal Australian Navy was the principal customer. The Commonwealth government was quite entitled to decide the future of the island and the dockyard (as it did in early 1987) but the implementation of that decision was badly managed. The future of the island was as uncertain in 1997 as it was in 1987. It would have been possible to bring the history of this remarkable dockyard to a close with less trauma to the employees, less disruption to the Australian submarine service, and much less cost to the Australian taxpayer.

A great deal was achieved during the long history of Cockatoo Dockyard, reflecting the skills and capability of the thousands of people who worked there. Today, few single organisations in the shipbuilding and ship repair industry in Australia have the same breadth of capability, as the nature of the industry changes and wider use is made of other industry to meet maritime needs.

POSTSCRIPT

On 4 June 1991, Rear Admiral Oscar Hughes AO, the Navy's project director for the new Collins class submarines, inspected and accepted the submarine HMAS *Orion* on behalf of the RAN after a major refit. It was the last submarine refit to be undertaken at Cockatoo. Addressing the dockyard employees and visitors assembled in the winter sunshine on the Destroyer Wharf,[158] he said:

> I am delighted to be present today to accept HMAS *Orion* on behalf of the Naval Support Commander.
>
> It is clear from my inspection this morning that many hours of dedicated work have gone into the refit of the boat.
>
> Cockatoo Dockyard management and workers have done a splendid job and have maintained their very good workmanship and quality. The submarine has been completed to a very high standard of which you should all be proud. I congratulate the Company on their splendid achievement.
>
> I am sure that the crew of HMAS *Orion* look forward to the coming three months of sea trials and their acceptance back into the fleet as a fully operational submarine unit.
>
> Sadly, today is the end of an era. It is more than the completion of the fourteenth Oberon refit — it is the end of submarine refitting at this historic facility and the end of Cockatoo Island's long and distinguished association with the Royal Australian Navy.
>
> Cockatoo Dockyard has a long and proud history of support to the Royal Australian Navy covering surface warship and auxiliary vessel construction and refitting, submarine refitting and, sometimes forgotten, a significant amount of specialist equipment repair work for naval stores.

The last submarine to be refitted at Cockatoo Island, HMAS *Orion*, drawing away from the Destroyer Wharf on 4 June 1991. (J C Jeremy)

I had the privilege of serving in HMAS *Vampire*, one of the many ships built at Cockatoo Island. *Vampire* was one of the great ships of the RAN.

I also had the privilege of seeing HMAS *Success* launched. This ship served with enormous distinction in the recent Gulf War.

I recall a conversation with John Jeremy during the difficult days that surrounded the construction of HMAS *Success*. He remarked that the Company and its workers intended to build a good ship and get it right — regardless of the difficulties and deficiencies of the contract and specifications.

I believe that approach underlined the relationship with Cockatoo Dockyard that the Navy enjoyed for so very long. It is an approach for others to follow as we go about the task of developing an ongoing Australian marine industry to support the Royal Australian Navy into the next century.

In appreciation of the support provided by Cockatoo Dockyard, it gives me much pleasure to present to the Company, on behalf of Vice Admiral I D G MacDougall AO, RAN, a long serving submariner, who has close personal links with the island, the Chief of Naval Staff's Commendation which reads as follows:

Commendation

Cockatoo Dockyard Pty Ltd has made a major contribution to the development and support of the Royal Australian Navy, and hence to the Defence capability of the Commonwealth of Australia. As this important phase in the history of Cockatoo Island itself comes to an end, it is appropriate to place on permanent record the satisfaction that the Royal Australian Navy has experienced from its productive and professional relationship with the Company.

Cockatoo Dockyard, the oldest dockyard in Australia, has a proud record of service to the Navy. Numerous surface ships have been built at, and supported from, the Island over the years, starting with HMAS HUON in 1916 and culminating with HMAS SUCCESS in 1986. The Company's involvement with submarines began in 1914 with the support of AE1 and AE2, followed by the J Class and subsequently by several classes of Royal Navy submarines. Cockatoo Dockyard's specialist expertise in submarine work was consolidated in 1967 when support for the six new Royal Australian Navy Oberon Class submarines began. In all, 14 major refits, including the complex Weapon Update Program, 15 Mid Cycle Survey Dockings, 39 Intermediate Dockings and 14 unprogrammed dockings have been successfully completed at Cockatoo Dockyard, all at a consistently high standard of workmanship and safety.

The Support which Cockatoo Dockyard and its employees have provided over a period of some 80 years, during times of peace and war, has contributed significantly to the high standards of operational availability regularly achieved by the Royal Australian Navy. This strong commitment and sense of identification with the Navy has been evident to all who have made their careers in the naval service, particularly those in the submarine arm who have special cause to recognise the Company's highest possible standards of quality in engineering. Accordingly, I am pleased to commend Cockatoo Dockyard Pty Ltd, and all of those who have given of their professionalism and skill over many years, for their outstanding performance in support of the Royal Australian Navy.

I. D. G. MACDOUGALL
Vice Admiral, RAN
Chief of Naval Staff

4 June 1991

APPENDIX 1

SELECTED PLANS AND SHIP DRAWINGS

There are many hundreds of drawings in the Cockatoo Dockyard records held by the National Archives in Sydney. A few have been selected for inclusion in this Appendix to illustrate the range and type of material available.

DRAWING 1
A considerable number of original drawings of the Fitzroy and Sutherland docks survive. This drawing 'Plan & sections of proposed new graving docks Cockatoo Island' is dated 5 June 1882 and is signed by Mr E O Moriarty, Engineer in Chief of the Harbours and Rivers Department. This is the drawing that shows the outlines of the ships that were used to set the parameters for the new dock—the *Great Eastern, City of Rome* and HMS *Inflexible*. The original drawing is coloured ink on linen-backed paper and measures about 1.5 by 3 metres. It is in the Archives at CRS C3579.

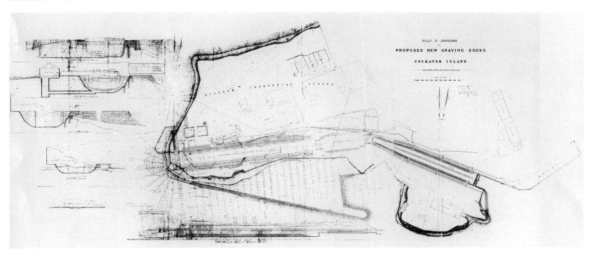

DRAWING 2
Another in the Sutherland Dock Series C3579, this drawing shows detail of the dock entrance.

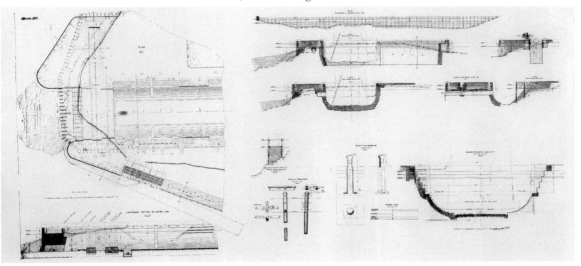

Drawing 3
This drawing is a
small-scale arrange-
ment drawing of the
power house built
during World War I.
The drawings of
this building are in
CRS C3539.

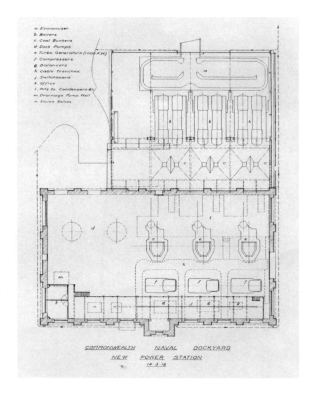

DRAWING 4
'HMAS *Huon* – General Arrangement, Profile, Upper & Forecastle Decks.' When new ships were completed, the
dockyard prepared a set of drawings that represented the ship as built, or 'as fitted'. These drawings were usually drawn in ink on linen, and copies were made for the ship, the owner, and the dockyard. They were often
coloured with ink washes, and were works of art in their own right. This is an 'as fitted' drawing of the first
wholly built Australian warship, HMAS *Huon*, which was completed in February 1916. This particular drawing
is a tracing of the original (less legible) drawing and was prepared by an apprentice draughtsman as an exercise
in the 1970s. The 'as fitted' plans of *Huon* are in CRS C3274, and those of her sister ships *Torrens* and *Swan* in
C3262 and C3275 respectively. The hull and electrical working drawings of these ships also survive.

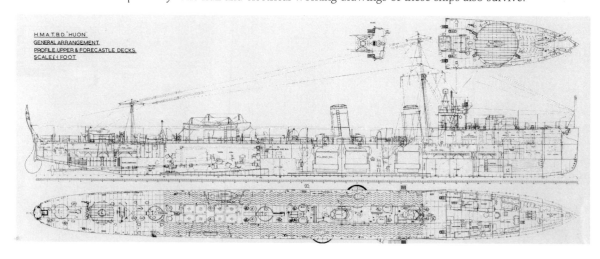

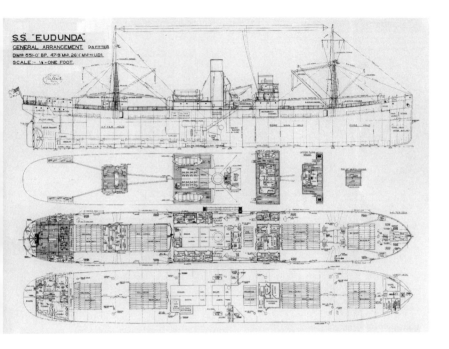

DRAWING 5
This is the general arrangement 'as fitted' of the Isherwood cargo ship SS *Eudunda*, completed in 1920. The working drawings of this ship are in CRS C3301. This particular plan is one of a number of 'as fitted' plans of these cargo ships that were held by the dockyard, from the time it was administered by the Australian Commonwealth Shipping Board.

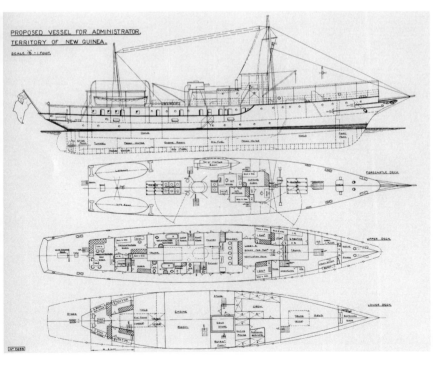

DRAWING 6
During the 1930s the dockyard tendered for many ships for a variety of customers, and designs were often prepared for the proposed vessels. This plan is one such design, for a vessel for the Administrator of the Territory of New Guinea. This drawing and other similar plans are in CRS C3368.

DRAWING 7
This drawing of
Cockatoo Island is one
of the most detailed
plans of the island on a
single sheet. It is dated
May 1932, and shows
the island very much
as it would have been
at the end of the World
War I. The original is
in CRS C3456, item
397.

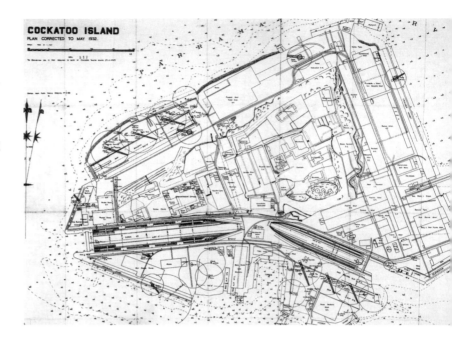

DRAWINGS 8A–C
The Bathurst class
minesweeper *Madras*
was completed for the
Royal Indian Navy in
1942. It was typical of
the 60 ships of this
type built in Australia
during World War II,
although the Indian
ships were slightly
modified for the spe-
cific requirements of
the RIN. The 'as fitted'
plans of HMIS *Madras*
and her sister ship
HMIS *Bengal* are held
in CRS M2857.

8A

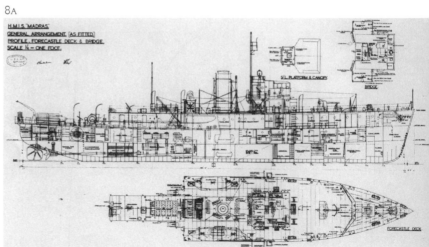

8B

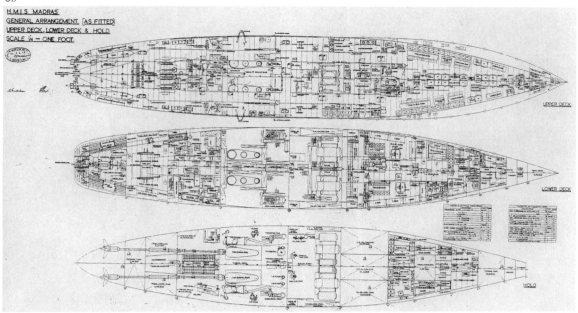

H.M.I.S. 'MADRAS'
GENERAL ARRANGEMENT. [AS FITTED]
UPPER DECK, LOWER DECK & HOLD.
SCALE ¼ = ONE FOOT.

UPPER DECK

LOWER DECK

HOLD

8C

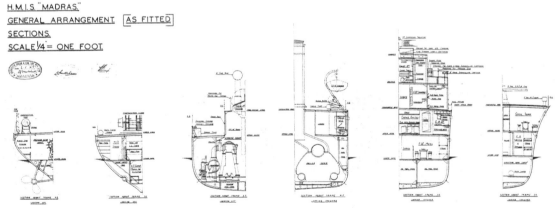

H.M.I.S. "MADRAS."
GENERAL ARRANGEMENT. [AS FITTED]
SECTIONS.
SCALE ¼ = ONE FOOT.

DRAWINGS 9A and B

The Liberty ship *William Ellery Channing* was converted to a troopship between February and April 1943. The conversion was basic but typical of the type of emergency troopship conversions carried out during World War II. The drawings of this ship are in CRS M2983.

9A

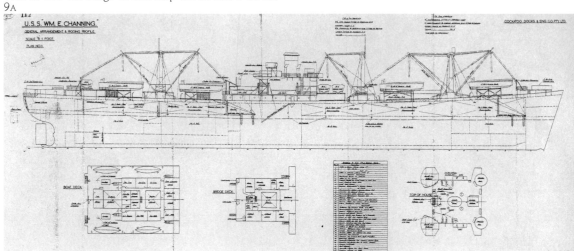

9B

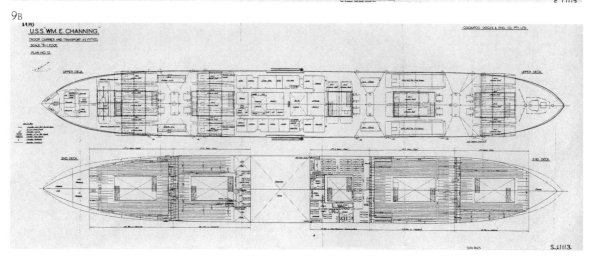

DRAWING 10

HMAS *Tobruk*, general arrangement profile ('as fitted'). *Tobruk* was completed in 1950 and was the last riveted destroyer built at Cockatoo. All surviving records of this ship have been retained in Archives. These drawings are in CRS M2835.

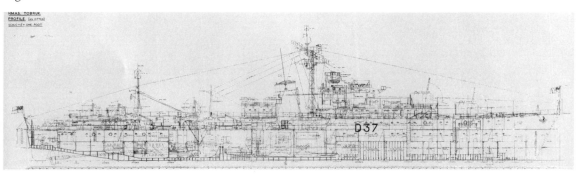

DRAWING 11

HMAS *Arunta* was the first of three Tribal class destroyers completed at Cockatoo during World War II. This drawing shows the ship after modernisation between 1950 and 1952. The 'as fitted' drawings of the modernisation are in CRS M2916. All surviving records from the original construction of *Arunta*, *Warramunga* and *Bataan* are also in Archives.

DRAWING 12

The destroyer HMAS *Queenborough* was converted to a Type 15 anti-submarine frigate at Cockatoo between 1950 and 1954. This drawing and others in the series are in CRS M2838.

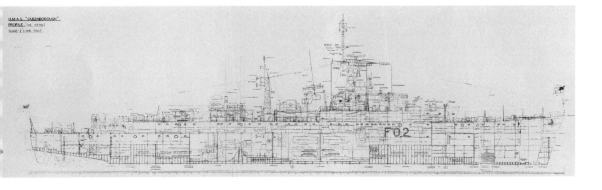

APPENDIX 2

SHIPS BUILT BEFORE 1913

Available records of the vessels built at Cockatoo Island before 1913 are incomplete, and this list has been compiled from the following sources:

Mitchell & Boden: D J Mitchell and C E B Boden, 'Some notes on the development of shipbuilding in Australia', presented to the Australian Branch of the Royal Institution of Naval Architects, 1960.

PWD 1926: New South Wales Public Works Department, Harbours and Drainage Branch, *Particulars of dredgers and attendant plant*, 24 May 1926.

PWD AR: New South Wales Public Works Department, *Annual report*, for the year indicated.

Govt D/Y AR: *Government Dockyard Biloela*, Report of the Management Committee, for the year indicated).

CRS M3081: National Archives series M3081, Folder listing vessels constructed from 1912 to 1991. (The author prepared this document in 1991 from information in the dockyard records.)

SMH of 5 May 1909: Article on shipbuilding in New South Wales in the *Sydney Morning Herald*, 5 May 1909.

Cutler: A E Cutler to Secretary Sydney Harbour Trust, letter dated 28 February 1912, advising of intention to launch, and a booklet of photographs in author's collection.

In this list, the information is given in the following format:

Name; type (and number of vessels where applicable); year completed; gross tonnage (each); dimensions (length x beam); remarks; and source (see above).

Clarence; dredger; 1871; 368; 148' x 33'; PWD 1926.
Orara; dredger; 1883; 168; 100' x 24'; PWD 1926.
Lansdowne; dredger; 1883; 122; 75' 3" x 25'; PWD 1926.
Hinton; tug; 1886; 56; 81' 7" x 14'; PWD 1926.
Wickham; dredger; 1890; 63; 59' 7" x 23' 6"; PWD 1926.
Chindera; dredger; 1892; 180; 81' x 30'; PWD 1926.
Harrington; dredger; 1892; 180; 81' x 30'; PWD 1926.
Groper; dredger; 1892; 115' x 50'; PWD AR 1892.
Poseidon; rock breaker; 1892; PWD AR 1892.
Morpeth; dredger; 1893; 510; 120' 3" x 50'; PWD 1926.
Ballina; dredger; 1893; 227; 101' 9" x 30'; PWD 1926.
Aurora; tug; 1893; PWD AR 1893–94.
Cardiff; steel steam tug; 1895; 90; 94' 6" x 17' 11"; PWD 1926.
Maclean; dredger; 1896; 141; 85' x 28'; PWD 1926.
Swansea; dredger; 1896; 86; 77' x 22' 6"; PWD 1926.
Macksville; dredger; 1896; 151; 91' x 28'; PWD 1926.
Octopus; anchor boat; 1896; steam engine taken from *Swift*; PWD AR 1895–96.
Galatea; tug; 1896; steam engine taken from *Little Nell*; PWD AR 1895–96.
Forster; dredger; 1897; 108; 81' x 22' 6"; PWD 1926.
Bellingen; dredger; 1897; 105; 81' x 22' 6"; PWD 1926.
Botany; dredger; 1897; 111; 83' x 22' 6"; PWD 1926.
Hexham; dredger; 1898; 504; 179' 6" x 24'; PWD 1926.
—— ; wooden crane barge; 1898; 80' x 42'; for construction of Darling Harbour sea wall; PWD AR 1897–98.
—— ; wooden pontoon; 1898; 54' x 26'; for dockyard plant; PWD AR 1897–98.
Casino; steel steam tug; 1899; 88; 92' 9" x 20'; PWD 1926.
Powerful; wood steam tug; 1899; 90' x 22'; PWD AR 1898–99.
Sol; wood steam launch; 1899; 50' x 10';PWD AR 1898–99.
—— ; 5 small pontoons; 1899; for dredge and survey work; PWD AR 1898–99.
Richmond; dredger; 1900; 200; 122' x 24'; PWD 1926.
Dooribang; steel steam ship; 1900; 85' x 20'; PWD AR 1898–99.
Phoenix; wood steam tug; 1900; PWD AR 1899–1900.
—— ; 2 motor launches; 1900; PWD AR 1899–1900.

—— ; 2 motor launches; 1901; PWD AR 1899–1900.

—— ; iron hopper barge; 1902; 136' x 25'; 350 ton capacity; PWD AR 1900–1901.

Mayfield; wooden steam tug; 1902; 26; 60' 8" x 12' 4"; PWD 1926.

Burunda; iron steam tug; 1902; 132; 108' 4" x 20' 2"; renamed *Waratah*, now owned by Sydney Maritime Museum; PWD 1926.

Wollumbi; wooden steam tug; 1902; PWD AR 1901–1902.

Yimmang; wooden steam tug; 1902.

Hamilton; wooden steam tug; 1903; 103; 100' x 21'; PWD 1926.

Seaham; dredger; 1903; 70; 57' x 27' 6"; PWD 1926.

—— ; steel hopper barge; 1903; 242; 136' 4" x 25' 6"; PWD 1926.

Glaucus; dredger; 1903; 1600; cutter gear and machinery from *Thetis*; PWD AR 1902–1903.

Stockton; dredger; 1905; 547; 153' x 36'; PWD 1926.

—— ; steel hopper barge; 1907; 310; 154' x 28'; PWD 1926.

Gosford; dredger; 1908; 123; 83' x 22' 6"; PWD 1926.

Endeavour; trawler; 1909; 331; 132' 2" x 23' 2"; keel laid 1 June 1908, completed January 1909; Govt D/Y AR 1908.

—— ; steel hopper barge; 1908; 136' x 25'; 600 ton capacity with hydraulic lifting gear for hopper doors; Govt D/Y AR 1908.

—— ; punt; 1909; 250; for Sydney Harbour Trusts; Govt D/Y AR 1908.

Jupiter; dredger; 1909; Govt D/Y AR 1909.

Poseidon; dredger; 1909; for Sydney Harbour Trust; Govt D/Y AR 1909.

Achilles; wooden steam tug; 1909; for Sydney Harbour Trust; Govt D/Y AR 1909.

Harwood; dredger; 1910; 89; 59' 6" x 26'; PWD 1926.

—— ; 3 steel hopper barges; 1910; 297; 144' 3" x 27' 6"; first laid down 22 March 1909 and launched 18 May 1909, second laid down 21 May 1909; Govt D/Y AR 1909.

Latona; dredger; 1911; 390; 166' x 35'; Govt D/Y AR 1910.

Warrego; destroyer for RAN; 700; 245' x 24' 3"; built in Scotland and reassembled at Cockatoo Island; CRS M3081.

Hydra; wooden steam tug; 1912; 90; launched on 3 March 1912; Cutler.

—— ; ferry punt; 1911; 200; for connection with tramway from Spit to Manly; Govt D/Y AR 1910.

Hunter; dredger; 1912; 461; 148' 6" x 32'; PWD 1926.

Groper; dredger; 1912; 1500; 120' x 50'; new hull for existing vessel; Mitchell & Boden.

Como; dredger; 1913; 161; 103' 3" x 24' 2"; PWD 1926.

John Stewart; dredger; 1913; 152' x 32'; for Melbourne Harbor Trust; Mitchell & Boden.

—— ; 24 dredgers; date unknown; 300; each named with a letter from the Greek alphabet; SMH 5 May 1909.

—— ; 6 tugs; SMH reported 12 tugs built at the Fitzroy Dock, 6 are listed above as completed before 1909; SMH 5 May 1909.

—— ; 50 hopper barges; 280–650 tons; the total may include some of the barges listed above; SMH 5 May 1909.

APPENDIX 3

SHIPS BUILT AFTER 1913

This Appendix lists in order of construction the ships and boats, generally over 30 feet length, that were built by (or under contract to) Cockatoo Dockyard after 1913.

Not all were allocated a 'Ship Number'. The Ship Number series is not continuous before 1924, as the numbers used in the dockyard were the project numbers allocated by Navy Office, Melbourne. Exceptions in this period include small craft built on other job numbers, or ships allocated class numbers. The latter include *Dundula, Eudunda, Fordsdale,* and *Ferndale,* which were Ships Numbers 6, 35, 47 and 48 in the series allocated by the Commonwealth Shipping Board to the Australian built ships of the Commonwealth Line.

After 1924, the dockyard allocated the Ship Number, and after Ship Number 101 the series is continuous. Some numbers were used for major conversions, modernisations or refits, and these have been included in the list for completeness.

In addition to the vessels listed, the dockyard built many small craft. The remaining records are not complete, as some boats were built against the job number of the ship for which they were intended, or on other job numbers for which there is no record. It is known, however, that at least the following boats have been built at Cockatoo Dockyard since 1913:

6	21-foot motor launches
17	lifeboats
18	cutters
10	whalers
30	dinghies
8	balsa rafts
665	life rafts
7	punts
60	bi-partite bridging pontoons.

SHIPS BUILT UNDER CONTRACT

In this list the information is given in the following format:

Name; builder; type and owner; date ordered (O); date laid down (LD); date launched (L); date completed (C); and remarks.

—— ; Morts Dock; cattle barge for Commonwealth Quarantine Department; O 30 Sept 1912; LD 25 Sept 1912; L 14 Mar 1913; C 19 Mar 1913; dimensions 40 feet x 21 feet x 5 feet depth.

OFL 1; Morts Dock; oil fuel lighter for RAN; O 20 Mar 1913; LD 8 Dec 1913; L 10 Nov 1913; C 25 Feb 1916; 550 tons deadweight, delivered to Thursday Island.

OFL 2; Morts Dock; oil fuel lighter for RAN; O 20 Mar 1913; LD 8 Dec 1913; L 4 Feb 1916; C 18 Mar 1916; 550 tons deadweight, delivered to Cairns.

OFL 3; Poole and Steel; oil fuel lighter for RAN; O 24 Jun 1913; LD 12 May 1914; L 28 Jul 1915; C 4 May 1916; 550 tons deadweight, delivered to Brisbane.

OFL 4; Poole and Steel; oil fuel lighter for RAN; O 24 Jun 1913; LD 4 Jun 1914; L 18 Jan 1916; C 19 Jun 1916; 550 tons deadweight, left Sydney on 2 Aug for Albany.

Ships built at Cockatoo Island

In this list the information is given in the following format:

Ship number; *name*; type and owner; date ordered (O); date laid down (LD); date launched (and by whom) (L); date completed (C); and remarks. When the building location is a slipway, it is identified with the date laid down by the number the slipway had at the time.

4; *Huon*; Torpedo boat destroyer for RAN; O 1 Aug 1912; LD 25 Jan 1913 on No. 2 slipway; L 19 Dec 1914 by Mrs J A Jensen, wife of the Assistant Minister for Defence; C 4 Feb 1916; ordered from the Government Dockyard Biloela before the sale of Cockatoo Island to the Commonwealth, allocated Ship No. 121 by the Government Dockyard.

5; *Torrens*; Torpedo boat destroyer for RAN; O 1 Aug 1912; LD 25 Jan on No. 3 slipway; L 28 Aug 1915 by Lady Helen Munro Ferguson, wife of the Governor General, C 8 Jul 1916; ordered from the Government Dockyard Biloela before the sale of Cockatoo Island to the Commonwealth, allocated Ship No. 122 by the Government Dockyard, commissioned 3 Jul 1916.

6; *Swan*; Torpedo boat destroyer for RAN; O 1 Aug 1912; LD 22 Jan 1915 on No. 2 slipway; L 11 Dec 1915 by Lady Creswell; C 22 Aug 1916; ordered from the Government Dockyard Biloela before the sale of Cockatoo Island to the Commonwealth, allocated Ship No. 123 by the Government Dockyard.

7; *Brisbane*; Town class cruiser for RAN; O 1 Aug 1912; LD 25 Jan 1913 on No. 1 slipway; L 30 Sept 1915 by Mrs Andrew Fisher, wife of Prime Minister; C 12 Dec 1916; ordered from the Government Dockyard Biloela before the sale of Cockatoo Island to the Commonwealth, allocated Ship No. 124 by the Government Dockyard, commissioned 30 Oct 1916.

21; *Greswell*; Steel steam launch for the Customs Department; O 26 Mar 1913; LD 3 Nov 1913 on the eastern shore slipway; L 7 Nov 1914; C 2 Jul 1915; drawings received 20 Feb 1913, left for Melbourne 2 Jul 1915 in charge of Mr J H Smith who had contracted with the Customs Department for the delivery voyage.

23; *Hercules*; Bucket dredger for the Sydney Harbour Trust; O 3 Feb 1913; LD 22 Sept 1913 on No. 5 slipway; L 15 Jan 1914; C 14 Apr 1915; left Cockatoo Dockyard 20 Apr 1915.

—— ; —— ; caisson for Cockatoo Dockyard; O 10 Feb 1915; LD 7 Apr 1915; C 30 Aug 1915; wooden caisson for No. 1 slipway.

32; *Moonbi*; Motor launch for Customs Department; O 5 May 1915; LD 20 Sept 1915 on No. 4 slipway; L 18 Oct 1916; C 26 Feb 1920; for use in the Port of Newcastle, hull completed 30 Oct 1916 then set aside awaiting delivery of main engines.

—— ; *Ruby*; Steam launch for Cockatoo Dockyard; O 9 Apr 1915; LD 21 Apr 1915; L 4 May 1915; C 6 Sep 1915; new hull for launch *Ruby*.

—— ; —— ; Loam punt for Cockatoo Dockyard; O 11 Feb 1915; LD 17 Feb 1915; L 2 Mar 1915; C 16 Mar 1915; to replace a condemned punt.

33; *C.N.D.2*; Bucket dredger for Commonwealth Navigation Department; O 16 Mar 1914; LD 4 Aug 1914 on No. 5 slipway; L 16 Feb 1915; C 21 Aug 1915; built in Britain and reassembled at Cockatoo Island, bucket capacity 25 cubic feet, 1275 tons/hour, left Cockatoo Dockyard for Western Australia on 16 Sept 1915.

35; —— ; Naval ordnance lighter for RAN; O 4 Jan 1915; LD 30 Mar 1915 on No. 4 slipway; L 30 Jun 1915; C 27 Jul 1915.

36; *Biloela*; Passenger ferry for Cockatoo Dockyard; O 4 Feb 1915; LD 3 Aug 1915 on No. 4 slipway; L 19 Jul 1916; C 23 Dec 1916; double-ended steel hull ferry to carry workmen between Cockatoo Island and the mainland.

37; —— ; Oil lighter for Cockatoo Dockyard; O 20 May 1915; LD 17 Jul 1915; L 4 Sept 1915; C 24 Sept 1915.

38; *Bustler*; Steam tug for Cockatoo Dockyard; O 25 Jun 1915; LD 11 Apr 1916 on No. 3 slipway; L 25 Jan 1917; C 31 Mar 1917.

—— ; —— ; Ferry pontoon for Parramatta Wharf Cockatoo Island; LD 16 Aug 1915; L 28 Sept 1915; C 29 Sept 1915.

—— ; *Sans Pareil*; Motor launch for Cockatoo Dockyard; O 18 Aug 1915; LD 20 Aug 1915; L 31 Dec 1915; C 13 Jan 1916; built on Shop Order No. 4325.

—— ; No. 2 Pontoon; Ferry pontoon for Cockatoo Dockyard; O 23 Oct 1915; LD 23 Oct 1915; L 3 Feb 1916; C 29 Aug 1916; provisional completion 3 Feb 1916.

44; *Adelaide*; Town class cruiser for RAN; O 7 Aug 1915; LD 20 Nov 1917 on No. 1 slipway; L 27 Jul 1918 by

Lady Helen Munro Ferguson, wife of the Governor General; C 31 Jul 1922; first drawings received 27 Sept 1916, first material received 2 Mar 1916, work suspended 10 Mar 1921, resumed 14 Jul 1921.

46; *Breaksea Spit No. 1*; Non-propelled lightship for Commonwealth Lighthouse Service; O 19 Jan 1916; LD 25 Apr 1916 on No. 2 slipway; L 16 Aug 1916; C 17 Aug 1917; Left Cockatoo Dockyard in tow of TSS *Karuah* on 25 May 1918.

47; *Carpentaria No. 1*; Non-propelled lightship for Commonwealth Lighthouse Service; O 19 Jan 1916; LD 1 May 1916 on No. 2 slipway; L 17 Aug 1916; C 15 Sept 1917; originally named *Proudfoot Shoal*, left Cockatoo Dockyard in tow of TSS *Karuah* on 19 Mar 1919.

50; *Ragleth*; Motor launch for RAN; O 24 Feb 1916; LD 27 Apr 1916; L 11 Nov 1916; C 18 Dec 1916; for the Royal Edward Victualling Yard, Sydney, work started in loft 2 Mar 1916.

—— ; —— ; Steam cutter for RAN; O 3 Mar 1916; LD 7 Mar 1916; C 6 Dec 1916; Registered number 208, for HMAS *Brisbane*.

51; *Waratah*; Steam driven lighter for RAN; O 4 Jul 1916; LD 20 Jun 1917 on No. 4 slipway; L 30 Jan 1918; C 24 Apr 1918; for Garden Island, Sydney, work started in drawing office 4 Jul 1916 and in yard 24 Nov 1916.

52; *Breaksea Spit No. 2*; Non-propelled lightship for Commonwealth Lighthouse Service; O 12 Apr 1916; LD 17 Aug 1916 on No. 2 slipway; L 4 Oct 1916; C 13 Oct 1917; originally named *Carpentaria*, left Cockatoo Dockyard in tow of TSS *Karuah* on 15 Jun 1918.

55; *Carpentaria No. 2*; Non-propelled lightship for Commonwealth Lighthouse Service; O 23 Sept 1916; LD 5 Nov 1917on No. 2 slipway; L 6 May 1918; C 17 Nov 1918; left Cockatoo Dockyard in tow of TSS *Karuah* on 7 Apr 1919.

57; *Titan*; 150-ton floating crane for Commonwealth of Australia; O 5 Oct 1916; LD 7 Mar 1917 on No. 5 slipway; L 5 Dec 1917; C 3 Dec 1919; for use by Cockatoo Dockyard, prefabricated by Gowans Sheldon and Company, Carlisle and assembled at Cockatoo Island.

60; —— ; Ammunition barge for RAN; O 17 Oct 1917; LD 12 Nov 1917 on No. 4 slipway; L 17 Jan 1918; C 5 Feb 1918; for use at Spectacle Island.

61; *Biloela*; Collier for RAN; O 20 Jun 1918; LD 21 Oct 1918 on No. 1 slipway; L 10 Apr 1919 by Mrs King Salter, wife of Dockyard General Manager; C 10 Jul 1920; first ship to be built with Australian produced steel plate.

—— ; *Dundula*; Cargo ship for the Commonwealth Line; O 20 May 1918; LD 8 Jul 1918 on No. 3 slipway; L 9 Jul 1919 by Mrs W A Holman; C 3 Nov 1919; Isherwood steamer No. 6, left dockyard 3 Nov 1919 for machinery completion and trials at Williamstown, Victoria, entered service May 1920.

62; —— ; Motor launch for RAN; O 26 Jul 1918; LD 28 Feb 1919; L 3 Jun 1919; C 5 Jul 1919; for use at Thursday Island.

63; —— ; Motor launch for RAN; O 11 Sept 1918; LD 26 Feb 1919; L 3 Jun 1919; C 29 Sept 1919; for use at Spectacle Island, Sydney.

—— ; *Eudunda*; Cargo ship for Commonwealth Line; O 24 Jun 1919; LD 22 Sept 1919 on No. 1 slipway; L 29 Mar 1920 by Lady Ryrie; C 14 Dec 1920; Isherwood steamer No. 35, left dockyard 14 Dec 1919, engines installed in Melbourne, ran trials in Port Phillip Bay 18 Aug 1921, commissioned for service Apr 1922.

—— ; —— ; Motor boat for RAN; O 14 Jul 1919; LD 17 Jul 1919; C 24 Jul 1922; Registered number 619, for HMAS *Adelaide*, work suspended 10 Mar 1921, resumed 3 Aug 1921.

65; *Mombah*; Coal storage vessel for RAN; O 4 Aug 1919; LD 21 Oct 1920 on No. 1 slipway; L 23 Apr 1921; C 20 Feb 1923; Non-propelled, work suspended 10 Mar 1921, resumed 29 Mar 1921 to enable ship to be launched, work again suspended 23 Apr 1921, and resumed 18 Jul 1921, left dockyard 20 Feb 1923.

—— ; *Fordsdale*; Refrigerated cargo steamer for Commonwealth Line; LD 29 Mar 1922 on No. 1 slipway; L 21 Jun 1923 by Mrs Oaks, wife of Acting Premier of NSW; C 13 Mar 1924; cargo steamer No. 47, work started in drawing office 27 Oct 1919, but cancelled on 29 Mar 1920, work restarted on 13 Apr 1920.

—— ; *Ferndale*; Refrigerated cargo steamer for Commonwealth Line; LD 28 Jun 1923 on No. 1 slipway; L 12 Jun 1924 by Mrs Earle Page, wife of the Federal Treasurer; C 20 Oct 1924; cargo steamer No. 48.

101; *Cape Leeuwin*; Lighthouse steamer for Commonwealth Government; LD 15 Jul 1924 on No. 1 slipway; L 10 Dec 1924; C 1 Jun 1925.

102; *Cape York*; Lighthouse steamer for Commonwealth Government; LD 17 Dec 1924 on No. 1 slipway; L 30 Jul 1925; C 10 Nov 1925.

103; —— ; Floating workshop barge for Cockatoo Dockyard; C 1925; later used as oxygen barge until replaced in 1979.

104; —— ; Hopper barge for Cockatoo Dockyard; 100 ton capacity.

105; *Codock*; Steam driven lighter for Cockatoo Dockyard; L 12 Feb 1926; C 22 Apr 1926; trials 22 Apr 1926, sold 1 Mar 1949 for £500.

—— ; *Fitzroy*; Motor launch for Cockatoo Dockyard; built in 1928 and sold about 1963.

106; *Albatross*; Seaplane carrier for RAN; O 2 Feb 1926; LD 5 May 1926 on No. 1 slipway; L 23 Feb 1928 by Lady Stonehaven, wife of the Governor General, C 21 Dec 1928; preliminary work started 4 Jan 1926.

107; *Dorlongco*; Barge for Dorman Long and Co.; L 12 Feb 1926; steel barge for use during construction of the Sydney Harbour Bridge.

108; Number reserved for Bunnerong Power Station Plant (cancelled).

109; *Cape Otway*; Lighthouse steamer for Commonwealth Government; O 1 Aug 1930; LD 22 Sept 1930 on No. 1 slipway; L 26 Jun 1931; C 3 Oct 1931.

110; *Aedes*; Motor launch for Department of Health; C 18 Aug 1931.

—— ; —— ; Caisson for Fitzroy Dock at Cockatoo Island; O 10 Sept 1931; L 19 Jul 1932; Shop Order No. 9799, establishment No. 1.

—— ; *Century Tire II*, Speedboat for Mr R Walder; L 14 Mar 1932; built by Aircraft Department, fast racing speedboat built of mahogany and Australian coachwood.

—— ; *Cettein*; Speedboat for Mr H McEvoy; L 22 Sept 1932; fast racing speedboat built by Aircraft Department.

—— ; *Clifton*; Fast ferry; C 20 Dec 1933; private venture double step planing hull high-speed ferry designed by L J Wackett and built by the Aircraft Department in mahogany and Queensland maple, intended to carry 35 passengers and proposed to Sydney Ferries Limited for service between Circular Quay and Clifton Gardens.

111; *Wattle*; Steam tug for RAN; L 27 Jun 1933; C 15 Feb 1934; built beside No. 1 slipway wharf as *Codeco* by the dockyard to employ apprentices, launched by floating crane *Titan*, used at Garden Island in Sydney.

112; *Sydney*; Steam launch for Cockatoo Dockyard; L 13 Apr 1934; C 20 Jun 1934; commonly known as *Prickly Heat II*.

113; Number reserved for Bunnerong Power Station (cancelled).

114; *Yarra*; Grimsby class sloop for RAN; O 22 Dec 1933; LD 24 May 1934 on No. 1 slipway; L 28 Mar 1935 by Mrs Parkhill, wife of Minister for Defence; C 12 Dec 1935; commissioned 21 Jan 1936.

115; *Swan*; Grimsby class sloop for RAN; O 27 Sept 1934; LD 1 May 1935 on No. 1 slipway; L 28 Mar 1936 by Mrs J A Lyons, wife of the Prime Minister, C 10 Dec 1936.

116; *Vivian*; Wood diesel tug for Sydney Ferries; O 3 Feb 1937; L 5 Aug 1937; C 18 Aug 1937.

117; Condensers for the Bunnerong Power Station.

118; *Hinton*; Steam tug for NSW Government; O 6 Nov 1935; LD 2 Apr 1936 beside No. 1 slipway wharf; L 4 Aug 1936; C 8 Sept 1936; hull only, launched by crane.

119; *Warang*; Steam tug for Waratah Tug Company; O 2 Mar 1936; LD 5 Aug 1936 beside No. 1 slipway wharf; L 19 Oct 1936; C 14 Dec 1936; launched by crane.

120; *Vigilant*; Patrol vessel for Commonwealth Department of Trade and Customs; O 12 Mar 1937; LD 30 Aug 1937 beside No. 1 slipway wharf; L 12 Feb 1938 by Mrs White, wife of Minister for Trade and Customs; C 25 Jul 1938; launched by *Titan*.

121; *Codock Jnr*; Motor launch for Cockatoo Dockyard; C 27 Jan 1938; fast launch for dockyard service, Thornycroft design.

122; *Shell 23*; Oil lighter for Shell Company of Australia; O 11 May 1937; LD 26 Dec 1937 on No. 1 slipway; L 10 May 1938; C 26 May 1938.

123; *Shell 24*; Twin screw motor tug for Shell Company of Australia; O 11 May 1937; LD 26 Feb 1938 beside No. 1 slipway wharf; L 30 Jun 1938; C 11 Aug 1938; launched by *Titan*.

124; Modernisation of cruiser HMAS *Adelaide*; O 12 Jan 1938; C 13 Mar 1939; work started 18 Jan 1938.

125; *Waree*; Steam tug for Waratah Tug Company; O 21 Dec 1937; LD 4 Jul 1938 beside No. 1 slipway wharf; L 21 Jan 1939; C 12 Apr 1939; launched by *Titan*.

126; *Kookaburra*; Boom defence vessel for RAN; O 9 Feb 1938; LD 4 Jul 1938 on No. 1 slipway; L 29 Oct 1938 by Mrs P E McNeil, wife of Rear-Admiral McNeil; C 28 Feb 1939.

127; *CA5, CA6, CA7*; Control launches for Civil Aviation Board; O 13 Jan 1938; C 1939; for Empire Flying Boat Service, hard chine timber construction to Thornycroft design.

128; *CA22* to *CA27*; Auxiliary launches for Civil Aviation Board, O 13 Jan 1938; C 1938; for Empire Flying Boat Service, based on Thornycroft design used for *Codock Jnr* (Ship No. 121).

129; *CA41* to *CA47*; Dinghies for Civil Aviation Board; O 13 Jan 1938; for Empire Flying Boat Service, clinker yacht type dinghies built of Queensland maple on spotted gum frames.

130; Modernisation of cruiser HMAS *Australia*; C 28 Sept 1939; work started 24 Apr 1938.

131; *Parramatta*; Grimsby class sloop for RAN; O 19 Jul 1938; LD 9 Nov 1938 on No. 1 slipway; L 10 Jun 1939 by Mrs G A Street, wife of Minister for Defence; C 4 Apr 1940.

132; *Warrego*; Grimsby class sloop for RAN; O 19 Jul 1938; LD 15 Mar 1939 on the new No. 2 slipway; L 10 Feb 1940 by Mrs R G Menzies, wife of Prime Minister; C 28 Aug 1940.

133; *No. 77*; 550-ton steel dumb hopper barge for NSW Department of Works and Local Government, Harbours and Rivers Office; O 18 May 1938; LD 15 Feb 1939 on a temporary slipway next to No. 1; L 17 Jul 1939; C 2 Sept 1939.

134; *No. 78*; 550-ton steel dumb hopper barge for NSW Department of Works and Local Government, Harbours and Rivers Office; O 18 May 1938; LD 15 Feb 1939 on a temporary slipway next to No. 1; L 17 Jul 1939; C 9 Sept 1939.

135; *Koala*; Boom defence vessel for RAN; O 28 Dec 1938; LD 21 Jun 1939 on No. 1 slipway; L 4 Nov 1940 by Mrs Custance, wife of Admiral Custance; C 27 Mar 1940.

136; *Koree*; Target towing launch for Royal Australian Engineers (Department of Defence); O 25 Nov 1938; L 4 Sept 1939; C 16 Jan 1940; timber construction, double skin, hard chine to Thornycroft design.

137; *Wadjemup*; Target towing launch for Royal Australian Engineers (Department of Defence); O 25 Nov 1938; L 6 Oct 1939; C 6 Dec 1939; timber construction, double skin, hard chine to Thornycroft design.

138; *Arunta*; Tribal class destroyer for RAN; O 6 Oct 1939; LD 15 Nov 1939 on No. 1 slipway; L 30 Nov 1940 by Lady Gowrie, wife of Governor General, C 30 Apr 1942.

139; *Warramunga*; Tribal class destroyer for RAN; O 6 Oct 1939; LD 10 Feb 1940 on No. 2 slipway; L 7 Feb 1942 by Mrs F M Forde, wife of Minister for the Army; C 22 Dec 1942.

140; Reserved for modernisation of the cruiser HMAS *Canberra* (cancelled).

141; *Kangaroo*; Boom defence vessel for RAN; O 11 Sept 1939; LD 15 Nov 1939 on No. 1 slipway; L 4 May 1940 by Mrs Boucher, wife of Commodore Boucher; C 26 Sept 1940.

142; Reserved for the modernisation of the cruiser HMAS *Sydney* (cancelled).

143; Conversion of the Commonwealth Line steamer *Moreton Bay* to armed merchant cruiser.

144; Conversion of *Changte* to victualling supply ship; C 9 Sept 1939.

145; Preparatory work for local defence vessels (LDV) later reclassified Australian minesweepers (AMS).

146; *Bathurst*; Minesweeper for RAN (Admiralty account); O 9 Dec 1939; LD 10 Feb 1940 on No. 3 slipway; L 1 Aug 1940 by Mrs A B Doyle, wife of the Engineering Manager, Garden Island; C 5 Dec 1940; LDV No. 1.

147; Manufacture of 34 boilers of 1750 IHP for Australian minesweepers and rehabilitation of two boilers taken from HMAS *Adelaide*.

148; *Bataan*; Tribal class destroyer for RAN; O 2 Feb 1940; LD 18 Feb 1942 on No. 2 slipway; L 15 Jan 1944 by Mrs Douglas MacArthur; C 26 Jun 1945; originally to have been named *Kurnai*, keel laid on No. 1 slipway 30 Nov 1940 by the Governor General on the launching day of *Arunta*, work delayed by war priorities and keel relaid on No. 2 slipway in Feb 1942.

149; *Goulburn*; Minesweeper for RAN (Admiralty account); O 8 Apr 1940; LD 9 Jul 1940 on No. 4 slipway; L 16 Nov 1940 by Mrs J G Grace, wife of Rear-Admiral Grace RN; C 27 Feb 1941; LDV No. 5.

150; *Bendigo*; Minesweeper for RAN (Admiralty account); O 8 Apr 1940; LD 12 Aug 1940 on No. 3 slipway; L 1 Mar 1941 by Dame Mary Hughes, wife of the Minister for the Navy; C 9 May 1941; LDV No. 6.

151; *Karangi*; Boom defence vessel for RAN; O 10 May 1941; LD 5 Feb 1941 on No. 1 slipway; L 16 Aug 1941 by Mrs G I D Hutcheson, wife of Engineer Manager, Garden Island; C 22 Dec 1941.

152; *Woollongong*; Minesweeper for RAN (Admiralty account); O 29 Jul 1940; LD 29 Jan 1941 on No. 4 slipway; L 5 Jul 1941 by Mrs J A Beasley, wife of the Minister for Supply and Shipping; C 22 Oct 1941; LDV No. 18.

153; *Cessnock*; Minesweeper for RAN (Admiralty account); O 29 Jul 1940; LD 16 Apr 1941 on No. 3 slipway; L 17 Oct 1941 by Lady Gordon, wife of dockyard director; C 29 Jan 1942; LDV No. 19.

154; Manufacture of 74 boilers of 2000 IHP for Australian minesweepers.

155; *Madras*; Minesweeper for Indian Navy; O 24 Sept 1940; LD 4 Aug 1941 on No. 4 slipway; L 17 Feb 1942 by Mrs Makin, wife of the Minister for the Navy; C 22 May 1942; LDV No. 38.

156; *Bengal*; Minesweeper for Indian Navy; O 24 Sept 1940; LD 3 Dec 1941 on No. 3 slipway; L 28 May 1942 by Mrs Curtin, wife of the Prime Minister; C 8 Aug 1942; LDV No. 39.

157; *Glenelg*; Minesweeper for RAN; O 24 Sept 1940; LD 2 Mar 1942 on No. 4 slipway; L 22 Sept 1942 by

Mrs H V Evatt, wife of the Minister for External Affairs; C 19 Nov 1942; LDV No. 40, was to have been *Bombay* for RIN, reallocated to RAN and renamed *Glenelg* 30 Jun 1941.

158; Preliminary work for Australian Standard A class steamers.

159; *River Clarence*; A class cargo steamer for Australian Shipbuilding Board; O 19 May 1941; LD 29 Jul 1941 on No. 1 slipway; L 2 Jan 1943 by Mrs McKell, wife of the NSW Premier; C 31 May 1943; Steamer A1.

160; *River Hunter*; A class cargo steamer for Australian Shipbuilding Board; O 19 Jul 1941, LD 29 Jul 1943 on No. 1 slipway; L 18 Oct 1945 by Mrs Chifley, wife of the Prime Minister; C 25 Jun 1946; Steamer A2.

161; Manufacture of exhaust steam turbines for A class standard steamships.

162; Preparatory work for Australian River class frigates.

163; *Barcoo*; River class frigate for RAN; O 16 Aug 1941; LD 21 Oct 1942 on No. 3 slipway; L 26 Aug 1943 by Mrs R V Keane, wife of the Minister for Trade and Customs; C 10 Feb 1944; River class frigate No. 1 (reciprocating machinery).

164; *Barwon*; River class frigate for RAN; O 16 Aug 1941; LD 31 May 1943 on No. 4 slipway; L 3 Aug 1944 by Mrs Scully, wife of the Minister for Commerce and Agriculture; C 12 Jan 1946; River class frigate No. 2 (reciprocating machinery).

165; Manufacture of 26 boilers for River class frigates.

166; Job number allocated for the modernisation of the cruiser HMAS *Canberra* (cancelled).

167; *Wollondilly*; River class frigate for the RAN; O 10 Dec 1942; Modified River class frigate No. 16 (turbine machinery), was to have been built on No. 2 slipway, cancelled 20 Apr 1944.

168; *Namoi*; River class frigate for the RAN; O 10 Dec 1942; Modified River class frigate No. 17 (turbine machinery), cancelled 20 Apr 1944.

169; *Wimmera*; River class frigate for the RAN; O 10 Dec 1942; Modified River class frigate No. 18 (turbine machinery), cancelled 20 Apr 1944.

170; *Campaspe*; River class frigate for the RAN; O 10 Dec 1942; Modified River class frigate No. 19 (turbine machinery), cancelled 6 Oct 1943.

171; Design of freighter 271' x 46' x 21' 6" for the Australian Shipbuilding Board.

172; Manufacture of Lentz type main engines for D class standard merchant ships.

173; Design of C class freighter for the Australian Shipbuilding Board.

174; Not used.

175; *ST17*; Fitting out only of US Army 75' tug, built by J & A Brown and Abermain Seaham Collieries Hexham, NSW.

176; Design of B class freighter for the Australian Shipbuilding Board.

177; O 8 Jun 1944; Design and preparatory work for 135' 6" ocean going A class tugs for the Australian Shipbuilding Board.

178; O 17 May 1944; Fitting out only of Modified River class frigate No. 11 HMAS *Shoalhaven*; (cancelled).

179; O 17 May 1944; Fitting out only of Modified River class frigate No. 21 HMAS *Condamine*; (cancelled).

180; —— ; Oceangoing tug for Australian Shipbuilding Board; O 24 Nov 1944; LD 21 Jun 1945 on No. 2 slipway; A class tug TA 1, cancelled 3 Sept 1945 when 46% steel erected on slipway, broken up 1947.

181; —— ; Oceangoing tug for the Australian Shipbuilding Board; O 24 Nov 1944; A class tug TA 2, cancelled 3 Sept 1945 when 57% steel fabricated.

182; —— ; Oceangoing tug for the Australian Shipbuilding Board; O 24 Nov 1944; A class tug TA 3, cancelled 3 Sept 1945 when 57% steel fabricated.

183; Manufacture of boilers for oceangoing tugs; cancelled and used for Ships 191 and 192.

184; Preparatory work for Australian Battle class destroyers.

185; *Tobruk*; Battle class destroyer for RAN; O 7 Oct 1944; LD 5 Aug 1946 on No. 1 slipway; L 20 Dec 1947 by Mrs W Riordan, wife of the Minister for the Navy; C 17 May 1950.

186; Manufacture of main machinery for Battle class destroyer HMAS *Anzac*.

187; Preparatory work for Daring class destroyers.

188; *Voyager*; Daring class destroyer for RAN; O 3 Dec 1946; LD 10 Oct 1949 on No. 1 slipway; L 1 march 1952 by Mrs R G Menzies, wife of the Prime Minister; C 10 Feb 1957; Daring class destroyer No. 1, work commenced in loft 1 Apr 1947 and in yard 1 Jun 1948.

189; *Vampire*; Daring class destroyer for RAN; O 3 Dec 1946; LD 1 Jul 1952 on No. 1 slipway; L 27 Oct 1956 by Lady Slim, wife of the Governor General; C 22 Jun 1959; Daring class destroyer No. 2.

190; Manufacture of turbines and boilers for Daring class destroyers *Voyager*, *Vampire*, *Vendetta* and *Waterhen*, and manufacture of fittings for *Vendetta* and *Waterhen*.

191; *Wonga*; Steam tug for Waratah Tug and Salvage Co.; O 6 Jan 1947; LD 25 Aug 1947 at the head of No. 2 slipway; L 3 Sept 1948; C 10 Jun 1949; Launched by *Titan*.

192; *Yelta*; Steam tug for Waratah Tug and Salvage Co.; O 6 Jan 1947; LD 25 Aug 1947 at the head of No. 2 slipway; L 18 Jun 1948; C 10 Feb 1949; Launched by *Titan*.

193; Not used.

194; Preparatory work for the modernisation of Q class destroyers and the manufacture of equipment and fittings for *Quadrant* and *Quickmatch* (Williamstown Dockyard).

195; Modernisation and conversion of HMAS *Queenborough* to Type 15 frigate.

196; Modernisation and conversion of HMAS *Quiberon* to Type 15 frigate; completed by Garden Island Dockyard.

197; Modernisation and conversion of HMAS *Quality* to Type 15 frigate; preparatory work and material ordering started but conversion cancelled.

198; Preparatory work for construction of Type 12 frigates.

199; *Parramatta*; Type 12 frigate for RAN; O 3 Oct 1951; LD 3 Jan 1957 on No. 1 slipway; L 31 Jan 1959 by Lady Dowling, wife of Vice Admiral Sir Roy Dowling, Chief of Naval Staff; C 4 Jul 1961; Hull number FSA RAN 01, work started in loft 8 May 1952 and in yard Dec 1955.

200; *Stuart*; Type 12 frigate for RAN; O 3 Oct 1951; LD 20 Mar 1959 on No. 1 slipway, L 8 Apr 1961 by Mrs J G Gorton, wife of the Minister for the Navy; C 27 Jun 1963; Hull number FSA RAN 02, work started in loft 8 May 1952, and in yard 3 Feb 1959, completed as IKARA trials ship.

201; Reserved for FSA RAN 03, order not placed.

202; Manufacture of Y100 turbines and Foster Wheeler boilers for Type 12 frigates FSA RAN 01, 02, 04, 05.

203; Manufacture of fittings (hull items) for Type 12 frigates building at Williamstown Dockyard (FSA RAN 04 and 05) and items supplied to Naval Board account for all ships.

204; —— ; Crane pontoon for Maritime Services Board of NSW; O 12 Nov 1956, L 27 Sept 1957; C 1957.

205 to 208; Refit of submarine HMS *Tabard*.

209 to 211; Refit of submarine HMS *Trump*.

212 to 214; Refit of submarine HMS *Taciturn*.

215 to 217; Second refit of submarine HMS *Tabard*.

218, 219; Not used.

220; *Empress of Australia*; Passenger vehicle ship for Australian Shipbuilding Board; O 21 Feb 1962; LD 11 Sept 1962 on No. 1 slipway; L 18 Jan 1964 by Catherine Sidney, daughter of the Governor General; C 8 Jan 1964; for the Australian National Line.

221; *Stalwart*; Destroyer tender for RAN; LD 23 Jun 1964 on No. 1 slipway; L 7 Oct 1966 by Lady Casey, wife of the Governor General; C 8 Feb 1968.

222; Preparatory work for the construction of Type 12 destroyer escort DE RAN 03.

223; Manufacture of Y136 turbines for Type 12 destroyer escorts DE RAN 03 and 06.

224; *Torrens*; Type 12 destroyer escort for RAN; O 14 Sept 1964; LD 18 Aug 1964 on No. 2 slipway; L 28 Sept 1968 by Dame Zara Holt; C 18 Jan 1971; Hull number DE RAN 03.

225; Manufacture of fittings for *Torrens* and *Swan* (DE RAN 06 built by Williamstown Dockyard).

226 to 228; Second refit of submarine HMS *Trump*.

229; Not used.

230; *AWL 304*; Aircraft/water lighter for RAN; O 7 Nov 1966; LD on No. 1 slipway 8 Sept 1967; L 26 Oct 1967; C 16 Nov 1967; Catamaran hull.

231; Preparatory work for the construction of flat top lighters.

232; *60101* to *60121*; 60-ton capacity flat top lighters for RAN; O 13 May 1970; LD 13 Jan 1971 (first lighter); L 30 march 1971 (first lighter); C 23 Nov 1971 (last lighter); Built on No. 1 slipway and launched by crane.

233; Preparatory work for construction of crane stores lighters.

234; *CSL 01*; Crane stores lighter for RAN; O 26 Aug 1971; LD 25 Feb 1972; L 12 Jul 1972; C 15 Aug 1972; Catamaran hull, built in plate yard, launched by *Titan*.

235; *CSL 02*; Crane stores lighter for RAN; O 26 Aug 1971; LD 4 May 1972; L 1 Sept 1972; C 29 Sept 1972; Catamaran hull, built in plate yard, launched by *Titan*.

236; *CSL 03*; Crane stores lighter for RAN; O 26 Aug 1971; LD 13 Jul 1972; L 29 Sept 1972; C 31 Oct 1972; Catamaran hull, built in plate yard, launched by *Titan*.

237; *SD 3201*; Slave dock for RAN; O 16 Feb 1973; LD 28 Mar 1973 on No. 1 slipway; L 18 Mar 1974; C 8 May 1975; For use at Cockatoo Island for refit of Oberon class submarines, construction completed in Oct 1974, handed over after trials in May 1975.

238; *Protector*; Fast combat support ship (AOE) for RAN; Project cancelled Aug 1973.

239; *A S Mayne*; Bucket dredger for Melbourne Harbor Trust; O 12 Sept 1974; LD 24 Feb 1975 on No. 1 slipway; L 29 May 1976 by Mrs A S Mayne; C 30 Mar 1977; Final assembly of bucket ladder completed in Melbourne after tow from Sydney.

—— ; —— ; Oxygen barge for Cockatoo Dockyard; Steel barge to carry bulk oxygen, registered number 1845, sold 1991.

240; *Bustler*; Steel workboat for Cockatoo Dockyard; L 12 Feb 1979; C 22 Feb 1979; Built as an apprentice project and named by shipwright apprentice Dennis Anning on 22 Feb 1979.

241; *Vickdock 30*; Floating dock for Cockatoo Dockyard as private venture; L 16 May 1980; C 11 Jul 1980; Prototype air-operated floating dock for small craft, construction commenced in Nov 1979, built on No. 1 slipway and launched by crane.

242; *Success*; Fleet underway replenishment ship (AOR) for RAN; O 26 Oct 1979; LD 9 Aug 1980 on No. 1 slipway; L 3 Mar 1984 by Lady Valerie Stephen, wife of the Governor General; C 15 Apr 1986; Modified Durance class design, largest naval ship built in Australia, the first built for the RAN to a French design, and the last ship built on Cockatoo Island.

APPENDIX 4

Major ship repairs and alterations during World War I

Ship	Type	Started	Completed	Work done
HMAS *Protector*	Gunboat	5 Aug 14	10 Aug 14	Overhaul and fitting gun supports
HMAS *Gayundah*	Gunboat	8 Jan 14	1 Aug 14	Conversion to training ship
Barcoo	Coal hulk	3 Apr 14	24 May 14	Rearrangement
Eastern	Steam ship	23 Feb 15	24 Mar 15	Repairs after grounding at Rabaul
HMS *Psyche*	Light cruiser	1 May 15	10 Jun 15	Overhaul before commissioned in RAN
HMS *Fantome*	Sloop	1 May 15	27 Jul 15	Overhaul before commissioned in RAN
HMAS *Huon*	Destroyer	29 Mar 16	3 May 16	Fitting torpedo tubes
Booral C7	Cargo steamship	12 Apr 16	19 Apr 16	General overhaul
HMAS *Una*	Sloop	17 Apr 16	2 May 16	Docking and fitting magazine flooding arrangements.
HMAS *Franklin*	Training ship	10 May 16	24 May 16	Docking, fitting new bilge keel
Karuah	Lighthouse ship	2 Jun 16	26 Jun 16	General overhaul
HMAS *Yarra*	Destroyer	13 Jul 16	20 Jul 16	General overhaul
HMAS *Parramatta*	Destroyer	31 Jul 16	19 Aug 16	General overhaul
HMAS *Encounter*	Light cruiser	18 Sept 16	26 Sept 16	Docking and overhaul
HMAS *Warrego*	Destroyer	7 Nov 16	18 Nov 16	Shell repairs and fitting searchlight platform
Carina C10	Cargo steamer	25 Oct 16	28 Feb 17	Grounding damage repairs
Albert	ex-gunboat	1 Nov 16	Not completed	Conversion to tug for Flinders Naval Depot
HMAS *Una*	Sloop	5 Dec 16	2 Feb 17	Alterations to mess decks
Araluen C5	Cargo steamship	29 Dec 16	19 Jan 17	General overhaul
HMAS *Yarra*	Destroyer	5 Jan 17	13 Jan 17	General overhaul
HMAS *Franklin*	Training ship	5 Jan 17	13 Jan 17	General overhaul
HMAS *Parramatta*	Destroyer	5 Jan 17	25 Jan 17	General overhaul
Conargo C8	Cargo steamship	5 Mar 17	15 Mar 17	Fitting wireless office
Parattah C6	Cargo steamship	22 Mar 17	16 May 17	General overhaul
Hirado	Light cruiser	7 May 17	9 May 17	Docking
Loongana	Troopship	15 May 17	29 Dec 17	Docking and turbine reblading
Chikuma	Light cruiser	28 May 17	30 May 17	Docking and machinery repairs
HMAS *Pioneer*	Light cruiser	28 Jun 17	5 Jul 17	Docking and overhaul
Cooee C3	Cargo steamship	13 Aug 17	3 Sept 17	Docking and overhaul
Araluen C5	Cargo steamship	21 Aug 17	6 Oct 17	General overhaul and repairs
Dongarra C4	Cargo steamship	3 Sept 17	25 Sept 17	General overhaul and repairs
Lindstol	Barquentine	6 Sept 17	10 Sept 17	Rudder repairs
Carawa C1	Cargo steamship	25 Sept 17	24 Oct 17	Repairs to complete survey
HMAS *Fantome*	Sloop	17 Oct 17	24 Oct 17	Docking and repairs
HMAS *Psyche*	Light cruiser	15 Nov 17	17 Nov 17	Docking

(*continued*)

Gilgai C11	Cargo steamship	20 Nov 17	12 Dec 17	Lloyds No. 1 special survey
Conargo C8	Cargo steamship	30 Nov 17	18 Dec 17	Lloyds survey
Bulga N1	Cargo steamship	5 Dec 17	7 Dec 17	General overhaul
Toromeo C2	Cargo steamship	11 Dec 17	7 Jan 18	General overhaul
HMAS *Brisbane*	Light cruiser	2 Feb 18	11 Mar 18	Docking and fitting search light platform
Barambah ex-A37	Cargo steamship	16 Jan 18	4 Feb 18	Lloyds No. 1 survey
Barungah ex-A43	Cargo steamship	8 Feb 18	27 Feb 18	General overhaul
Carina C10	Cargo steamship	19 Feb 18	2 Mar 18	Docking and annual survey
Parattah C6	Cargo steamship	21 Feb 18	15 Mar 18	General overhaul and repairs
Boonah ex-A36	Cargo steamship	12 Mar 18	19 Mar 18	General overhaul
HMAS *Una*	Sloop	11 Mar 18	18 Mar 18	Docking and repairs
Booral C7	Cargo steamship	2 Apr 18	19 Apr 18	Lloyds No. 3 survey
Bulla ex-A45	Cargo steamship	3 Apr 18	16 Apr 18	Lloyds No. 3 survey
Carina C10	Cargo steamship	25 Apr 18	8 May 18	General repairs
Bulla ex-A45	Cargo steamship	29 Apr 18	6 May 18	Completion of refit
Meklong	Cargo steamship	14 May 18	31 Jul 18	Hull repairs
Dongarra ex-C4	Cargo steamship	23 Jul 18	28 Aug 18	General overhaul and hull repairs
Bakara ex-A41	Cargo steamship	6 Aug 18	16 Aug 18	General overhaul and deck repairs
HMAS *Encounter*	Light cruiser	26 Sept 18	10 Oct 18	Docking and fitting para-vane gear
Cethana	Wood motor ship	11 Sept 18	14 Oct 18	Overhaul and caulking decks and bottom
Nautilus	Steamship	12 Sept 18	23 Oct 18	Overhaul, new bulkheads, tanks and fittings
Yahagi	Light cruiser	25 Sept 18	26 Sept 18	Docking
Australplain	Cargo steamship	9 Oct 18	14 Oct 18	General overhaul and repairs
Australpool	Cargo steamship	21 Oct 18	8 Nov 18	General overhaul and repairs
Siar	Cargo steamship	18 Dec 18	31 Jan 19	Docking and repairs
Challamba	Wood motor ship	19 Dec 18	18 Jan 19	General overhaul, topsides and bottom caulked.

APPENDIX 5

Transports converted during World War I

Ship	Started	Finished	Fit to carry:	
			MEN	HORSES
Aorangi	10 Aug 14	17 Aug 14		
Berrima (A35)	12 Aug 14	18 Aug 14	1500	
Argyllshire (A8)	22 Aug 14	9 Sept 14	845	392
Marere (A21)	29 Aug 14	12 Sept 14	85	475
Star of England (A15)	29 Aug 14	12 Sept 14	524	511
Anglo Egyptian (A25)	10 Sept 14	19 Sept 14	127	552
Armadale (A26)	11 Sept 14	22 Sept 14	284	388
Ajana (A31)	9 Nov 14	10 Dec 14	427	304
Clan MacGillivray (A46)	29 Dec 14	23 Jan 15	1107	
Ascanius (A11)	19 Apr 15	12 May 15	1820	12
Afric (A19)	21 Apr 15	13 May 15	549	500
Medic (A7)	3 May 15	21 May 15	531	500
Uganda (A66)	17 May 15	29 May 15	136	180
Kanowna (A61)	1 Jun 15	6 Jun 15	1100	
Clan MacEwan (A65)	8 Jun 15	26 Jun 15	126	450
Aeneas (A60)	14 Jun 15	23 Jun 15	1820	
Anchises (A68)	9 Aug 15	14 Aug 15	1520	
Makarini	30 Aug 15	6 Sept 15	1010	
Benalla (A24)	1 Oct 15	14 Oct 15	1395	
Hawkes Bay	14 Oct 15	21 Oct 15	1395	
Canberra	16 Oct 17	16 Nov 17	1080	
Wyreema	24 Sept 18	14 Oct 18	926	
Mahana	21 Ja. 19	10 Feb 19	1250	
Orari	7 Feb 19	21 Feb 19	1014	

APPENDIX 6

TRANSPORTS REFITTED DURING WORLD WAR I

The following transports were refitted at Cockatoo Dockyard during World War I, listed in alphabetical order. The number of times each ship was refitted is given in brackets.

Adolph Woermann (1)
Aeneas (4)
Afric (1)
Ajana (4)
Alexander Woermann (1)
Anchises (3)
Anglo Egyptian (3)
Argyllshire (4)
Armadale (4)
Armagh (1)
Ascanius (4)
Ayrshire (2)

Bahia Castillo (1)
Bakara (5)
Balmoral Castle (1)
Barambah (4)
Barunga (2)
Benalla (1)
Berrima (1)
Boonah (3)
Boorara (3)
Borda (1)
Botanist (1)
Bulla (1)

Ceramic (3)
Chemintz (1)
City of Exeter (1)
City of Poona (1)
City of York (1)
Clan MacCorquodale (4)

Clan MacEwan (2)
Clan Macgillivray (3)
Cluny Castle (1)
Commonwealth (1)

Dongola (2)
Dunluce Castle (2)
Durham (1)

Eastern (1)
Euripides (2)
Fieldmarshall (1)
Frankfurt (1)
Friedrichsruh (1)
Geelong (1)

Hawkes Bay (later Port
    Napier) (2)
Hororata (4)
Hymettus (2)

Itonus (2)
Itria (4)

Kabinga (1)
Kaiser I Hind (1)
Kanowna (2)
Karmala (1)
Karoola (1)
Katuna (1)
Kigoma (1)
Konigin Luise (1)

Kursk (1)

Leicestershire (1)
Lucie Woermann (1)

Main (1)
Makarini (later Port
    Nicholson) (2)
Marathon (1)
Marere (2)
Margha (1)
Medic (4)
Militiades (1)

Nestor (2)

Oxfordshire (1)

Pera (1)
Persic (3)
Port Darwin (1)
Port Denison (1)
Port Lincoln (1)
Port Lyttleton (2)
Port Macquarie (1)
Port Stephens (1)

Rio Negro (1)
Rio Pardo (1)
Rugia (1)
Runic (4)

Saldanha (3)

Sardinia (2)
Seang Bee (1)
Seang Choon (1)
Seuvic (2)
Shropshire (4)
St. Albans (1)
Star of England (later Port
    Sydney) (9)
Star of Victoria (later Port
    Melbourne) (6)
Suffolk (6)
Surada (2)
Swakopmund (1)

Thermistocles (2)
Tras os Montes (2)

Uganda (3)
Ulysses (2)

Valencia (1)
Vestalia (2)

Wahene (1)
Wandilla (3)
Warwickshire (1)
Willochra (1)
Wiltshire (9)
Windhuk (1)
Wyreema (2)

Ypiranga (1)

APPENDIX 7

Ships reconverted for merchant service after World War I

Transports partly reconditioned by Cockatoo Dockyard

Troop fittings in the following ships (listed in alphabetical order) were dismantled and stowed on board or taken ashore.

Adolf Woermann	City of Exeter	Madras	Port Napier
Aeneas		Mahana	Port Sydney
Ajana	Demosthenes	Mahia	
Alexander Woermann	Devon	Main	Raranga
Anchises	Durham	Marathon	Runic
Argyllshire		Medic	
Ayrshire	Ellenga	Megantic	Seuvic
	Essex	Militiades	Shropshire
Bahia Castillo	Euripides		Somerset
Bakara		Nestor	Swakopmund
Barambah	Freidrichsruh	Norman	
Bellerophon		Northumberland	Thermistocles
Beltana	Hororata		
Benalla	Indarra	Orari	Ulysses
Boorara	Irishman	Oxfordshire	
Borda			Wahene
Bremen	Kigoma	Persic	Wiltshire
Burma	Konigin Luise	Port Denison	Windhuk
		Port Lincoln	
Cap Verde	Leicestershire	Port Lyttleton	Ypiranga
Chemintz	Lucie Woermann	Port Macquarie	Zealandic

Ships fully reconditioned at Cockatoo Dockyard

Ship	Type	Started	Completed
Wandilla A62	Transport	29 May 19	9 Sept 19
Karoola A63	Transport	30 Jun 19	8 Nov 19
Zealandia	Transport	5 Jun 19	1 Aug 19
Wyreema	Transport	20 May 20	11 Oct 20
Katoomba	Transport	3 Oct 19	8 Mar 20
Ulimaroa	Transport	1 Sep 19	8 Mar 20
Canberra	Transport	2 Dec 19	21 Jun 20
Kanowna A61	Transport	1 Mar 20	29 Jul 20
Heroic	Tug	20 Feb 20	23 Sep 20
Heroine	Tug	29 Mar 20	3 Aug 20

(Source: *Record of work done from 1913 to 31 July 1921 at the Commonwealth Naval Dockyard, Cockatoo Island*, CRS C3445.)

APPENDIX 8

SHIP REFITS AND REPAIRS DURING WORLD WAR II

SHIP	STARTED	FINISHED	WORK DONE
Moreton Bay	31 Aug 39	19 Oct 39	Conversion to armed merchant cruiser
Changte	1 Sep 39	17 Sep 39	Conversion to victualling issue ship, fitting of paravane gear and gun stiffening
Otranto	6 Sep 39	20 Sep 39	Fitting of paravane gear, gun stiffening and bow protection
Maimoa	8 Sep 39	17 Sep 39	Gun stiffening
Janeta	12 Sep 39	21 Sep 39	Gun stiffening
Ormonde	21 Sep 39	8 Oct 39	Gun stiffening and bow protection
Awatea	22 Sep 39	7 Oct 39	Gun stiffening
Oronsay	4 Oct 39	21 Oct 39	Gun stiffening and bow protection
HMS *Kanimbla*	16 Oct 39	21 Oct 39	Fitting of paravane shoe
Niagara	23 Oct 39	2 Nov 39	Gun stiffening
Orion	8 Dec 39	28 Dec 39	Fitted as troopship, bow protection
Heros	14 Dec 39	20 Dec 39	Underwater fitting
St Giles	14 Dec 39	20 Dec 39	Underwater fitting
HMAS *Manoora*	18 Dec 39	22 Dec 39	Underwater fitting, bow protection
HMAS *Sydney*	23 Dec 39	29 Dec 39	Temporary repairs at stern
Orcades	29 Dec 39	8 Jan 40	Fitted as troopship, bow protection
Orford	31 Dec 39	8 Jan 40	Fitted as troopship
Otranto	3 Jan 40	8 Jan 40	Tourist saloon converted for troop dining
Strathnaver	4 Jan 40	9 Jan 40	Fitted as troopship
Dumont d'Urville	1 Feb 40	18 Mar 40	French Navy, general repairs
Empress of Japan	12 Mar 40	26 Mar 40	Additional accommodation for troops on A, B, C and boat decks
Battle practice target	15 Mar 40	29 Jul 40	Conversion to high speed target
Dunera	19 Mar 40	9 Apr 40	Additional accommodation for troops on Promenade, Shelter, Upper and Lower decks
HMS *Ramillies*	19 Mar 40	9 Apr 40	Repairs to boats, machinery etc.
Strathaird	25 Mar 40	5 Apr 40	Additional accommodation for troops on B, C, D, E, F, G, and H decks
Empress of Canada	25 Mar 40	5 Apr 40	Additional accommodation for troops on A, B, C and D decks
Aquitania	12 Apr 40	16 Apr 40	Additional accommodation for troops on A, B, C, D, E, F, and G decks
Queen Mary	17 Apr 40	3 May 40	Additional accommodation for troops on sun, main, A, B, C, D, and E decks
Orcades	18 Apr 40	19 Apr 40	Dismantling fittings in troops' mess space for carriage of cargo.
Mauretania	27 Apr 40	3 May 40	Additional accommodation for troops on sun, main, A, B, C, and D decks
Manunda	27 May 40	31 Jul 40	Conversion to hospital ship, fitting of paravane gear and degaussing
Zealandia	21 Jun 40	30 Jun 40	Fitted to carry 1000 troops, holds 2 and 4 fitted as mess decks and promenade deck enclosed to form mess deck, fitted with paravane gear and additional galley equipment
2nd target towing skid	25 Jun 40	18 Dec 40	Wooden construction, 51 feet long, complete with coils

(*continued*)

1st target towing skid	25 Jun 40	14 Oct 40	Wooden construction, 51 feet long, complete with coils
Orontes	8 Jul 40	12 Jul 40	Section of permanent accommodation reerected, including wiring and fittings, section of portable accommodation erected
Cape Horn	10 Jul 40	15 Jul 40	Fitted with paravane gear
SS *Ulysses*	29 Jul 40	2 Aug 40	23 additional bunks fitted in cabins, first class saloon divided into first, second and third class
Strathallan	2 Aug 40	9 Aug 40	100 additional bunks fitted in cabins
Nieuw Holland	12 Aug 40	7 Sep 40	Fitted to carry 1000 troops, four mess decks, new galley and bakery equipment, paravane gear and bridge protection fitted
Orcades	12 Aug 40	17 Aug 40	No. 6 Section re-erected, including electrical and plumbing work
Aquitania	15 Aug 40	30 Aug 40	Extensive machinery, boiler, electrical and plumbing repairs
Indrapoera	19 Aug 40	14 Sep 40	Fitted for 1000 troops, one mess deck in hold, and weather deck enclosed for troops, fitted with new galley equipment, bridge protection and paravane gear
Zealandia	29 Aug 40	30 Aug 40	Two mess decks stripped, including electrical and plumbing work
Nieuw Zeeland	4 Sep 40	26 Sep 40	Fitted for 1000 troops, four mess decks fitted out, new galley and bakery equipment, bridge protection and paravane gear fitted
Koree	12 Sep 40	27 Dec 40	Target towing launch, extensive alterations
Johann De Witt	20 Sep 40	26 Sep 40	Paravane gear fitted
Queen Mary	25 Sep 40	15 Oct 40	Completion of troop decks fitted out at Singapore, engine and electrical repairs
Zealandia	4 Oct 40	10 Oct 40	Replaced troop fittings in 2 and 4 between decks, built new galley in No. 2 upper between deck
Aquitania	8 Oct 40	18 Oct 40	Alterations to accommodation for troops in third class cabins, engine and electrical repairs.
Stratheden	21 Oct 40	28 Oct 40	Stem extension for paravane gear
Strathmore	28 Oct 40	4 Nov 40	Stem extension for paravane gear
Aquitania	24 Nov 40	24 Dec 40	Accommodation increased by 500, minor alterations and repairs
Queen Mary	25 Nov 40	24 Dec 40	Minor alterations to accommodation
Manunda	17 Dec 40	24 Dec 40	Alterations to fittings and illumination as hospital ship
Boissevain	18 Dec 40	20 Dec 40	Paravane gear fitted
Wadjemup	19 Dec 40	25 Feb 41	Extensive alterations
Nieuw Amsterdam	8 Jan 41	23 Jan 41	Alterations to troop fittings, messing arrangements, canteens etc., additional galley equipment fitted
Ruys	8 Jan 41	14 Jan 41	Paravane gear fitted
Zealandia	14 Jan 41	17 Jan 41	Fitted forced ventilation into No. 2 mess space, built dispensary in cabin 93, minor repairs to accommodation
3rd target towing skid	15 Jan 41	30 May 41	Wooden construction, 51 feet long, complete with coils

(*continued*)

Queen Elizabeth	25 Jan 41	31 Mar 41	Alterations to troop messes, canteens, etc., completion of ship's engine and electrical work, general engineering, electrical and boiler repairs
Queen Mary	28 Jan 41	3 Feb 41	Alterations to troop fittings, messing arrangements etc., engineering, electrical and boiler repairs
Aquitania	29 Jan 41	4 Feb 41	Repairs to troop fittings etc., extra galley equipment fitted, engineering, electrical and boiler repairs
SS *Ulysses*	29 Jan 41	31 Jan 41	Extra bunks in cabins, divisional screens in dining room and lounge
Queen Mary	1 Mar 41	8 Mar 41	Deck, engineering and electrical repairs
Zealandia	1 Mar 41	7 Mar 41	Minor alterations to troop accommodation
Katoomba	7 Mar 41	10 Mar 41	Fitted hammock racks and spurnwater around promenade deck, suite B fitted out for nurses, alterations to messing arrangements
Mauretania	22 Mar 41	28 Mar 41	Alterations to canteens, spare propellers stowed in hold
Nieuw Amsterdam	22 Mar 41	28 Mar 41	Alterations to canteens, stores, black-out screens and latrines, new galley equipment fitted
Diomede	1 Apr 41	7 Apr 41	Fitted out gun crew's accommodation
Oranje	4 Apr 41	30 Jun 41	Fitted out as hospital ship for 676 patients
Ile de France	4 Apr 41	10 Apr 41	Alterations to messing arrangements, repairs to canteens, dispensary, black-out screens and galley equipment
Manunda	15 Apr 41	21 Apr 41	Minor repairs and alterations to wards, duty rooms etc.
Oranje	16 Apr 41	27 Apr 41	26 foot motor boat fitted
Glenogle	9 May 41	24 May 41	Fitted out gun crew's accommodation
Perseus	10 May 41	16 May 41	Fitted out gun crew's accommodation
Sarpedon	14 May 41	17 May 41	Fitted out gun crew's accommodation
Wanganella	15 May 41	22 Jul 41	Fitted 26 foot motor boat
Katoomba	27 May 41	28 May 41	Removal of troop fittings
Queen Mary	27 May 41	15 Jun 41	General deck, engine and electrical repairs
Gleniffer	12 Jun 41	16 Jun 41	Fitted out gun crew's accommodation
Queen Elizabeth	16 Jun 41	27 Jun 41	General deck, engine and electrical repairs
Aquitania	16 Jun 41	21 Jun 41	General deck, engine and electrical repairs
Manunda	27 Jun 41	15 Jul 41	Fitted electrical cot lift, minor alterations to wards etc.
Zaanland	1 Jul 41	4 Jul 41	Fitted out gun crew's accommodation
Katoomba	24 Jul 41	25 Jul 41	Fitted out E suite for officers
Johan van Oldenbarneveldt	26 Jul 41	29 Jul 41	Minor repairs to accommodation, plumbing etc.
Queen Mary	15 Aug 41	3 Sep 41	Hull and engine repairs
HMAS *Perth*	18 Aug 41	24 Sep 41	Repairs to tanks and shaft alignment due to bomb damage
Aquitania	23 Aug 41	4 Sep 41	Hull, engine and electrical repairs, rebuilding of firemen's quarters
Queen Elizabeth	23 Aug 41	2 Sep 41	Hull and engine repairs
Oranje	4 Sep 41	30 Sep 41	Alterations and additions to wards, dispensaries, etc., and repairs to waste heat boilers
Hertford	15 Sep 41	19 Jan 42	Renewed insulation in No. 2 lower hold and between decks and Nos 3, 4 and 5 lower holds, renewed approximately half brine piping in No. 2 lower hold and between decks

(*continued*)

Manunda	22 Sep 41	24 Oct 41	Minor additions and repairs to fittings
Queen Mary	14 Oct 41	31 Oct 41	Hull, engine and boiler repairs, extensive alterations to life boats
Queen Elizabeth	16 Oct 41	24 Oct 41	Hull, engine and boiler repairs, extensive alterations to life boats
Le Triomphant	11 Nov 41	11 Dec 41	French destroyer, extensive hull, engine and electrical repairs
Katoomba	26 Nov 41	26 Nov 41	Minor repairs to troop accommodation
Aquitania	1 Dec 41	15 Dec 41	Extensive repairs to life boats, officer's and crew's accommodation, altered and rebuilt steward's accommodation
Largs Bay	1 Dec 41	10 Dec 41	Turbine repairs
Oranje	15 Dec 41	2 Jan 42	Minor repairs and additions to hospital accommodation
Queen Elizabeth	16 Dec 41	16 Jan 42	Deck repairs, fitting additional tanks in lifeboats
Republic	2 Jan 42	7 Jan 42	Docking repairs and stem extension
Taiping	3 Jan 42	21 Jan 42	Conversion to victualling supply ship and fitting of bridge protection
HMAS *Bungaree*	13 Jan 42	21 Jan 42	Docking and fitting of A/S gear
Wanganella	2 Feb 42	18 Feb 42	Alterations to crew's accommodation and repairs to hospital fittings
Aquitania	2 Feb 42	9 Feb 42	Repairs to deck and lifeboats
Katoomba	4 Feb 42	7 Feb 42	Installed fittings for 408 hammocks on promenade deck.
HMAS *Rockhampton*	5 Feb 42	9 Feb 42	Docking and change of propellers
HMAS *Rockhampton*	12 Feb 42	14 Feb 42	Completion of minor details
HMS *Kanimbla*	13 Feb 42	2 Mar 42	Extensive hull, engine and electrical repairs, bridge protection fitted
Le Triomphant	14 Feb 42	16 Feb 42	French destroyer, repairs to A/S gear
Warwick Castle	20 Feb 42	25 Feb 42	Repairs to troop fittings
Tromp	6 Mar 42	19 Apr 42	Dutch cruiser, extensive hull, engine and electrical repairs
HMAS *Canberra*	9 Mar 42	22 Apr 42	Building A/S compartment, fitting of pitometer log, rudder straightened, and structural repairs to forepeak, extensive turbine repairs
Koree	17 Mar 42	1 Jun 42	Extensive engine repairs
USS *William B Preston* (AVD 7)	27 Mar 42	2 Jun 42	Extensive hull and engine repairs following bomb damage, restoration of crew accommodation and armament modifications
Queen Mary	30 Mar 42	6 Apr 42	Boiler repairs and cleaning
USS *Whipple* (DD 217)	31 Mar 42	3 Apr 42	Bow repairs
HMAS *Swan*	17 Apr 42	29 Apr 42	Completion of two Oerlikon gun positions, hull and machinery repairs
HMAS *Australia*	22 Apr 42	29 Apr 42	Repairs to A-bracket bushes, starboard side, and fitting of seven Oerlikon guns
Tromp	4 May 42	16 May 42	Dutch cruiser, re-arrangement of crew space, storerooms, bridge etc., fitting of two 3-inch high angle guns
USS *Chicago* (CA 29)	15 May 42	24 May 42	Hull and machinery repairs, fitting of 12 Oerlikon guns

(continued)

HMAS *Warrego*	18 May 42	29 May 42	Removal and realignment of shafting
Wanganella	18 May 42	26 May 42	Alterations and additions to accommodation, fitting forced ventilation to No. 4 hold
K XII	26 May 42	9 Aug 42	Dutch submarine, extensive hull machinery and electrical repairs
Tromp	8 Jun 42	13 Jun 42	Dutch cruiser, minor hull and machinery repairs, completion of RDF installation
USS *Helm* (DD 388)	9 Jun 42	24 Jun 42	Extensive bow repairs
Oranje	11 Jun 42	17 Jul 42	Repairs to waste heat boilers and renewal of insulation in coal room after fire damage
Marina	14 Jul 42	12 Aug 42	Extensive bow damage repairs and fitting of two Oerlikon guns and two 0.5-inch machine guns
HMAS *Kybra*	28 Jul 42	30 Jul 42	Shell and tank repairs
USS *Phoenix* (CL 46)	6 Aug 42	13 Aug 42	Rudder and hull repairs
HMAS *Townsville*	9 Aug 42	24 Aug 42	Renewal of top half of sonar gear
HMAS *Westralia*	10 Aug 42	22 Aug 42	Fitting out of additional accommodation for officers and ratings
HMAS *Castlemaine*	14 Aug 42	22 Aug 42	Collision damage repairs
HMS *Kanimbla*	18 Aug 42	20 Aug 42	Gun mountings
HMAS *Stuart*	27 Aug 42	2 Sep 42	Machinery and sonar repairs
USS *Chicago* (CA 29)	29 Aug 42	19 Sep 42	Torpedo damage repairs
HMAS *Cessnock*	2 Sep 42	4 Sep 42	Sonar and deck repairs
HMAS *Innisfail*	4 Sep 42	6 Sep 42	Repairs to ship's side fittings
HMS *Ban Hong Liong*	7 Sep 42	9 Sep 42	Hull repairs
USS *Mugford* (DD 389)	9 Sep 42	12 Sep 42	Hull repairs
HMAFA *Kurumba*	21 Sep 42	24 Sep 42	Hull and engine repairs and fitting of Oerlikon gun seats
USS *Tulsa* (PG 22)	22 Sep 42	10 Oct 42	Extensive repairs and alterations
HMAS *Tamworth*	22 Sep 42	24 Sep 42	Minor repairs and sonar repairs
Le Triomphant	5 Oct 42	8 Oct 42	French destroyer, hull repairs.
HMAS *Swan*	7 Oct 42	28 Oct 42	Extensive hull and engine repairs
HMAS *Hobart*	16 Oct 42	20 Oct 42	Hull and engine repairs
Tromp	20 Oct 42	28 Oct 42	Dutch cruiser, shell and engine repairs
HMAS *Australia*	28 Oct 42	23 Nov 42	Extensive turbine and hull repairs
USS *San Juan* (CL 54)	9 Nov 42	17 Nov 42	Hull and engine repairs, new rudder fitted
USS *Chester* (CA 27)	18 Nov 42	23 Dec 42	Extensive battle damage repairs
HMAS *Rockhampton*	18 Nov 42	19 Nov 42	Sonar repairs
HMAS *Yandra*	1 Dec 42	3 Dec 42	Rudder and engine repairs
USS *Portland*(CA 33)	2 Dec 42	10 Feb 43	Extensive battle damage repairs
USS *Phoenix* (CL 46)	9 Dec 42	24 Dec 42	Repairs and alterations
HMAS *Vendetta*	12 Dec 42	15 Dec 42	Repairs to machinery and propellers
USS *New Orleans* (CA 32)	28 Dec 42	6 Mar 43	Extensive action damage repairs
USS *Southard* (DMS 10)	29 Dec 42	7 Jan 43	Repairs to tanks and propeller
USS *Hopkins* (DMS 13)	7 Jan 43	9 Jan 43	Repairs to tanks and hull
Yunnan	11 Jan 43	16 Jan 43	Extensive alterations and repairs
USS *Zane*	14 Jan 43	16 Jan 43	Repairs to tanks and shell
HMAS *Moresby*	21 Jan 43	22 Jan 43	Repairs to deck and fittings
HMAS *Mildura*	22 Jan 43	23 Jan 43	Sonar repairs
USS *Bagley* (DD 386)	27 Jan 43	28 Jan 43	Repairs to sonar
HMAS *Moresby*	28 Jan 43	29 Jan 43	Repairs to deck and fittings
HMAS *Arunta*	1 Feb 43	5 Feb 43	Machinery and hull repairs and alterations

(continued)

Wanganella	1 Feb 43	4 Feb 43	Repair and renewal of fittings
HMAS *Bundaberg*	3 Feb 43	19 Feb 43	Sonar repairs
USS *Hovey* (DMS 11)	8 Feb 43	10 Feb 43	Hull repairs
USS *Henley* (DD 391)	10 Feb 43	12 Feb 43	Fuel tank repairs
USS *William Ellery Channing*	12 Feb 43	12 Apr 43	Fitted out to carry 1500 troops
USS *Sumner* (AGS 5)	18 Feb 43	21 Feb 43	Engine repairs
Jacob Van Heemskerk	1 Mar 43	6 Apr 43	Dutch destroyer, fitting of sonar and radar and general overhaul
USS *Helena* (CL 50)	10 Mar 43	18 Mar 43	Machinery repairs and catapult overhaul
USS *Selfridge* (DD 357)	18 Mar 43	25 Mar 43	Machinery repairs and repairs to oil fuel tanks
USS *Nashville* (CL 43)	2 Apr 43	8 Apr 43	Machinery and hull repairs, re-wooding of A-brackets
HMAS *Townsville*	5 Apr 43	7 Apr 43	Sonar repairs
HMAS *Hobart*	9 Apr 43	14 Apr 43	Fitting of sonar
Van Galen	12 Apr 43	26 Apr 43	Dutch destroyer, machinery repairs and modifications to rudder.
USS *Henry T Allen* (AP 30)	19 Apr 43	15 May 43	Modifications to accommodation and hull machinery and electrical repairs
HMAS *Stuart*	1 May 43	20 Jun 43	General refit, fitting of RDF and bridge modifications
HMAS *Australia*	10 May 43	18 May 43	Minor deck repairs and repairs to A-brackets
HMAS *Nepal*	10 May 43	14 May 43	Rudder stiffening
HMAS *K IX*	17 May 43	8 Jun 43	All tanks cleaned, re-coated and tested; hydroplanes and torpedo tubes overhauled
HMAS *Westralia*	19 May 43	22 May 43	Sea tubes fitted
USS *Vestal* (AR 4)	24 May 43	30 May 43	New radar fitted and machinery repairs
Reynella	7 Jun 43	10 Jun 43	Repairs to lube oil tanks
USS *LST 464*	9 Jun 43	30 Jun 43	Fitted out to carry 66 hospital cases, hull machinery and electrical repairs
HMAFA *Kurumba*	10 Jun 43	19 Jun 43	Repairs to broken shaft coupling
HMAS *Warramunga*	16 Jun 43	18 Jun 43	Minor hull and machinery repairs
USS *Victoria* (AO 46)	25 Jun 43	30 Jun 43	Repairs to oil fuel tanks and rudder fittings
Tjerk Hiddes	1 Jul 43	3 Jul 43	Dutch destroyer, hull and sonar repairs
Peter H Burnett	2 Jul 43	13 Aug 43	Liberty ship, temporary repairs to torpedo damage in way of No. 5 hold
USS *LST 469*	12 Jul 43	16 Feb 44	Extensive reconstruction following action damage
USS *Flusser* (DD 368)	2 Aug 43	13 Aug 43	Re-alignment of starboard shaft and minor hull repairs
Taron	9 Aug 43	11 Aug 43	Minor hull and machinery repairs
HMAS *Arunta*	25 Aug 43	14 Sep 43	Fitting of sonar gear and new RDF installation
HMAS *Kanimbla*	26 Aug 43	28 Aug 43	Repair to rudder and fitting of sea tubes
HMAS *Hobart*	6 Sep 43	6 Feb 45	Major damage repairs and modernisation
HMAS *Warramunga*	21 Oct 43	29 Oct 43	Hull, machinery, boiler, electrical and radar repairs
Taroona	29 Nov 43	18 Feb 44	Turbine repairs
USS *LST 471*	2 Dec 43	17 Aug 44	Reconstruction after extensive action damage
Birchgrove Park	29 Dec 43	4 Jan 44	Engine, boiler and minor hull repairs
HMAS *Warramunga*	12 Jan 44	3 Feb 44	Electrical repairs, stiffening in sonar compartment, radar refit, A-bracket bushes re-metaled

(continued)

HMAS *Arunta*	5 Feb 44	25 Feb 44	Electrical repairs, stiffening in sonar compartment, radar refit
USS *Mullany* (DD 528)	15 Feb 44	23 Feb 44	Repairs to oil fuel tanks
HMAS *Australia*	21 Feb 44	2 Mar 44	Extensive hull repairs at stern and minor hull repairs forward
Nairana	22 Feb 44	5 Apr 44	Re-blading of turbines, removal of guns and minor hull alterations
USS *Gilmer* (APD 11)	23 Feb 44	28 Feb 44	Repairs to oil fuel tanks, A-bracket bushes re-wooded
USS *Sea Star*	24 Feb 44	25 Apr 44	Electrical repairs and repairs to turbines and gears
Sussex	13 Mar 44	19 Mar 44	Preparation of between decks for carrying butter
Hororata	21 Mar 44	26 Mar 44	Preparation of between decks for carrying butter
Agnes	13 Apr 44	15 Apr 44	Minor hull repairs
Straat Soenda	19 Apr 44	22 Apr 44	Minor repairs to rudder
Colina	26 Apr 44	29 Apr 44	Minor hull and engine repairs
Ponce	1 May 44	4 May 44	Minor hull repairs
Muliama	1 May 44	4 May 44	Minor hull and rudder repairs
HMAS *Westralia*	17 May 44	7 Jun 44	Hull, machinery and electrical repairs
HMAS *Norman*	23 May 44	7 Jun 44	Renewal of two shell plates, renewal of sonar hull outfit, machinery and electrical repairs
Medusa	9 Jun 44	18 Jun 44	Renewal of insulation in cool room, repairs to bilge keel and renewal of rivets in oil fuel tanks
HMAS *Shropshire*	14 Jun 44	22 Jun 44	Part turbine re-blading
Rimu Paka	9 Aug 44	28 Aug 44	Extensive repairs to hold insulation
HMAS *Burdekin*	9 Aug 44	15 Aug 44	Condenser repairs
HMAS *Arunta*	13 Aug 44	24 Aug 44	Hull, machinery and electrical repairs
Army tug 454	24 Aug 44	12 Sep 44	Repairs to hauling winch etc.
USS *Venus* (AK 135)	25 Aug 44	28 Sep 44	Torpedo damage repairs
HMAS *Vendetta*	28 Aug 44	29 Dec 44	Re-tube and repairs to boilers
HMS *Challenger*	15 Sep 44	20 Sep 44	Repairs to hull in way of oil fuel tanks
HMAS *Nepal*	20 Sep 44	25 Sep 44	Sonar overhaul and re-metal of A-bracket bushes
USS *Octans* (AF 26)	5 Oct 44	15 Oct 44	Minor hull repairs and renewal of top rudder bearing
Orari	9 Oct 44	15 Oct 44	Rudder repairs
USS *Gold Star* (AG 12)	21 Oct 44	24 Oct 44	Minor hull repairs
Reijnst	25 Oct 44	31 Oct 44	Minor shell repairs and renewal of scupper pipes
HMAS *Quickmatch*	1 Dec 44	12 Dec 44	General hull examination, stern tubes remetaled and A-brackets re-rubbered
Glenbeg	4 Dec 44	29 Dec 44	Insulation of holds
Hororata	12 Dec 44	18 Dec 44	Insulation of holds
HMS *Quadrant*	27 Dec 44	29 Dec 44	Minor shell repairs
HMS *Glenearn*	2 Jan 45	6 Feb 45	Hull and machinery repairs
HMS *Queenborough*	9 Jan 45	12 Jan 45	Internal standpipes and cofferdams fitted
HMAS *Australia*	30 Jan 45	24 May 45	Action damage repairs, new shell plates, funnels and standpipes fitted, radar mess and magazines built and fitted out, engine and boiler repairs
HMS *Illustrious*	11 Feb 45	25 Feb 45	Action damage repairs, rudder repairs and turbine bearings re-metaled

(*continued*)

HMS *Euryalus*	13 Feb 45	18 Feb 45	Rivets renewed, sonar examination
HMS *Grenville*	13 Feb 45	16 Feb 45	Minor hull repairs
HMS *Indomitable*	15 Feb 45	26 Feb 45	Construction of admiral's staff cabin and fitting out
HMS *Undaunted*	16 Feb 45	21 Feb 45	General hull repairs
HMAS *Burnie*	26 Feb 45	3 Mar 45	Minor hull repairs
HMS *Quilliam*	5 Mar 45	9 Mar 45	Additional stiffening and oil fuel tanks repaired
HMAS *Stuart*	10 Mar 45	19 Mar 45	Minor hull and propeller repairs
HMAS *Arunta*	16 Apr 45	26 Apr 45	Action damage repair, three new shell plates and sonar examination
HMAS *Shropshire*	1 May 45	11 May 45	Aft peak stiffened and four sea tubes fitted, sonar examination
HMS *Pioneer*	17 May 45	20 May 45	Boiler brickwork repaired
HMS *Voracious*	28 May 45	2 Jun 45	A-bracket bushes re-metaled, propellers repaired
HMS *Formidable*	31 May 45	26 Jun 45	Action damage repair to flight deck, erection of admiral's staff cabin
HMS *Urania*	5 Jun 45	9 Jun 45	Minor general repairs
HMS *Grenville*	5 Jun 45	8 Jun 45	Minor general repairs
HMAS *Quickmatch*	9 Jun 45	13 Jun 45	Minor repairs
HMAS *Napier*	9 Jun 45	23 Jun 45	General repairs
HMNZS *Gambia*	14 Jun 45	20 Jun 45	Minor general repairs and shaft bushes
HMAS *Warramunga*	20 Jun 45	25 Jun 45	Minor repairs and new rope guards fitted, sonar examination
HMS *Tumult*	26 Jun 45	8 Aug 45	Grounding damage repairs, A-brackets re-bored, shafts realigned, general hull, machinery and electrical repairs
HMS *Guardian*	27 Jun 45	6 Jul 45	General repairs
HMAS *Burdekin*	27 Jun 45	6 Jul 45	Type 147 B sonar fitted
HMS *Kempenfelt*	11 Jul 45	21 Jul 45	Repairs to forepeak tanks
HMAS *Arunta*	23 Jul 45	16 Oct 45	Refit, new foremast and ventilation improvements
HMS *Resource*	23 Jul 45	29 Jul 45	Minor repairs
Agnes	24 Jul 45	28 Jul 45	New tail shaft and stem shoes fitted
HMS *Venerable*	26 Jul 45	10 Aug 45	Reading room and dormitory fitted out
HMAS *Stuart*	28 Jul 45	2 Aug 45	A-bracket bushes re-metaled
HMS *Swiftsure*	31 Jul 45	7 Aug 45	Minor repairs to tanks
HMAS *Ping Wo*	3 Aug 45	8 Aug 45	Minor hull repairs
HMS *Bermuda*	7 Aug 45	15 Aug 45	Minor hull, machinery and electrical repairs, new staff accommodation fitted out
HMAS *Warrego*	8 Aug 45	27 Aug 45	Joiners and general repairs
HMS *Lothian*	12 Aug 45	17 Aug 45	Minor repairs
HMAS *Hawkesbury*	18 Aug 45	23 Aug 45	Minor repairs and sonar examination
HMS *Ulysses*	22 Aug 45	21 Sep 45	Bow repairs, new plating fitted, general repairs
HMAS *Manoora*	22 Aug 45	25 Aug 45	Minor engine repairs
HMS *Formidable*	25 Aug 45	19 Sep 45	Joiners and structural repairs.
HMS *Implacable*	25 Aug 45	10 Sep 45	Renewal of insulation in cold and cool rooms, minor engine repairs

APPENDIX 9

SHIP'S BOILERS BUILT DURING WORLD WAR II

Type	No.	H.P.	Evaporation (lbs/hour)	Shipyard	Ships
Yarrow water tube	4	2 750	53 100	Cockatoo	*Barcoo Barwon*
Yarrow water tube	8	2 750	53 100	Mort's Dock	*Gascoyne Hawkesbury Lachlan Macquarie*
Yarrow water tube	6	2 750	53 100	Walkers	*Burdekin Diamantina Shoalhaven*
Yarrow water tube	4	2 750	53 100	Evans Deakin	*Murcheson Warburton*
Yarrow water tube	4	2 750	53 100	Williamstown	*Culgoa Murrumbidgee*
Yarrow water tube	9	15 000	133 000	Cockatoo	*Arunta Warramunga Bataan*
Yarrow water tube	4	1 000	17 800	Cockatoo	*Parramatta Warrego*
Babcock & Wilcox	2	1 750	21 500	Cockatoo	*River Clarence River Hunter*
Scotch	6	425	20 250	Cockatoo	*Koala Karangi Kangaroo*
Water tube	14	1 000	14 000	various	D Class freighters
Yarrow water tube	6	875	16 700	Cockatoo	*Bathurst Bendigo Goulburn*
Yarrow water tube	10	875	16 700	Mort's Dock	*Lismore Burnie Lithgow Mildura Warrnambool*
Yarrow water tube	4	875	16 700	MHT	*Ballarat Geelong*
Yarrow water tube	6	875	16 700	Walkers	*Maryborough Toowoomba Rockhampton*
Yarrow water tube	4	875	16 700	BHP Whyalla	*Whyalla Kalgourlie*
Yarrow water tube	2	875	16 700	Poole & Steel	*Katoomba*
Yarrow water tube	2	875	16 700	Evans Deakin	*Townsville*
Yarrow water tube	10	1 000	20 800	Cockatoo	*Wollongong Cessnock Madras Bengal*
Yarrow water tube	20	1 000	20 800	Mort's Dock	*Glenelg Deloraine Wagga Colac Armidale Dubbo Punjab Bombay Inverell Latrobe*
Yarrow water tube	8	1 000	20 800	Evans Deakin	*Launceston Ipswich Broome Bundaberg Gympie Fremantle Ararat Kiama*
Yarrow water tube	8	1 000	20 800	Poole & Steel	*Geraldton Wallaroo Kapunda Cootamundra*
Yarrow water tube	10	1 000	20 800	MHT	*Castlemaine Echuca Horsham Shepparton Benalla*
Yarrow water tube	4	1 000	20 800	BHP Whyalla	*Pirie Gawler*
Yarrow water tube	6	1 000	20 800	Walkers	*Tamworth Cairns Bowen*

APPENDIX 10

NAVAL SURFACE SHIP REFITS AND REPAIRS AFTER 1945

SHIP	TYPE	WORK DONE	STARTED	FINISHED
HMAS *Arunta*	Destroyer	Modernisation refit	1 Sep 50	12 Nov 52
HMAS *Bataan*	Destroyer	Refit	18 Jun 51	Aug 52
HMAS *Swan*	Training frigate	Refit	25 Sep 61	24 Nov 61
HMAS *Supply*	Fleet tanker	Refit	11 Dec 62	Jan 63
HMAS *Melbourne*	Aircraft carrier	Collision damage repair	12 Feb 64	27 Apr 64
HMAS *Sydney*	Troop carrier	Refit	4 Jul 67	23 Feb 68
HMAS *Vampire*	Destroyer	Refit	27 Oct 67	16 Apr 68
HMAS *Stalwart*	Destroyer tender	Occasional docking	28 Mar 68	10 Apr 68
HMAS *Queenborough*	Frigate	Refit	14 Jun 68	16 Sep 68
HMAS *Ibis*	Minesweeper	Refit	26 Aug 68	1 Apr 69
HMAS *Supply*	Fleet tanker	Refit	1 Nov 68	8 Apr 69
HMAS *Vendetta*	Destroyer	Refit	17 Feb 69	3 Jul 69
HMAS *Ardent*	Patrol boat	Fire damage repairs	22 May 69	9 Sep 69
HMAS *Sydney*	Troop carrier	Refit	17 Jun 69	3 Nov 69
HMAS *Attack*	Patrol boat	Refit	27 Jun 69	5 Sep 69
HMAS *Melbourne*	Aircraft carrier	Collision damage repair	16 Jul 69	11 Oct 69
HMAS *Aitape*	Patrol boat	Refit	4 Aug 69	25 Nov 69
HMAS *Advance*	Patrol boat	Refit	9 Sep 69	19 Dec 69
HMAS *Queenborough*	Frigate	Refit	1 Oct 69	2 Feb 70
HMAS *Supply*	Fleet tanker	Refit	28 Nov 69	24 Apr 70
HMAS *Aware*	Patrol boat	Refit	30 Dec 69	9 Mar 70
OFL 2	Oil fuel lighter	Refit	15 Jan 70	3 Nov 70
HMAS *Lae*	Patrol boat	Refit	2 Feb 70	17 Apr 70
HMAS *Ardent*	Patrol boat	Refit	9 Mar 70	25 Aug 70
HMAS *Arrow*	Patrol boat	Refit	20 Mar 70	28 May 70
HMAS *Barbette*	Patrol boat	Refit	27 Apr 70	13 Aug 70
MWL 254	Motor water lighter	Refit	18 May 70	26 Nov 70
HMAS *Assail*	Patrol boat	Refit	1 Jun 70	16 Sep 70
HMAS *Ladava*	Patrol boat	Refit	6 Jul 70	15 Oct 70
HMAS *Adroit*	Patrol boat	Refit	14 Sep 70	16 Nov 70
HMAS *Queenborough*	Frigate	Refit	14 Oct 70	30 Mar 71
HMAS *Barricade*	Patrol boat	Refit	19 Oct 70	3 Mar 71
HMAS *Madang*	Patrol boat	Refit	23 Nov 70	22 Mar 71
HMAS *Supply*	Fleet tanker	Refit	16 Dec 70	16 Nov 71
HMAS *Bombard*	Patrol boat	Refit	14 Jan 71	10 May 71
HMAS *Ardent*	Patrol boat	Refit	9 Feb 71	2 Jun 71
HMAS *Buccaneer*	Patrol boat	Refit	29 Mar 71	31 Aug 71
HMAS *Attack*	Patrol boat	Refit	21 Jun 71	26 Oct 71
HMAS *Aitape*	Patrol boat	Refit	10 Aug 71	20 Jan 72
HMAS *Aware*	Patrol boat	Refit	5 Oct 71	3 Mar 72
HMAS *Hawk*	Minesweeper	Refit	1 Nov 71	Never finished
HMAS *Advance*	Patrol boat	Refit	29 Nov 71	29 Mar 72
HMAS *Bandolier*	Patrol boat	Refit	17 Jan 72	14 Mar 72
HMAS *Arrow*	Patrol boat	Refit	28 Feb 72	23 May 72
HMAS *Kimbla*	Oceanographic ship	Refit	4 Apr 72	21 Aug 72
HMAS *Lae*	Patrol boat	Refit	17 Apr 72	31 Jul 72
HMAS *Assail*	Patrol boat	Refit	16 Jun 72	31 Aug 72
HMAS *Paluma*	Survey ship	Refit	16 Jun 72	14 Sep 72

(continued)

HMAS *Ladava*	Patrol boat	Refit	31 Jul 72	10 Oct 72
HMAS *Adroit*	Patrol boat	Refit	4 Sep 72	14 Nov 72
HMAS *Archer*	Patrol boat	Refit	25 Sep 72	15 Dec 72
HMAS *Teal*	Minesweeper	Intermediate docking	27 Nov 72	21 Dec 72
HMAS *Bombard*	Patrol boat	Refit	4 Dec 72	16 Mar 73
HMAS *Madang*	Patrol boat	Refit	26 Apr 73	14 Aug 73
HMAS *Buccaneer*	Patrol boat	Refit	10 Jul 73	6 Sep 73
HMAS *Bandolier*	Patrol boat	Refit	22 Aug 73	19 Oct 73
HMAS *Ardent*	Patrol boat	Refit	5 Nov 73	25 Jan 74
HMAS *Aware*	Patrol boat	Refit	18 Feb 74	11 Jun 74
HMAS *Arrow*	Patrol boat	Refit	29 Apr 74	25 Jul 74
HMAS *Archer*	Patrol boat	Refit	8 Jul 74	19 Sep 74
HMAS *Adroit*	Patrol boat	Refit	8 Oct 74	19 Dec 74
HMAS *Snipe*	Minesweeper	Intermediate docking	2 Dec 74	20 Jan 75
HMAS *Curlew*	Minesweeper	Intermediate docking	2 Dec 74	20 Jan 75
HMAS *Bombard*	Patrol boat	Refit	6 Feb 75	24 Apr 75
HMAS *Buccaneer*	Patrol boat	Refit	30 Jun 75	12 Sep 75
HMAS *Duchess*	Destroyer	Refit	6 Oct 75	6 Jan 76
HMAS *Ardent*	Patrol boat	Refit	2 Feb 76	2 Apr 76
HMAS *Duchess*	Destroyer	Refit	5 Jul 76	24 Sep 76
HMAS *Stalwart*	Destroyer tender	Intermediate docking	5 Jul 76	28 Jul 76
HMAS *Aware*	Patrol boat	Refit	30 Aug 76	4 Nov 76
HMAS *Yarra*	Destroyer escort	Half-life refit	11 Oct 76	1 Feb 78
HMAS *Stalwart*	Destroyer Tender	Refit	21 Feb 77	26 May 77
HMAS *Supply*	Fleet tanker	Refit	18 Apr 77	24 Aug 77
HMAS *Bombard*	Patrol boat	Refit	10 Apr 78	24 Jul 78
HMAS *Swan*	Destroyer escort	Intermediate docking	6 Jun 78	14 Aug 78
HMAS *Jervis Bay*	Training ship	Refit	26 Jun 78	26 Sep 78
HMAS *Buccaneer*	Patrol boat	Refit	3 Oct 78	5 Dec 78
HMAS *Derwent*	Destroyer escort	Intermediate docking	10 Nov 78	20 Dec 78
HMAS *Yarra*	Destroyer escort	Intermediate docking	5 Feb 79	23 Mar 79
HMAS *Jervis Bay*	Training ship	Refit	25 Jun 79	10 Sep 79
HMAS *Stalwart*	Destroyer tender	Intermediate docking	12 Nov 79	21 Dec 79
HMAS *Jervis Bay*	Training ship	Refit	17 Jun 80	3 Oct 80
USNS *Yukon*	Tanker	Collision damage repair	11 Feb 82	14 Mar 82
HMAS *Canberra*	Frigate	Occasional docking	30 Nov 82	20 Dec 82
HMAS *Supply*	Fleet tanker	Intermediate docking	16 Nov 84	25 Jan 85
HMAS *Adelaide*	Frigate	Occasional docking	9 Jan 86	31 Jan 86
HMAS *Tobruk*	Amphibious heavy lift ship	Refit	20 Jan 86	3 Jul 86
HMAS *Stuart*	Destroyer escort	Mid-cycle docking	21 May 86	4 Jun 86
HMAS *Success*	Fleet underway replenishment ship	Post-delivery availability	9 Oct 86	27 Feb 87
HMAS *Stuart*	Destroyer escort	Refit	28 Feb 87	23 Oct 87
HMAS *Jervis Bay*	Training ship	Occasional docking	24 Apr 87	29 May 87
HMAS *Stalwart*	Destroyer tender	Intermediate docking	11 Jun 87	5 Aug 87
HMAS *Parramatta*	Destroyer escort	Intermediate docking	17 Aug 87	25 Sep 87
HMAS *Jervis Bay*	Training ship	Assisted maintenance period	16 Nov 87	18 Dec 87
HMAS *Tobruk*	Amphibious heavy lift ship	Intermediate docking	23 Nov 87	18 Dec 87
HMAS *Torrens*	Destroyer escort	Intermediate docking	21 Mar 88	6 May 88
HMAS *Jervis Bay*	Training ship	Refit	15 Mar 89	23 Aug 89

APPENDIX 11

SUBMARINE REFITS

SUBMARINE	STARTED	COMPLETED	REMARKS
HMAS J 5	8 Aug 19	1 May 20	General overhaul and docking
HMAS J 4	11 Aug 19	12 Feb 20	General overhaul and docking
HMAS J 1	16 Aug 19	29 Dec 19	General overhaul and docking, in conjunction with Garden Island Dockyard
HMAS J 2	9 Dec 19	17 Jan 20	General overhaul and docking, in conjunction with Garden Island Dockyard
HMAS J 3	11 Dec 19	23 Mar 21	General overhaul and docking, in conjunction with Garden Island Dockyard, work suspended 23 Mar 1921, all shop orders closed 22 Jul 1921
HMAS J 7	13 Jan 20	23 Mar 21	General overhaul and docking, work suspended 23 Mar 1921 and all shop orders closed 28 Jun 1921
HMAS J 7	14 Jul 21	15 May 22	Completion of refit cancelled 28 Jun 1921
HMAS J 3	18 Jul 21	27 Sep 21	Refit and battery repairs
HMAS J 2	9 Aug 21	29 Apr 22	General overhaul and docking
K XIII	26 May 42	9 Aug 42	Extensive hull, engine and electrical repairs
HMS Tabard	9 Jan 61	26 Mar 62	First T class submarine refit undertaken at Cockatoo Dockyard
HMS Trump	19 Jan 62	8 Apr 63	Extensive weld repairs to pressure hull plates with Araldite coating to prevent further deterioration
HMS Taciturn	15 Jan 63	28 Mar 64	Last refit for this submarine, pressure hull plate 27 ft x 5 ft replaced, extensive repairs to systems due to generally poor condition
HMS Tabard	9 Oct 64	10 Dec 6	Last refit for this submarine, extensive repairs to aluminium fin and casings and salt water systems, commissioned at Cockatoo Island on 10 December 1965
HMS Trump	28 Aug 65	10 Oct 66	Last refit for this submarine. Work extensive but routine, commissioned at Cockatoo Island on 10 October 1966
HMAS Oxley	29 Mar 71	23 Mar 73	First Oberon class submarine refit at Cockatoo Dockyard
HMAS Otway	28 Jun 72	12 Jun 74	
HMAS Ovens	10 Sep 73	30 Oct 75	
HMAS Onslow	24 Mar 75	21 Apr 77	Navy budget control procedure (mandatory/non-mandatory system), tried for this refit, resulted in considerable work growth during tests and trials due to failure of equipment not included in work package
HMAS Oxley	4 Oct 77	18 Dec 79	Submarine arrived 25 July 1977 for pre refit work, effective start was 4 October 1977, first Submarine Weapons Update Programme (SWUP) refit
HMAS Otway	8 Jan 79	30 Apr 81	Major fire in February 1979, refit affected by shorter working week campaign, SWUP modernisation

(*continued*)

HMAS *Ovens*	10 Mar 80	12 Aug 82	Refit adversely affected by the shorter working week campaign, including six week strike in August and September 1981, SWUP modernisation
HMAS *Orion*	11 May 81	12 Aug 83	Refit affected by shorter working week campaign including six week strike in August and September 1981, SWUP modernisation
HMAS *Onslow*	23 Aug 82	21 Sep 84	SWUP modernisation refit
HMAS *Otama*	26 Jul 83	12 Sep 85	Work included rearrangement of Gyro Compass room, full SWUP weapons fit, and renewal of bow torpedo tube runners
HMAS *Oxley*	7 Jan 85	12 Feb 87	Work included fitting seat to forward escape tower for DSRV, upgrading SFCS to Mod 1 status, and fitting of sonar analysis system
HMAS *Otway*	17 Jun 86	9 Sep 88	Refit extended by major pressure hull repair over generator room, and shortage of spares, major work on bow tube runners, comcentre and blanking of countermeasure tubes
HMAS *Ovens*	23 Sep 87	11 Apr 90	Refit included comcentre rebuild, pressure hull repair over generator room, blanking counter measure tubes, bow tube runners, 3 and 5 main ballast tanks conversion, and DSRV fit, delayed by 14-week strike in 1989 over pending government decisions on future of submarine refitting
HMAS *Orion*	28 Nov 88	4 Jun 91	Comcentre rebuild and sonar/ESM changes. delayed by 14-week strike in 1989 over pending government decisions on future of submarine refitting

APPENDIX 12

DOCKING AND SLIPPING OF SHIPS AT COCKATOO DOCKYARD

FITZROY DOCK

DIMENSION	AS COMPLETED	FINAL
Length from caisson (inner fit)	260 ft (approx)	474 ft 7 in
Length from caisson (outer fit)	282 ft (approx)	496 ft 11 in
Maximum width of entrance	58 ft 8 in	58 ft 8 in
Width of sill at entrance	44 ft	44 ft
Depth of water over sill, ISLW	14 ft 11.5 in	14 ft 11.5 in

(ISLW = Indian Spring Low Water, zero on the Fort Denison tide gauge after 1 January 1954.)

SUTHERLAND DOCK

Dimension	AS COMPLETED	FINAL
Length, caisson in inner fit	638 ft	720 ft
Length, caisson in outer fit	608 ft	690 ft
Maximum width at entrance	84 ft	87 ft 11 in
Depth of water over sill, ISLW	25 ft 10.5 in	25 ft 10.5 in

ADMIRALTY FLOATING DOCK *AFD 17*

Built by Devonport Dockyard, 1942

Lifting capacity	2 750 tons
Overall length over platforms	380 ft
Overall length of dock	350 ft
Overall width of dock	72 ft
Clear width between fenders	50 ft
Overall depth of pontoon	8 ft 6 in
Overall length of side wall	325 ft
Overall height of side wall	26 ft 6 in
Overall width of side wall	8 ft
'Tween deck height	9 ft 6 in

SLAVE DOCK *SD 3201*

Built by Cockatoo Dockyard, 1975

Lifting capacity	1 900 tons
Overall length	320 ft
Length, between bulkheads	288 ft
Beam, moulded	55 ft
Beam, extreme (over fenders)	56 ft 8 in
Depth, at centre line	9 ft 6 in

DOCKING RECORDS

In 1865 Gother Mann, the engineer in chief of the Fitzroy Dry Dock reported to the under secretary of Public Works on progress at the dock. He included a return of vessels docked from the opening of the Fitzroy Dock to 30 April 1865. As shown below, 163 vessels were docked in that period.

	1857	1858	1859	1860	1861	1862	1862	1864	1865
Warships	1	7	7	5	5	14	8	13	6
Merchant vessels	0	0	1	11	8	39	13	16	9
TOTAL	1	7	8	16	13	53	21	29	15
									(to 30 April)

For the period 1891 to 1910 the number of ships docked each year are recorded in most of the Annual Reports of the Public Works Department. These figures are shown in the table below.

	1891	1892	1893	1898	1899	1900	1901	1902
HM Ships	17	20	17	27	29	24	22	23
Foreign warships	0	1	1	0	0	0	4	4
Government vessels	44	65	61	92	96	88	84	101
Merchant ships	8	4	5	31	30	46	51	32
TOTAL	69	90	84	150	155	158	161	160

	1903	1904	1905	1906	1907	1908	1909	1910
HM Ships	30	20	21	18	15	15	19	14
Foreign warships	0	0	0	0	0	0	0	0
Government vessels	70	60	50	68	60	55	74	78
Merchant ships	2	10	2	2	6	9	6	3
TOTAL	102	90	73	88	83	79	99	95

John Bastock in *Ships on the Australia Station* provides information that can be used to determine the number of ships on the Australia Station between 1856 and 1914. Using these numbers and the actual number of warships docked in each year for which records exist, an average number of dockings per ship on the Station can be calculated. Some ships would have been docked away from Sydney after 1874 (when the Alfred Graving Dock was opened in Melbourne). Some would have been hauled down or slipped elsewhere in earlier years. The average docking rate can therefore be applied to the period for which records are unavailable without risk of overestimating the number of dockings. Such an analysis does not include the dockings of visiting ships, or indeed of Colonial Navy ships, and so is likely to be conservative.

A major source of docking work for the Fitzroy Dock would have been government vessels such as dredges, barges, tugs and other Colonial Government ships, particularly after the Public Works Department took control of the Fitzroy Dock. It seems reasonable to assume a gradual build-up in the number of such dockings in the years leading up to the first recorded figure of 44 in 1891.

The conditions on the use of the docks at Cockatoo during the nineteenth century stated that Cockatoo was not to compete with private docks. A commercial graving dock of a similar size to the Fitzroy Dock was available in Sydney (Mort's Dock in Balmain) as well as floating docks and slipways. Therefore the number of dockings each year might not have exceeded the figure of about five per year that occurred in the early 1890s.

These assumptions suggest that some 3400 ships could have been docked at Cockatoo Island between 1857 and 1911, including about 825 naval vessels.

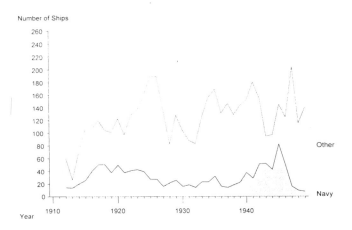

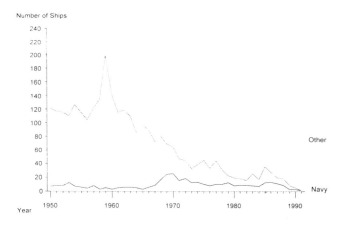

The dockings in the period 1912 to 1991 are well documented in the Docking Books. These books record 3614 ships as having docked in the Sutherland Dock, 2304 in the Fitzroy Dock, 641 in *AFD 17*, 1009 on the patent slipway on the eastern shore, 509 on the patent slipway in Timber Bay, and 510 on the boat slip. A further eight are recorded as having been lifted out by crane and placed on a wharf, or in the northern of the old coal bunkers at the power station, which was used for that purpose for a number of years. The total is therefore 8595.

The records for the boat slip are not complete. This slipway was used for small craft, such as dockyard launches. It was very busy in the early decades of this century slipping many small craft for the dockyard and other customers. The records are intermittent after 1933, suggesting either much less use, or more likely, a change in record keeping practices.

The total number of dockings and slippings at Cockatoo Island between 1857 and 1991 would appear to be about 12 000. Charts indicating the total number of dockings each year since 1912 and 1991 and the number of naval dockings in the same period are shown at left.

APPENDIX 13

CORPORATE INFORMATION

CHIEF EXECUTIVE OFFICERS OF THE DOCKYARD AFTER 1913

Mr A E Cutler (acting)	1913–1914
Mr John J King Salter RCNC	1914–1920
Mr James W Clark (acting)	1920–1923
Mr Robert Farquhar MINA	1923–1928
Mr Jack Payne MIEAust MIMarE MINA	1928–1932
Mr John Wilson (acting)	1932–1933
Mr Norman Frazer	1933–1947
Engr Captain G I D Hutcheson CBE BE FIEAust RAN (Retd)	1947–1962
Captain Roger Parker OBE RAN (Retd)	1962–1971
Captain R R W Humbley BEc RAN (Retd)	1971–1981
Mr John C Jeremy BE CPEng FIEAust FRINA	1981–1991

DIRECTORS OF THE COMPANY

Cockatoo Docks & Engineering Company Limited	1933–1937
Cockatoo Docks & Engineering Company Pty Limited	1937–1972
Vickers Cockatoo Dockyard Pty Limited	1972–1984
Cockatoo Dockyard Pty Limited	after 1984

NAME	POSITION	FROM	TO
Maurice Davis		Feb 1933	Mar 1947
Norman Frazer	Managing Director 1933–47 Chairman 1947–49	Feb 1933	Sep 1949
Sir George Francis Davis +	Chairman 1933–47	Feb 1933	Aug 1947
Frederick David Michaelis +		Feb 1933	Nov 1937
Edward Hallenstein +		Feb 1933	Apr 1946
Victor Herbert Barr-Smith		Feb 1933	Feb 1938
Sir Thomas Stewart Gordon		Nov 1933	Jun 1948
Charles Christopher Davis +		Jan 1934	Sep 1949
Sir Keith Smith KBE +	Chairman 1949–55	Nov 1937	Dec 1955
Commander Sir Robert Micklem CBE RN (Retd)		Mar 1947	Apr 1952
Engr Captain G I D Hutcheson CBE RAN (Retd) +	Managing Director 1948–62 Chairman 1962–65	Sep 1947	Sep 1965
Sir Alan G Potter		Jun 1948	Dec 1962
Sir James Reid Young		Mar 1949	Dec 1954
Archibald Campbell		Nov 1951	Sep 1963
Major General Sir Charles Dunphie CB CBE DSO		Jul 1952	Jun 1962
Henry Edward Morgan +		Jan 1953	Mar 1959
Charles Inglis		Jan 1953	Jun 1955
George H Houlden MBE		Jan 1955	Feb 1966
Aubrey R L Wiltshire CMG DSO MC VD	Chairman 1956–62	Apr 1956	Nov 1962
Captain Roger G Parker OBE RAN (Retd)	Managing Director 1962–71	Mar 1959	Oct 1971
Arthur P Wickens		Jun 1962	Jun 1972
Ronald William Joselin		Feb 1963	Jan 1976
Stanley J Fisher		Oct 1963	Sep 1969
Edward Patrick Mawbey Harty	Chairman 1965–81	Sep 1965	May 1981
Albert Haig Thompson		Nov 1965	Aug 1971

(*continued*)

Peter Douglas Scott Maxwell DSC		Jun 1967	Mar 1986
Captain Richard Rex Wells Humbley RAN (Retd)	Managing Director 1971–81	Feb 1971	Dec 1984
Ronald Francis Jones		Dec 1971	Aug 1986
Sir John Gardner Wilson CBE		Jan 1972	Oct 1984
Sir Gregory Blaxland Kater +		Jan 1972	Jul 1978
Gavin Macrae Bunning		Jan 1972	May 1981
Sir Leonard Redshaw		Jan 1972	Jun 1976
John Christopher Jeremy	Managing Director 1981–86	Jan 1976	Aug 1986
Jack Coleman		Jan 1976	Jun 1978
Peter John Pannell	Chairman 1981–86	Aug 1976	Mar 1986
·Colin James Harper		Aug 1976	Mar 1986
William Richardson CBE DL		Mar 1977	Mar 1984
Thomas Charles Nicol Yandell		Oct 1981	Aug 1986
Roger Ian Seymour		Apr 1982	Mar 1986
John B Reid AO		May 1984	Mar 1996
Sidney John Hines		May 1984	Aug 1986
D. Jock Dalziel		Aug 1984	Aug 1986
Ian R Russell		Dec 1984	Mar 1986
Neil Ross Jones	Chairman 1986–89	Jan 1986	Jun 1989
Robert James Cox		Jan 1986	Feb 1990
John Philip Maher		Jan 1986	Jun 1989
Michael J E Houghton		Dec 1986	Jun 1989
Henry Evan Rees		Oct 1988	Feb 1996
Donald Woolgar Bourke		Jun 1989	Sep 1991
Paul George Reading		Feb 1990	Jul 1995
Peter George Edward Fitch		Jul 1995	Sep 1996
Peter William Stancliffe		Feb 1996	
Russell Langtry Chenu		Nov 1995	
Ross Murdoch Bunyon		Sep 1996	

(+ Died in office)

FINANCIAL RESULTS 1933 TO 1991

FINANCIAL YEAR (ENDING)	SALES	NET PROFIT (BEFORE TAX)
Feb 1934	(£) 139 870	(£) 743
Feb 1935	249 154	5 838
Feb 1936	366 472	6 819
Feb 1937	341 763	7 021
Feb 1938	354 965	24 217
Feb 1939	673 554	30 470
Feb 1940	1 050 078	42 381
Feb 1941	1 837 329	43 420
Feb 1942	1 930 320	42 939
Feb 1943	1 872 838	48 330
Feb 1944	1 659 141	45 656
Feb 1945	1 246 912	37 880
Feb 1946	1 283 544	38 334
Feb 1947	Not available	Not available
Feb 1948	Not available	Not available
Feb 1949	Not available	Not available
Oct 1949 (8 mths)	1 445 808	26 710
Oct 1950	2 349 164	37 355
Oct 1951	2 399 531	41 758
Oct 1952	2 887 945	43 852
Oct 1953	3 060 896	42 587
Oct 1954	2 365 654	37 535
Oct 1955	2 595 130	47 813
Oct 1956	3 035 975	65 390
Oct 1957	2 735 383	55 370
Oct 1958	2 969 234	63 471
Oct 1959	2 923 528	63 610
Oct 1960	3 002 616	67 907
Oct 1961	2 977 319	69 885
Oct 1962	2 911 988	57 617
Oct 1963	3 494 663	67 729
Oct 1964	3 323 697	(243 554)
Oct 1965	3 495 604	46 846
Oct 1966	($) 7 681 076	($) 123 974
Oct 1967	8 870 159	136 904
Oct 1968	8 027 291	152 738
Dec 1969 (14 mths)	10 548 825	161 641
Dec 1970	9 074 876	112 968
Dec 1971	10 061 477	149 752
Dec 1972	17 281 000	173 417
Dec 1973	9 916 000	210 969
Dec 1974	13 403 000	219 513
Dec 1975	14 860 000	336 262
Dec 1976	16 135 000	305 835
Dec 1977	29 394 000	821 318
Dec 1978	22 425 000	703 237
Dec 1979	22 885 000	552 058
Dec 1980	30 251 000	905 603
Dec 1981	29 472 000	1 146 422
Dec 1982	41 046 000	1 809 952

(*continued*)

Dec 1983	($) 44 041 000	($) 4 000 205
Jun 1984(six months)	22 199 985	1 144 377
Jun 1985	47 338 994	3 333 232
Jun 1986	197 304 629	4 123 626
Jun 1987	66 974 257	2 850 537
Jun 1988	65 413 577	4 624 353
Jun 1989	55 467 727	4 111 896
Jun 1990	52 973 267	4 444 652
Jun 1991	43 507 656	6 295 443

NUMBER OF EMPLOYEES

Records of the number of employees at Cockatoo Dockyard are not readily available before 1913. Since then the number of employees has varied greatly from year to year, reflecting the lack of continuity of the work-load and the nature of the shipbuilding and ship repair business. The greatest number ever on the dockyard's books was 4085 on 31 December 1919. The approximate average total number of employees each year since 1913 is shown in the graph below.

ENDNOTES

CHAPTER ONE

1. 'Cockatoo Island', *Sydney Gazette and New South Wales Advertiser*, no. 4140, 23 February 1839.
2. James Semple Kerr, *Cockatoo Island, penal and institutional remains*, National Trust of Australia (NSW), 1984.
3. *Report of Select Committee on public prisons in Sydney and Cumberland*, New South Wales Leglislative Assembly, 9 May 1861, p. 6.
4. Kerr, *op. cit.*, p. 11.
5. *Last of Biloela: old time gaol to be pulled down*, 1 February 1908, (extract from Biloela Gaol: Newspaper cuttings, Volume 9, pp. 85–87, held at Mitchell Library).

CHAPTER TWO

6. *Historical records of Australia*, vol. XXIV, p. 611.
7. This communicataion from the Admiralty is included in: *Report of the Royal Commission of Inquiry into the workings and administration of the government docks and workshops at Cockatoo Island*, Leglislative Assembly of New South Wales, 1903, p. 2.
8. *ibid.*
9. Emery Balint, *Construction of the Fitzroy Dock, Cockatoo Island*, Engineering Heritage, 1985.
10. The original caisson remained in service until 1932, and was kept at the island for a number of years. It can been seen at the Sutherland Wharf in the excellent series of aerial photographs of the island taken on 23 February 1944.
11. *Report from the Select Committee on the Fitz Roy dry dock*, Legislative Assembly of New South Wales, 22 May 1860, p. 17.
12. *Report of the Royal Commission* etc., 1903, *op. cit.*
13. *ibid.*
14. Gother Mann died at Greenwich (Sydney) on 1 January 1889, at the age of 89 years and 10 months.
15. E O Moriarty, *Docks: Report of Engineer in Chief for Harbours and Rivers on the subject of docks generally, bearing upon the proposal of the government to construct a new first class dock at Cockatoo Island*, Leglislative Assembly, New South Wales, 10 March 1874.
16. *ibid.*, p. 11.
17. *ibid.*, p. 12.
18. *Report of the Royal Commission* etc., 1903, p. 3.
19. Erich Gröner, *Die deutschen Kriegsschiffe 1815–1945*, J F Lehmanns Verlag, München, 1966.
20. *Report of the Royal Commission* etc., 1903, p. 3.
21. Charles F Morris, *Origins, Orient and Oriana*, Teredo Books, Brighton, 1980.
22. Oscar Parkes, *British Battleships*, Seeley Service & Co., London, 1966.
23. Edward William Young, 'Biloela Graving-Dock, Cockatoo Island, Sydney Harbour, NSW', *Minutes of Proceedings of the Institute of Civil Engineers*, vol. CXI.
24. See *Plan of Alteration of Sutherland Dock*, 1911, National Archives, CRS C3539/1, item E212.

CHAPTER THREE

25. *Report from the Select Committee on the Fitz Roy* etc., 1860.
26. *ibid.*, p. 3.
27. Access to the docks at Cockatoo Island by other ship repair firms in Sydney remained a contentious issue for life of the dockyard. They claimed that the priority given to naval ships denied them reasonable access, as the docks were always extensively booked out by the Navy. In fact, they were usually able to book the docks like any ship owner, but tended to seek bookings at short notice whereas the Navy program was often established many months in advance.
28. *Docks, slips, and engineering establishments of Port Jackson*, p. 1, extract of a publication held at Mitchell Library at 627.3/1A1. This document includes the 'Fitzroy Dock Conditions and Scale of Charges', dated 20 January 1864.

29. *ibid.*, p. 2. The name of the French ironclad is correctly spelled *Atalante*.

30. John Bach, *Australia Station: a history of the Royal Navy in the south west Pacific 1821–1913*, University of New South Wales Press, 1986, p. 219.

31. *ibid.*, p. 219. Bach says: 'The commander-in-chief was able to describe the docking facilities available to him at Sydney, Melbourne, Auckland, Lyttleton, Dunedin and other places as "extremely good", all of them belonging to government or port trusts and available free of charge.' The 'Fitzroy Dock Conditions etc.', of January 1864 (see note 28 above), p. 2, included: '1. All vessels belonging to H M Navy, the Colonial Government, and men-of-war of other nations, will be admitted to repair in the Fitzroy Dock, Sydney Harbour, free of any dock dues or rates, but they will be required to repay all actual expenditure of stores, wages, and material.'

32. Ross Gillett and Michael Melliar-Phelps, *A century of ships in Sydney Harbour*, Rigby, 1980, p. 24; Issey Wyner, *With banner unfurled: the early years of the Ship Painters and Dockers Union*, Hale & Ironmonger, Sydney, 1983, p. 54; Morris, *op. cit.*, p. 64.

33. See: *Annual reports of the Public Works Department: Harbours and Rivers Branch*, for the period 1891–1903; and *Reports of the managing committee of the Government Dockyard, Biloela*, for 1904–1910.

34. There may be some duplication in the numbers of barges and punts in this total. Some indication of the number of ships built before 1912 is given by the allocation by the Government Dockyard of Ship Nos 121, 122, 123 and 124 to the torpedo boat destroyers and the cruiser *Brisbane*.

35. *Annual report of the Department of Public Works for the year 1892*, Legislative Assembly, New South Wales, 1893, p. 23.

36. *Report of the Royal Commission* etc., 1903, *op. cit.*

37. *ibid.*, p. 3.

38. Government Dockyard, Biloela, *Report of the managing committee for year ended 30th June, 1909*, (contained in the *Annual report of the Public Works Department* etc., for that year).

39. John Mortimer, 'HMAS *Huon*: Australia's first locally constructed destroyer', *The Navy*, July 1984.

CHAPTER FOUR

40. Engineer Captain Clarkson to Secretary Department of the Navy, Letter 11/059, 3 November 1911, CRS MP1049/1.

41. *Report of the Joint Committee of Public Accounts upon the Commonwealth Naval Dockyard, Cockatoo Island, New South Wales*, Parliament of the Commonwealth of Australia, October 1915.

42. T R Frame, *Garden Island*, Kangaroo Press, 1990, p. 169.

43. *Defence: Cockatoo Island Dockyard: papers re. boilers etc.*, Parliament of the Commonwealth of Australia, September 1913.

44. *Report of the Joint Committee* etc., 1915, *op. cit.*, p. 12.

45. *ibid.*

46. *ibid.*

47. This report is cited in Robert Hyslop, *Australian naval administration 1900–1939*, Hawthorn Press, 1973, p. 137.

48. *Report of the Joint Committee* etc., 1915, *op. cit.*, p. 19. The remaining Cockatoo Dockyard records show three different figures for the final cost of the *Brisbane*: £576 504, £556 253/5/1 and £746 454. These figures may simply reflect the inclusion of different categories of cost.

49. *Cockatoo Island Dockyard, Report of Royal Commission*, Parliament of the Commonwealth of Australia, 12 July 1921.

50. *ibid.*, p. 4.

51. *ibid.*, p. 10.

52. *Cockatoo Island Dockyard, Report of Royal Commission* etc., *Minority report*, p. 3.

53. *ibid.*

54. Joint Committee of Public Accounts, *Report on the Commonwealth Government shipping activities including Cockatoo Island Dockyard*, Parliament of the Commonwealth of Australia, November 1927 p. 25.

55. *ibid.*, p. 27.

56. Commonwealth vs Australian Commonwealth Shipping Board (1926) 39 CLR 1, p. 4.

57. *ibid.*, p. 9.

58. The Attorney-General, the Hon. John Latham CMG KC in debate 17 March 1927 on the Supply Bill (No. 1) 1927–28, *Commonwealth of Australia parliamentary debates*, vol. 115, p. 545.

59. J D Scott, *Vickers: a history*, Weidenfeld and Nicholson, London, 1963.

60. This is as described in P-E Consulting Group (Australia), *Overall plan for development of Cockatoo Island Dockyard*, 6 September 1967.
61. Peter Scott Maxwell's wartime experiences in the submarine service were typical of his determined approach to everyday problems. Some of his experiences as engineering officer in the submarine HMS *Tally-Ho* are described in Ian Trenowden, *Hunting submarine, the fighting life of HMS* Tally-Ho, William Kimber and Co., 1974.
62. Harold Evans, *Vickers: against the odds 1956/77*, Hodder and Stoughton, 1978.
63. Minister for Defence, *Defence shipbuilding decisions*, media release NO41/87, 1 April 1987.
64. *ibid.*
65. Pers. com. Treasurer, Paul Keating, to author, June 1990.
66. The Cockatoo Dockyard legal team was led initially by R J Ellicott QC, and later by T E F Hughes QC. Both had been Attorneys General of the Commonwealth of Australia during their political careers. They were assisted by T G R Parker and instructed by Allen Allen and Hemsley. Senior Counsel for the Commonwealth included C R Einstein QC, T K Tobin QC, D M Bennett QC, D F Jackson QC, B W Rayment QC and R Burbidge QC. With supporting junior counsel they were instructed by the Australian Government Solicitor.
67. Cockatoo Dockyard Pty Ltd vs Commonwealth of Australia (No. 3) 35 NSWLR 5, pp. 689–703.
68. Australian National Industries Limited, *Interim Report*, for the six months ended 31 December 1996, p. 21.
69. Senator Newman (in response to a question by Senator Margetts of the Minister for Defence, upon notice, on 11 June 1996), Senate, Tuesday 20 August 1996.

CHAPTER FIVE

70. *Report of the Joint Committee* etc., 1915, *op. cit.*, p. 17.
71. Balint Godden Whittaker Associates, *Cockatoo Island Dockyard, Historical Equipment and Facilities*, report for the Department of Housing and Construction, 1981.
72. *Cockatoo Docks war record 1939–1945*, Cockatoo Docks and Engineering Company, c. 1950.
73. See P-E Consulting Group (Australia) reports: *Proposed refitting facilities for Oberon class submarines, Cockatoo Island, New South Wales*; and *Proposed facilities for modernisation of the shipyard, Cockatoo Island, New South Wales*.
74. J C Jeremy, *Design and construction of a slave dock for submarine refitting*, Royal Institution of Naval Architects, Australian Branch, May 1975.
75. The crane was much less reliable after this conversion. It became known around the yard as the 'London fog' — because it rarely lifted.
76. J C Jeremy, *Naval shipbuilding, some Australian experience*, Strategic and Defence Studies Centre, Australian National University, working paper no. 205, 1990.

CHAPTER SIX

77. Navy Office, *Specification of hull for the 26-knot torpedo boat destroyers to be named* Torrens, Swan, *and* Derwent, Melbourne, July 1912.
78. John Mortimer, 'HMAS *Huon*: Australia's first locally constructed destroyer', *The Navy*, July 1984.
79. The last ship built at Cockatoo with extensive use of rivets was HMAS *Stalwart*, launched in 1966, which had the frames riveted to the shell plating. Rivet-like connections are still sometimes used today for light structures like minor bulkheads in warships, although these employ cold-drawn rivets like Huckbolts or Avdelbolts (similar to a pop rivet).
80. Australian Commonwealth Shipping Board, *Circumstances under which HMAS* Adelaide *was built*, Cockatoo Island Dockyard, August 1924. Details of the delays are also set out in the Commonwealth Hansard, no. 66, 7 May 1921.
81. See *Shipbuilding in Australia: launch of HMA Fleet Collier* Biloela, The Commonwealth Engineer, 1 May 1919.
82. Captain R McDonell, *Build a fleet, lose a fleet*, Hawthorn Press, 1976.
83. Statement by the Prime Minister, W M Hughes at the Shipbuilding Conference, Parliament House, Melbourne, 12 June 1917.
84. B A Wilkinson, 'Burns Philp's SS *Mangola*', *The Log*, vol. 9, no. 1, 29 February 1976.
85. Minutes of Conference held in Board Room, Cockatoo Island, on Friday 9 November 1923, CRS C3389,

item NH. In addition to the dockyard management, the meeting was attended by Engineer Rear-Admiral Sir William Clarkson.

86. Department of Defence to the General Manager, Australian Commonwealth Line of Steamers, letter T.C. 603/248/1/2069, 3 July 1924, CRS C3389, item 9.

87. J Monash, 'Cost of construction in Australia of a 100,000 ton cruiser', report to the Prime Minister, 19 August 1924, CRS C3389, item 3.

88. The development of the County class cruiser, of which the Kent class comprised the ships of the British 1924–25 programme, is described in Alan Raven and John Roberts, *British cruisers of World War II*, Arms and Armour Press, 1980. On p. 107 they state: 'The first mention of guns appears in a memorandum dated 13 November 1922, from Admiral Backhouse, the DNO, when the question of available funds for the design of single, twin and triple 8in mountings is mentioned. ... The triple was dismissed because of the complexity of such a mounting; it would also take considerable time to prepare a design and because the other navies were known to be pressing ahead with their own cruiser design, the need for speed overrode the increased fire-power that a layout of triple mountings might give. The twin was decided on, and by April 1923, design was well underway at Vickers.' It is interesting to note that the drawings of the cruiser on which Cockatoo prepared their first estimate in July 1924 show an armament of nine 8-inch guns in three triple turrets.

89. *Sydney Morning Herald*, 25 March 1925.

90. Group Captain Keith Isaacs, 'First of the Line', *Defence Force Journal*, no. 3, March/April 1977: 'The Government's announcement also caused embarrassment to the RAN because, apparently, an aircraft carrier specification had not been prepared. This confused situation resulted in a cryptic cable being received by the Admiralty Director of Naval Construction which stated, in effect, that it was politically desirable to build a "seaplane carrier" in Australia. The cable then provided the two only known specifications — a speed of 21 knots, and a cost of one million pounds! The Naval Constructor in charge of the Admiralty's Aircraft Carrier Section is on record as retorting "a more unsatisfactory way of producing an aircraft carrier I do not know, and cannot imagine".'

91. Isaacs, *op. cit.*

92. Curiously, the request for tender specifically forbade the dockyard from sub-contracting any part of the ship's electrical installation.

93. *Wattle* is still afloat in steaming condition in Melbourne.

94. Secretary of the Naval Board to Managing Director Cockatoo Docks and Engineering Co., 21 September 1939.

95. Director of Engineering, Navy Office to Managing Director Cockatoo Docks and Engineering Co., 30 June 1941. *LDV 42*, built by Mort's Dock, and intended to be *Glenelg*, was completed for the RIN as *Bombay*.

96. *History of the Australian Shipbuilding Board, March 1941 to 31 December 1945*, written for the Australian Shipbuilding Board, author unknown, 1947.

97. Address of Prime Minister R G Menzies at the keel laying of *River Clarence* on 29 July 1941, cine film in the National Archives, CRS M3285.

98. The deadweight of *River Clarence* was 9293 tons, *River Hunter* 8601 tons.

99. Tim Ryan, 'River class frigates', *The Navy*, January–March, 1989.

100. These ships are sometimes incorrectly referred to as 'Bay class', due to the similarity of their armament with the British ships of that later frigate class. The Australian ships were based on the earlier River class.

101. This was probably just as well. In the author's opinion these ships would have been a liability rather than an asset in the post-war years.

102. Department of the Navy to Cockatoo, 18 December 1946.

103. Edgar J March, *British destroyers, a history of development 1892–1953*, Seeley Service & Co., London, 1966.

104. H P Weymouth, *David S Carment: His life and times*, the first David Carment Memorial Lecture, Royal Institution of Naval Architects, Australian Division, 9 May 1979.

105. The story of this project is told in some detail in J C Jeremy, *Naval shipbuilding, some Australian experience*, Strategic and Defence Studies Centre working paper no. 205, Australian National University, February 1990.

106. Roger Parker described the condition of the boilers to Arthur Storey, General Manager of the engineering works at Barrow in a letter of 10 July 1967. The author happened to be in Barrow at the time and heard of the pilchards on 19 July.

107. J C Jeremy, *Naval shipbuilding* etc., *op. cit.*

108. Joint Committee of Public Accounts, *Report No. 243, Review of defence project management: project analyses*, Parliament of the Commonwealth of Australia, 1986, vol. 2, p. 69.

CHAPTER SEVEN

109. John Bastock, *Ships on the Australia Station*, Child and Associates Publishing, 1988. HMS *Drake*, 14,100 tons displacement, 533 feet LOA, 71 feet beam, two 9.2-inch and sixteen 6-inch guns, completed at Pembroke Dockyard January 1903.
110. HMAS *Australia* was a battle cruiser, 22,000 tons displacement (full load), 590 feet LOA, 80 feet beam, eight 12-inch and sixteen 4-inch guns, completed by John Brown and Co., Scotland in 1913.
111. *Hirado, Chikuma* and *Yahagi*, second class cruisers, 4950 tons displacement, eight 6-inch, two 3-inch, completed 1912.
112. Mark Richards, *Workhorses in Australian waters*, Turton and Armstrong, 1987.
113. RMS *Cathay*, 15,225 tons gross, 573 feet 5 inches LOA, Peninsular & Oriental Steam Navigation Co., built by Barclay Curle and Co., Glasgow, 1925.
114. *Vardaas* was a twin screw motor tanker, 8176 tons gross, Agedesidens Rederi A/s, completed by Deutsche Werke AG, Kiel, 1931.
115. See M A Payne, *HMAS* Australia *1928–1955*, Naval Historical Society of Australia.
116. See Steve Harding, *Gray ghost, the RMS* Queen Mary *at war*, Pictorial Histories Publishing Company, 1982.
117. See Chris Konings, Queen Elizabeth *at War, his majesty's transport 1939–1946*, Patrick Stephens, 1985.
118. USS *Chicago* (CA 29), heavy cruiser, 9300 tons displacement, 600 feet 3 inches LOA, nine 8-inch and four 5-inch guns, completed Mare Island Navy Yard, 1931.
119. USS *Chester* (CA 27), heavy cruiser, 9200 tons displacement, 600 feet 3 inches LOA, 66 feet beam, nine 8-inch and four 5-inch guns, completed by New York Shipbuilding Company, 1930.
120. USS *Portland* (CA 33), heavy cruiser, 11,574 tons displacement, 610 feet 3 inches LOA, 66 feet beam, nine 8-inch and eight 5-inch guns, completed Bethlehem Steel, Quincy, 1932.
121. USS *New Orleans* (CA 32), heavy cruiser, 11,515 tons displacement, 588 feet LOA, 61 feet 9 inches beam, nine 8-inch and eight 5-inch guns, completed New York Navy Yard, 1933.
122. See Norman Friedman, *US cruisers, an illustrated design history*, Naval Institute Press, 1984.
123. *History of the Australian Shipbuilding Board* etc., *ibid*.
124. From text of COMSOWESPACFOR 0002/2, in Australian Commonwealth Naval Board's signal 0614Z/6 Feb 43, to Naval Officer in Charge, Sydney.
125. HMS *Formidable*, Illustrious class aircraft carrier, 28,210 tons displacement, 740 feet LOA, 95 feet 9 inches beam, completed Harland and Wolff, 1940.
126. HMS *Indomitable*, Illustrious class aircraft carrier, completed Vickers, 1941.
127. Commanding Officer, HMS *Indomitable* to Flag Officer in Charge, Sydney, letter 4504/170 dated 22 July 1945, author's copy.
128. *ibid*.
129. The largest merchant ship ever docked at Cockatoo was the liner *Dominion Monarch* (27,155 tons gross) in 1945.
130. *Palana* (ex-*Sussex* -46), 11,063 tons gross, built by John Brown & Co., Clydebank, 1937.
131. See J C Jeremy, 'Collision damage repairs of HMAS *Melbourne*', *Proceedings of the Second Commonwealth Welding Conference*, Institute of Welding, London, 1965.
132. FOCAF signal 150241Z September 69.

CHAPTER EIGHT

133. See John Mortimer, 'HMAS *Huon* Australia's first locally constructed destroyer', *The Navy*, July 1984.
134. A N Harrison, *Development of HM Submarines from Holland No. 1 (1901) to Porpoise (1930)*, (BR 3043) Ministry of Defence, Ship Department, 1979.
135. John Bastock, *Australia's ships of war*, Angus and Robertson, 1975.
136. Commander (S/M), Fourth Submarine Squadron to Captain R G Parker, 4 April 1962, author's copy.
137. J C Jeremy, 'Submarine refitting in Australia', *Transactions of the Royal Institution of Naval Architects*, London, 1981.
138. Vickers Cockatoo Dockyard Pty Ltd, *Submarine construction feasibilty study report*, CRS M3080, items 2–10.

CHAPTER NINE

139. Gother K Mann, *Fitz Roy Dry Dock – report from the Engineer-in-Chief to Under Secretary for Public Works*, 8 May 1865 in Journal of the Legislative Council of New South Wales, Session 1865–6, vol. 13, pp. 309–312.

140. See *Government Dockyard, Biloela: report of the managing committee for the year ended 30th June 1904*.
141. D J Mitchell papers.
142. See *Government Dockyard, Biloela* etc., *ibid*.
143. See Mike Richards, *Workhorses in Australian waters*, Turton and Armstrong, 1987, p. 133.
144. *ibid.*, p. 76.
145. W D Dinnie, 'Some unusual rotor repairs', unpublished paper, July 1978.

CHAPTER TEN

146. See J D Scott, *Vickers: a history*, Weidenfeld and Nicholson, London 1962.
147. See Hans Georg Prager, *Blohm+Voss – Ships and machinery for the world*, Brassey's Publishers, 1977.
148. See Lawrence James Wackett, *Aircraft pioneer,* Angus and Robertson, 1972.
149. See Pedr Davis, *Charles Kingsford Smith: World's greatest aviator*, Summit Books, 1977.
150. Wackett, *op. cit.*, p. 105.
151. Don Fraser (ed.), *Sydney from settlement to city, an engineering history of Sydney*, Engineers Australia, 1989.
152. See *Departmental investigation into the capsize of the crane barge* Titan *off Smoky Cape, on 25 December 1992 and the subsequent sinking of the barge off Camden Head, on 29 December 1992*, Inspector of Marine Accidents, Department of Transport and Communications, Canberra, 18 October 1993.

CHAPTER ELEVEN

153. *Report of the Royal Commission* etc., 1903, *op. cit.*, p. 12.
154. *Report of the Joint Committee* etc., 1915, *op. cit.*, p. 15.
155. H E Morgan to Managing Director Hutcheson, 7 Aug 1957: memorandum re. RAN letter 3406/114/34 (5 Aug 1957), copy with the author.
156. H E Morgan to Managing Director Hutcheson, 2 May 1956: memorandum, copy with the author.
157. See Douglas Beck and John Lord, *Design and production of ANZAC frigates for the RAN and RNZN: Progress towards international competitiveness*, presented at the Society of Naval Architects and Marine Engineers 1997 Ship Production Symposium, New Orleans.

POSTSCRIPT

158. Address of Rear Admiral Hughes, 4 June 1991, transcript in author's collection.

INDEX

Page numbers in *italics* refer to illustrations.

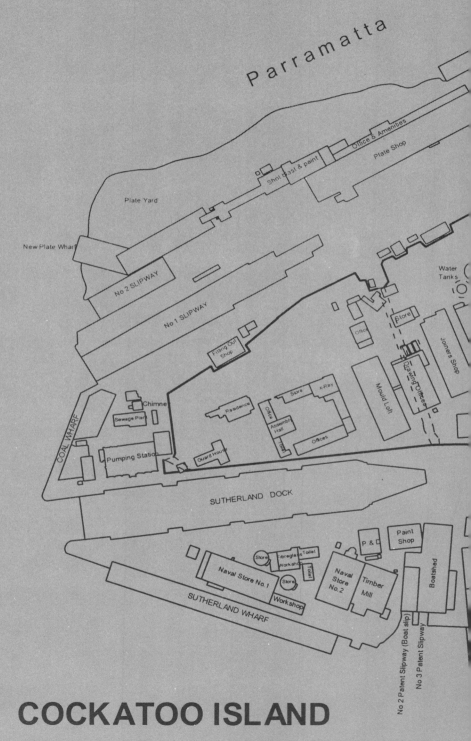

COCKATOO ISLAND

JUNE 1991